Contents

P9-CER-964

FLORIDA

Acknowledgments

Chelle Koster Walton and Sara Kennedy—both well-known to me for many years—did a great job of kicking this book off. It's been updated over the years and much has changed. I wish to thank Adele Woodyard, who partners with me on various travel-writing projects including past projects for Globe Pequot and the previous update of this book. I would also like to thank the many, many fellow Floridians who work so hard to make every visitor's stay here in Florida a pleasant, comfortable, and informative adventure, and who took the time to talk to me and show me around. Last, I thank Globe Pequot Press, and editor Amy Lyons, for putting up with my questions and for giving me this opportunity to further showcase my favorite place to live and to visit.

–Stephen Morrill

Special thanks go to Chelle Koster Walton and Sara Kennedy, coauthors of the first *Fun with the Family in Florida* in the late '90s. With the help of contacts too numerous to mention, it's now my pleasure to add what's new and worth a visit in the Sunshine State. As a transplanted Yankee, it's been a lot of fun to explore and write about such a diverse state over the years. I've especially enjoyed the times my youngest son, Scott, and I pitched a tent in several of Florida's great state parks, when he was 10 to 13 years old.

–Adele Woodyard

Introduction

Florida is a natural for families, and not only because of the universal attraction of Disney World and the countless theme parks that have cropped up in its wake. In the Orlando area alone, there are kids' attractions enough to delight families for days. Many concentrate on pure showbiz or get-wet entertainment; others enrich with lessons on nature, science, history, and outer space. The Disney influence has spread throughout Florida, and here you'll find the widest assortment of twisting, twirling, often enlightening, sometimes frightening diversions in any one state.

On the quieter side of things, however, visitors are often surprised to discover all that Florida has to offer in terms of wilderness and adventure experiences that the whole family can enjoy. Below the surface of glossy brochure items dwells another Florida for families to discover, one that outweighs in sheer volume and enrichment value the artificial high-dollar-ticket Florida.

Of course your children will probably insist on visiting the artificial attractions. One day at an amusement park can easily be balanced with something more physically and mentally challenging, however. This book, a result of my many years as a mother doing the balancing act, takes you to both extremes, but with emphasis on discovery opportunities.

Fortunately for everyone, government agencies at all levels have worked to preserve Florida's special spectrum of fragile environments. City, county, state, and national parks and preserves strive to ensure that our children and theirs will know the teeming wildlife and habitat that once dominated the state—the rare panthers, alligators, manatees, roseate spoonbills, torreya trees, mangroves, and coral reefs. Many of the parks provide recreational opportunities that allow families to play while immersing themselves ecologically. Florida's excellent and extensive state park system is a good place to begin your adventures. If you plan on exploring these parks to any extent, consider purchasing an annual family pass for $120 ($60 for individuals).

LODGING AND RESTAURANT RATES

In the "Where to Eat" section and for other stand-out family restaurant listings, prices are indicated by dollar signs. The range is figured per adult meal of one typically priced dinner (unless dinner is not served, then lunch) entree, beverage (nonalcoholic), and dessert or appetizer:

Rates for Restaurants

$	under $10
$$	$10 to $20
$$$	$21 to $30
$$$$	over $30

Dining recommendations usually avoid the family and fast-food chains, which are in abundance throughout most of Florida. Instead we concentrate on restaurants that can be enjoyed by the entire family. (Mom and Dad shouldn't be subjected to burger-doodle boredom just because they're on a family vacation.)

Under the "Where to Stay" section and for other lodging recommendations, room rates are based on double occupancy of a typically priced room, per night, before tax or service charge. The range covers the lowest rates during off-peak season to the highest rates in peak season. Many large resorts offer family packages throughout the year and have a "kids stay free" policy. Where rates include meals, it is so indicated in the lodging description.

Rates for Lodging

$	under $90
$$	$90 to $150
$$$	$151 to $200
$$$$	over $200

Again, we generally leave out the less expensive chain motels and hotels that travelers find along highways, although these are great for overnight stops and tight budgets. Included are most of Florida's great family destination resorts, which offer kids programs and often some kitchen facilities. Florida is known for these, but they can be pricey.

Attractions Key

The following is a key to the icons found throughout the text.

SWIMMING		FOOD	
BOATING/BOAT TOUR		LODGING	
HISTORIC SITE		CAMPING	
HIKING/WALKING		MUSEUM	
FISHING		PERFORMING ARTS	
BIKING		SPORTS/ATHLETICS	
AMUSEMENT PARK		PICNICKING	
HORSEBACK RIDING		PLAYGROUND	
SKIING/WINTER SPORTS		SHOPPING	
PARK		PLANTS/GARDENS/NATURE TRAILS	
ANIMAL VIEWING		FARM	

Northwest
Florida

Northwest Florida folks talk with a twang and invite you in with Dixie hospitality. Oaks and pines, not palms and orange trees, grace roadsides brightened by magnolia, camellia, and azalea blossoms. Restaurants serve fried catfish and hush puppies. This may be northern Florida, but it's still the Deep South, sure as neighboring Alabama—and much surer than Florida's southern reaches, where influences from the Yankee states hold sway.

Sometimes known as the Redneck Riviera, Florida's Panhandle holds the most prideful beaches in the entire state. Created over the centuries from quartz rock flushed westward from the Appalachian Mountains, these sandy beaches sparkle the whitest, feel the softest, and drift the most mountainous of any in Florida. Trouble is, winters are too cold to fully enjoy them year-round, as you can in southern regions. The tourist season here begins at spring break, then slacks off until summer, when families converge on resorts known for their value.

Of the seven sections of Florida covered in this book, the Northwest boasts the most state parks, recreation areas, historic sites, and national wildlife refuges, affording the adventurous family endless latitude for fun and meaningful vacations.

Tallahassee and Area

On I-10.

Home of Florida State University, Tallahassee boasts fine museums and well-dressed streets, all decked in enough trees to earn the city a listing among the Top Ten Scenic Byways in America. At its southern doorstep, Florida reverts to its natural tendencies and holds some secrets of times past.

NORTHWEST FLORIDA

Alfred B. Maclay State Gardens (ages 8 to 12)

3540 Thomasville Rd., Tallahassee; (850) 487-4556. Gardens open from 9 a.m. to 5 p.m. daily, state park open 8 a.m. to sunset daily, house open 9 a.m. to 5 p.m. from Jan through Apr, when entrance to the gardens, house, and park is $4 for adults, $2 for children under 12. Park entrance is $4 per car year-round.

One of the Quail Trail's most important sites bursts into bloom January through April with camellias and azaleas. It's a lovely place for a stretch of the legs anytime. The state park, which contains the gardens, offers swimming, nature trails, canoe rentals, fishing, and boating. You can tour the gardens' historic home and botanical exhibits in season.

Bradley's Country Store (all ages)

10655 Centerville Rd., Tallahassee; (850) 893-1647; www.bradleyscountrystore.com. Open 8:00 a.m. to 6 p.m. Mon through Fri and 8:00 a.m. to 5 p.m. Sat.

Homemade sausage is the claim to fame at this circa-1920 vestige of yesteryear. It holds all the sweetness of childhood days, moon pies, and old-time sugarmaking.

Challenger Learning Center and IMAX Theatre (ages 5 to 12)

Kleman Plaza, 200 South Duval St. and College Avenue; (850) 644-4629; www.challengertlh .com. IMAX: $8.00 for adults, $7.00 for seniors and students, $6.00 for children 5 to 12; planetarium: $5.00 for adults, $4.75 for seniors and students, $4.25 for children 5 to 12.

TopPicks for Family Fun in Northwest Florida

1. Beaching and ruins-ruminating at Fort Pickens National Park, Pensacola Beach

2. Spotting animals in the wilds and watching nineteenth-century farmers at Tallahassee Museum of History and Natural Science, Tallahassee

3. Going underground at Florida Caverns State Park, Marianna

4. Swimming and boat touring at Wakulla Springs State Park, Wakulla Springs

5. Taking cockpit controls at the National Museum of Naval Aviation, Pensacola

6. Tubing at Ichetucknee Springs State Park, Fort White

7. Sunday-driving the canopy roads of Tallahassee

8. Seeing trees and bushes aflutter with monarch butterflies in migration, St. Marks National Wildlife Refuge, St. Marks

9. Strolling through time at Pensacola Historic Village, Pensacola

Amazing
Tallahassee Facts

- Tallahassee is closer to Alabama, Louisiana, Georgia, Kentucky, Tennessee, Mississippi, Texas, Arkansas, North Carolina, and South Carolina than it is to Key West, Florida.
- America's largest concentration of original plantations—seventy-one plantations comprising 300,000 acres—exists between Tallahassee and Thomasville, Georgia, 28 miles away.

With its K through 12 outreach program, the simulated "Mission Control" requires groups of fourteen or more, but the 50-foot planetarium and IMAX theater bring space adventures to all.

Civic Center (ages 5 to 12)
505 West Pensacola St., Tallahassee; (850) 487-1691 or (800) 322-3602; www.tlccc.org.

Check out ice shows, concerts, sports events such as Florida State University basketball games, and Broadway musicals at this modern, multipurpose convention and entertainment center.

Downtown Historic District (ages 4 to 13)
A brochure for a self-guided walking tour of downtown is available through the Tallahassee Area Convention and Visitors Bureau; (850) 606-2305 or (800) 628-2866, or view or order online at: www.seetallahassee.com.

The 10-block area contains two districts listed on the National Register of Historic Places: Calhoun Street and Park Avenue. Highlights include the Old and New Capitol complexes.

Goodwood Plantation (ages 9 to 12)
1600 Miccosukee Rd., Tallahassee; (850) 877-4202; www.goodwoodmuseum.org. Main house tour 10 a.m. to 4 p.m. Mon through Fri and 10 a.m. to 2 p.m. Sat. Admission is $6 for ages 3 and older. The gardens are open 9 a.m. to 5 p.m. Mon through Fri and 10 a.m. to 2 p.m. Sat; free.

The gardened grounds and restored nineteenth- and early-twentieth-century buildings are open for touring.

Mary Brogan Museum of Art and Science (ages 5 to 12)
Kleman Plaza, 350 South Duval St., Tallahassee; (850) 513-0700; www.thebrogan.org. Open 10 a.m. to 5 p.m. Mon through Sat, 1 to 5 p.m. Sun. Admission is $6.00 for adults; $3.50 for seniors, college students, and children ages 3 through 17.

This three-story family attraction has interactive exhibits on the second floor and an art gallery on the third. Changing exhibits feature art collections and themed hands-on experiences.

Mission San Luis Archaeological and Historic Site
(ages 7 to 12)

2100 West Mission Rd., Tallahassee (near the intersection of Tennessee Street and White Drive); (850) 487-3711; www.missionsanluis.org. Open 10 a.m. to 4 p.m. Tues through Sun. Living history program available daily. Admission is free (suggested donation $5 adult and $2 child).

As in California, Catholic Spanish missions once spread across the northern part of Florida. San Luis survives as the only reconstructed Spanish mission in the state. Living history re-creates the days when the mission was built in the mid-seventeenth century to convert the Apalachees to Christianity. Archaeological digs are ongoing here, and you can watch and question archaeologists at work. The kids will enjoy seeing the Apalachees' ball game plaza, where Indians played a competitive, ritualistic sport that combined elements of soccer and handball.

Museum of Florida History (ages 5 to 12)

500 South Bronough St., Tallahassee; (850) 245-6400; www.museumoffloridahistory.com. Open 9 a.m. to 4:30 p.m. Mon through Fri, 10 a.m. to 4:30 p.m. Sat, and noon to 4:30 p.m. Sun. Free.

The kids will marvel at the 12,000-year-old skeleton of the 9-foot-tall mastodon affectionately known as Herman and a display of Spanish doubloons. The comprehensive museum chronicles the state's bygones from the days of prehistoric settlement and European invasion to more modern eras of pioneer settlement and the "Tin Can Tourist" (trailer traveler) invasion.

Natural Bridge Battlefield Reenactment (ages 7 to 12)

Natural Bridge Battlefield State Historic Site, 15 miles southeast of Tallahassee off Rte. 363; 1022 DeSoto Park Dr., Tallahassee; (850) 922-6007; www.floridastateparks.org/natural bridge/. Open 8 a.m. to sunset daily. Park entrance is $3 per vehicle.

Florida **Trivia**

Panhandle beaches are so white and crunchy underfoot because, unlike other Florida beaches, made from pulverized shell matter, Panhandle beaches are quartz based. The quartz sand has been buffed smooth, whereas most other sand has rough edges. That's what makes it sound as if you're walking on fresh, cold snow.

Canopy Roads

For detailed directions to trails and their attractions, download a copy of the *Driving Guide to Scenic Leon County* from www.co.leon.fl.us/PUBWORKS/ oper/canopy/crcl/index.htm. (Just print the Web page; it's the old, discontinued printed brochure.) Among arboresque Tallahassee's best features are the five oak-tunnel routes once followed by Native Americans and Spanish conquistadors. They are Old St. Augustine, Miccosukee, Meridian, Centerville, and Old Bainbridge Roads. Many of the area's most worthwhile sites lie along these routes. Four peaceful trails to the past have been devised to incorporate the sites along these routes.

The Cotton Trail A 50-mile eastward loop visits the *Gone with the Wind* era of plantations. It begins on lovely Miccosukee Road (Route 0347), where red earth and live oaks draped dreamily with ghostlike Spanish moss create an antebellum mood. The trail turns north onto Crump Road, then left onto Roberts Road and follows Centerville Road (Route 151) to Moccasin Gap Road.

The Quail Trail This northern loop of about 50 miles leaves town via Thomasville Road (Hwy. 319) and takes in Meridian Road.

The Native Trail Beginning downtown, it leads to archaeological sites of ancient civilizations along both Old Bainbridge and Old St. Augustine Roads.

Old St. Augustine Road A designated canopy road, it dates back to the 1600s, when it linked the colonial settlements of Tallahassee and the earlier Florida capital of St. Augustine.

Natural Bridge is where the St. Marks River drops into a sinkhole and flows underground for one-quarter of a mile before reemerging. In the final weeks of the Civil War, Confederate troops kept Union soldiers at bay and prevented the capture of Tallahassee in 1865. Thus Tallahassee remained the only uncaptured Confederate capital east of the Mississippi. The battle comes to life each March with a staged reenactment. The park is open for picnicking year-round.

New Capitol (ages 4 to 12)

South Monroe and Apalachee Parkway; 400 South Monroe St., Tallahassee; (850) 488-6167. Open 8 a.m. to 5 p.m. Mon through Fri except holidays. Forty-five-minute guided tours must be booked in advance; call ahead for times. Admission is free.

The centerpiece of the Tallahassee historic section is the Capitol Complex, which juxtaposes the classic domed structure of 1845 against the sleek new high-rise built in the late 1970s. Begin at the New Capitol, where you can tour the town in a few steps by circling the gallery on the twenty-second floor, or sit in on legislative sessions. Stop at the Visitor Information Center to learn more about what the city has to offer.

Old Capitol (ages 8 to 12)

South Monroe Street and Apalachee Parkway; 400 South Monroe St., Tallahassee; (850) 487-1902. Open 9 a.m. to 4:30 p.m. Mon through Fri, 10 a.m. to 4:30 p.m. Sat, and noon to 4:30 p.m. Sun. Closed Thanksgiving and Christmas. Admission is **free.**

You can tour the restored legislative chambers and view exhibits on the state's political history.

Springtime Tallahassee Parade and Jubilee (ages 4 to 12)

209 East Park Ave., Tallahassee; (850) 224-5012; www.springtimetallahassee.com.

The town's big event each year begins in late March or early April, an extravaganza of parades, a kids' park, and fairs that runs for three weeks during prime azalea-blooming time.

Tallahassee Automobile Museum (all ages)

3550 Mahan Dr., Tallahassee; (850) 942-0137; www.tacm.com. Open 8 a.m. to 5 p.m. Mon through Fri, 10 a.m. to 5 p.m. Sat, and noon to 5 p.m. Sun. Admission is $16.00 for adults ($13.50 each for two or more), $10.75 for students, $7.50 children 5 to 8, kids 4 and under **free.**

Vehicles from Abraham Lincoln's 1860s hearse to Hollywood's Batmobiles, a Bat Boat, and the Penguin's Duck join rooms crammed with collectibles of every description that will fascinate young and old.

Tallahassee Museum of History and Natural Science
(ages 4 to 12)

Near the airport off Rte. 371 at 3945 Museum Dr., Tallahassee; (850) 576-1636; www.talla hasseemuseum.org. Open 9 a.m. to 5 p.m. Mon through Sat and 12:30 to 5 p.m. Sun. Admission is $9.00 for adults, $8.50 for seniors and students, $6.00 for children ages 4 to 15, and **free** to those 3 and under.

Florida **Trivia**

How Tallahassee Became Capital Before Florida became a U.S. territory, it was split in two parts. St. Augustine served as East Florida's governmental seat, while Pensacola ruled West Florida. When the two became one, a new centrally located capital was needed. Legend says envoys were sent by horseback from St. Augustine and by boat and foot from Pensacola to see where they'd meet. And so backwoods Tallyhassee, as it was known, became capital of Florida.

A Panhandle **Undiscovered Treasure**

Possibly the tiniest state park is also a fine beach. Deer Lake State Park, off CR 30A in Santa Rosa Beach, has one small parking lot, no ranger at all (that we saw, there's a $3 "honor" admission fee per car, so someone must come by to empty the cashbox), and a loooong, loooong boardwalk over the dunes, skirting Deer Lake itself, and out to the beach. That's the park. We hoofed it out to the beach which was gorgeous and totally empty. In fact we passed a man walking back who said he came there often because he almost never saw anyone else on the beach.

If you do nothing else in the capital city, you must make it to this attraction. Part zoo, part hands-on museum and living history arena, it gives you fifty-two acres and a half-day's worth of activities, including a re-created nineteenth-century farm, boardwalks through panther and red wolf habitat, historical buildings, and a Discovery Center. The animal exhibits are conscientious in the way they allow Florida's native critters to roam freely within low-impact barriers. Kids love the indoor Discovery Center—especially the feel-and-identify box and crawl-through tree—and the old schoolhouse once attended by the children of former slaves. Go when guides dress and act the part of nineteenth-century settlers, usually every day but Monday, but for sure on weekends.

Tallahassee–St. Marks Historic Railroad State Trail
(ages 7 to 12)

Along Rte. 363; for access points and information call 850-487-7989 or visit www.dep.state .fl.us/gwt/guide/regions/panhandleeast/trails/tallahassee_stmarks.htm.

Follow the 20 miles of paved and unpaved trail from Tallahassee to St. Marks by foot, horseback, bike, or in-line skates.

Where to Eat

Eating and lodging are inexpensive in and around Tallahassee.

Andrew's Capital Grill and Bar. 228 South Adams St., Tallahassee; (850) 222-3444; www.andrewsdowntown.com/capital-grill.html. Popular with state politicians and university sports fans. Sandwiches and casual entrees for lunch Mon through Sat, dinner daily, Sun brunch. $$

Barnacle Bill's. 1830 North Monroe St., Tallahassee; (850) 385-8734; www.barnaclebills .com. Florida seafood raw, grilled, steamed, smoked, or fried; casual atmosphere. Big-screen and cable TVs. Lunch and dinner daily. $$

Where to Stay

Most of the lodging choices in town are of the chain variety.

DoubleTree Hotel Tallahassee. 101 South Adams St., Tallahassee; (850) 224-5000 or (800) 222-TREE; www.doubletree.com. An old downtown hotel luxuriously renovated with 242 well-appointed units, restaurant, pool, and **free** chocolate chip cookies upon check-in. $

For More Information

Tallahassee Area Convention and Visitors Bureau. 106 East Jefferson St., Tallahassee 32301; (850) 606-2305 or (800) 628-2866; www.seetallahassee.com.

Nature Attractions along I-10

The Panhandle's main northern route, I-10, strings together natural wonder gems with tons of recreational adventures for families.

Adventures Unlimited (ages 8 to 12)

Off Hwy. 87, 12 miles north of Milton; 8974 Tomahawk Landings, Milton; (850) 623-6197 or (800) 239-6864; www.adventuresunlimited.com. Open daily; hours vary according to the season. Prices vary according to length of trip.

The town of Milton is the self-proclaimed Canoe Capital of Florida. Adventures Unlimited, an eighty-eight-acre privately owned park, launches canoeing, kayaking, rafting, paddle-boating, and tubing expeditions into the spring-fed wilderness streams of Coldwater, Blackwater, Sweetwater, and Juniper Creeks. It also provides cabins and campsites.

Blackwater River State Park (ages 8 to 12)

15 miles northeast of Milton off Hwy. 90; 7720 Deaton Bridge Rd., Holt; (850) 983-5363; www.floridastateparks.org/blackwaterriver. Open 8 a.m. to sunset daily. Park entrance is $4 per vehicle of eight persons or fewer, $1 per extra passenger, cyclist, or pedestrian.

Named for one of the Panhandle's great natural rivers, it gives outdoor types the opportunity to revel in canoeing, hiking, camping, and biking opportunities.

Florida Trivia

Clock Watch Panhandle Florida has two time zones. The Apalachicola River runs from Georgia to the Gulf of Mexico and divides Eastern from Central time except for the Gulf County capital of Port St. Joe which, while on the west bank of the river, is on Eastern time. Panhandle residents refer to Eastern time as "fast" time and Central as "slow" time, and Gulf County is the only Florida county with both fast and slow time. Just remember, as you drive east or west in the Florida panhandle, that when you cross the Apalachicola River you change your watch too.

Falling Waters State Park (ages 7 to 12)

1130 State Park Rd., Chipley; (850) 638-6130; www.floridastateparks.org/fallingwaters/default.cfm. Open 8 a.m. to sunset daily. Park entrance is $5 per vehicle of eight persons or fewer, $1 per extra passenger, cyclist, or pedestrian.

A dramatic, 73-foot waterfall tumbles over the edge of a 100-foot stovepipe sinkhole. The water goes underground and no one knows where it comes out; this part of Florida is one vast karst formation of subterranean water-filled caverns. Explore this and other sinks along 945 feet of boardwalks. Have a swim and a picnic while you're there.

Florida Caverns State Park (ages 5 to 12)

Off Hwy. 167; 3345 Caverns Rd., Marianna; (850) 482-9598 (recorded message) or (850) 482-1228; www.floridastateparks.org/floridacaverns/default.cfm. Open 8 a.m. to sunset daily (you must buy tour tickets before 1 p.m.). Tour hours are 9:30 a.m. to 4:30 p.m. Park entrance is $5 per car of eight persons or fewer, $1 per extra passenger, cyclist, or pedestrian. Guided one-hour cave tours cost $8 for visitors age 13 or older and $5 for children 3 to 12.

Take your explorations 50 feet underground at an unusual network of classic limestone formations. Spelunking tours are ranger guided. Aboveground you can hike, camp, fish, swim, golf, and canoe.

Ponce de Leon Springs State Park (ages 5 to 12)

Off Hwy. 98, 12 miles north of de Funiak Springs; 2860 Ponce de Leon Springs Rd., Ponce de Leon; (850) 836-4281; www.floridastateparks.org/PoncedeLeonSprings. Open 8 a.m. to sunset daily. Park entrance is $4 per vehicle, $1 per cyclist or pedestrian.

All right, Ponce did not actually visit this spring but it's named after him. Hot, with irritable kids? Take a quick detour for a cool plunge into the clear springs pool with its 68-degree water. Have a picnic and a nature hike while you're at it.

Road Markers

This Panhandle Express begins in Tallahassee, capital of Florida and its Southern culture. From there it follows scenic and brisk I-10 westward to the Alabama border, where it drops south to Pensacola, western gateway to the shimmering emerald coastline.

Here begins the most scenic portion of the trip—along Hwy. 98 and its offshoots—to Florida's top-shelf beaches. The route rounds the so-called Big Bend, where Hwy.s 98 and 19 merge, and ends at the pristine shores of historic Cedar Key. Hwy. 98 becomes congested in places, especially in the summer and especially where it narrows to two lanes.

Torreya State Park (ages 6 to 12)

**Route C1641 off Rte. 12; 2576 Northwest Torreya Park Rd., Bristol; (850) 643-2674; www
.floridastateparks.org/torreya/. Open 8 a.m. to sundown daily. Park entrance is $3 per
vehicle; admission to the Gregory House is $2 for adults, $1 for children 12 and under.
Visit www.Reserveamerica.com or call 1-800-326-3521 for camping reservations in the
family campground or the park's yurt.**

Named for a rare species of evergreen that grows in abundance here, the 12,000-acre
park is also unusual for its towering bluff formations along the Apalachicola River. Yew
and winged elm trees and other vegetation reminiscent of the Appalachian Mountains
add to the park's mystique. Avid hikers take to the 15 miles of Florida's most strenuous
(read: hilly) trail. History lovers tour the antebellum Gregory House.

Pensacola Area

I-10 forms the northern border of Pensacola, where Florida history takes a turn toward
salt and swashbuckling as wilderness meets the sea. This is the very brink of Florida, and
Pensacola's close proximity to Alabama has a decided effect upon the temperament and
tradition of the city. Things move at the pace of a southern drawl, music goes country,
and hospitality is steeped in the graciousness of eras past.

This route takes you into Pensacola's historic downtown district, so prettily restored
and valuable for its history lessons and antiques shopping. Three oak-lined districts hold
the town's treasures: Seville, Palafox, and North Hill.

Pensacola and much of the Panhandle coastline have been pervaded with military
history since the days when the Spaniards first arrived and built forts to protect the deep
harbor. More recently, Pensacola is home to the Pensacola Naval Air Station and its Blue
Angel daredevil flyers.

In the westernmost part of town, off the beaten path, lies an island whose name
means "lost," which is what you'll be if you don't get good directions. Perdido Key is a
quiet, little-known island that is partly the property of Alabama and a part of the Gulf
Islands National Seashore system. The beaches here present lightly developed dunes-
capes, where a peculiar sort of maritime ecology persists despite the effects of salt-
battering waves and hurricane winds.

To the east, looping back along the coast, a bridge
crosses from downtown Pensacola to the community
of Gulf Breeze, then another takes you to Pensacola Beach. Historic attractions aside, the best
part of Pensacola lies there, on Santa Rosa Island,
with its 22 miles of brilliant, fluffy, dunes-drifted
sand. Most of these beaches are also protected
by the U.S. government under the auspices of the
Gulf Islands National Seashore.

Big Lagoon State Park (ages 5 to 12)

12301 Gulf Beach Hwy, Pensacola (at the intersection of Bauer Road); (850) 492-1595; www
.floridastateparks.org/biglagoon/. Open 8 a.m. to sunset daily. Park entrance is $5 per
vehicle of eight persons or fewer, $1 per extra passenger, cyclist, or pedestrian.

Camp, hike, fish, and commune with nature. Gray foxes, cardinals, and nuthatches inhabit
this 698-acre world of coastal ecology. Nature study programs familiarize you with life on
the bay beach and along the trails.

Fiesta of Five Flags (various events)

An annual celebration in Pensacola each June, this includes activities for all ages and
ranks as one of the oldest and largest festivals in the state. It commemorates Pensacola's
rich history and culture under five governmental powers—Spain, France, England, the
United States, and the Confederacy. It is celebrated throughout the community, including Pensacola Beach, with costumed revelry, parades, music, antiques shows, and sports
activities. For a detailed calendar of events, visit its Web site, www.fiestaoffiveflags.org,
or call (850) 433-6512.

Fort Barrancas (ages 5 to 10)

1801 Gulf Breeze Parkway, Gulf Breeze; (850) 934-2600; www.nps.gov/guis/historyculture/
fort-barrancas-visitor-center.htm. Self-guided tours available; daily guided tours at 2 p.m.
Admission is **free.**

Some Pensacola **Historic Village Sites**

The Museum of Industry. 200 East Zaragoza St. It exhibits old sawmill
machinery from the area's lumber boom.

The Museum of Commerce. 201 East Zaragoza St. Static displays depict an
1890s streetscape, complete with trolley car, barbershop, print shop, hard-
ware store, leather shop, toy store, and early-1900s newsroom and pressroom.

Julee Cottage. 210 East Zaragoza St. This circa-1804 home of a **free** African-
American woman houses a museum on local black history.

1810 Lavalle House. Behind Julee Cottage. Here you find a prime example of
old Pensacola's French-Creole architecture.

Manuel Barrios Cottage. East Zaragoza Street, in front of the Museum of
Industry. Exhibits depict the 1920s lifestyle.

Dorr House. This beautifully ornate home is filled with Victorian antiques.

The Barkley House. Florida Blanca Street. Another fine example of French-
Creole architecture.

Seashore Pristine

Gulf Islands National Seashore, 1801 Gulf Breeze Parkway, Gulf Breeze (850-934-2600; www.nps.gov/guis), holds in its protective embrace a total of 52 miles of Florida Panhandle barrier islands. Most of it lies in and around Pensacola, on Perdido Key and Santa Rosa Island (Pensacola Beach). Bird-watchers have counted more than 280 different species of birds in these areas. Another small section of the Seashore is found on Okaloosa Island, home of Fort Walton Beach.

Built between 1839 and 1844 to protect Pensacola Harbor and once a Confederacy strong-hold. Bring a picnic lunch and spend some time exploring the fort ruins at its elevated site (*barranca* means "bluff" in Spanish). The fort is part of the Gulf Islands National Seashore.

Gulf Islands National Seashore, Fort Pickens (ages 4 to 12)
West end of Fort Pickens Road; 1400 Fort Pickens Rd., Pensacola Beach; (850) 934-2635; www.nps.gov/guis/planyourvisit/fort-pickens.htm. Park and fort are open 7 a.m. to 10 p.m. daily. Guided tours of the fort at 2 p.m. daily. Park entrance is $8 per car for a seven-day permit into the park, good also for Perdido Key National Seashore and Santa Rosa Day Use Area.

Part of the above-mentioned Seashore system, these extensive fort ruins, ca. 1830, add to the attraction of the pristine beachfront. The park is a definite must-see because of the variety of activities offered within its vast acreage. The drive through the park is sheer entrancement with its otherworldly terrain of undulating sand dunes and salt-dwarfed maritime vegetation. Adjuncts to the fort pop up around this corner and that and at beach recreational areas, where you can camp, hike, fish, or bike. The main fort complex occupies the island's west end with a natural history museum, terrific book and gift shop, fishing pier, and administration buildings. You can see the fort, which operated during the Civil War (it was held by Yankee troops while Fort Barrancas, across the bay, was occu-pied by Confederates) and once imprisoned Apache chief Geronimo, by a self-guided or guided tour (offered at 2 p.m. seven days a week, except Christmas Day).

Bike Path
Seven miles of bike path travel along Fort Pickens Road and Via de Luna, plus Fort Pickens National Seashore holds miles of unpaved bike trails through ruins and natural flora.

Main Beach (ages 8 to 12)
On Via de Luna near the Bob Sikes Bridge.

Look for the beachball water tower. Sometimes still referred to by locals as Casino Beach, this was renovated with new, expanded facilities and restaurants at the center of town. It appeals to water-sports enthusiasts, fun lovers, and older children.

Quietwater Beach (all ages)

Quietwater Beach Road.

At the island's doorstep, this protected bay beach in the crook of the causeway greets you with shopping, restaurants, and calm, tot-friendly waters. In this area and around the main beach to the west, you will find all manner of water-sports facilities. Fishing is popular at the Bob Sikes Fishing Pier, which parallels the causeway.

Key Sailing (ages 9 to 12)

500 Quietwater Beach Rd., Suite 14, Pensacola Beach; (850) 932-5520; www.keysailing.com/keysail/. Open usually 9 a.m. to 6 p.m. daily.

Rents pontoons, catamarans, and parasail equipment.

The National Naval Aviation Museum (ages 6 to 12)

Pensacola Naval Air Station, off Rte. 292A on Blue Angel Parkway; 1750 Radford Blvd., NAS Pensacola; (850) 452-3604 or (800) 327-5002. Open 9 a.m. to 5 p.m. daily. Admission to museum is free. Admission to simulator is $5.00 per person; IMAX costs $8.00 for adults, $7.50 for seniors and ages 5 through 12.

This immense facility preserves the history of military aircraft. It contains more than 150 specialized aircraft in all, including the A-4 Skyhawks once used by the world-famous Blue Angels. Kids can manipulate controls in a test cockpit trainer and antiaircraft gun battery. A motion-based, fifteen-seat flight simulator ride re-creates a Desert Storm aircraft engagement and barnstorming flight. In the IMAX theater, you feel as though you're flying an F-18 fighter jet. Guided tours of the museum run four times daily led by retired military volunteers. The Blue Angels Air Show highlights a November visit.

Naval Live Oaks (ages 5 to 12)

East of the Three-Mile Bridge at 1801 Gulf Breeze Parkway, Gulf Breeze; (850) 934-2600; www.nps.gov/guis/planyourvisit/naval-live-oaks.htm. Open 8 a.m. to 5:30 p.m. year-round. Free.

Live oaks were excellent ship-building material and the trunk-branch joints were cut to make the "knees" joining keel to sides in sailing vessels. Gulf Islands National Seashore has its local headquarters here, along with an informative visitor center and 5 miles of nature trails. Bobcats and red foxes survive among nearly 1,400 acres of live oaks, Southern magnolia, and sand pines.

Pensacola Historic Village (ages 6 to 13)
330 South Jefferson St., Pensacola; (850) 595-5985; www.historicpensacola.org. The parking lot for the village is located at the intersection of South Tarragona Street and Zaragoza Street. All attractions open 10 a.m. to 4 p.m. Tues through Sat. Admission is $6 for adults, $5 for seniors, and $3 for children ages 4 to 16.

This 4-block complex contains several museums and historic sites, all of which you can enter for one admission fee. Daily guided tours are held at 11 a.m., 1 p.m., and 2:30 p.m.

Florida **Trivia**

In the First Place En route to Fort Pickens, you may notice a white cross perched atop one of the dunes. It marks the location of the first religious service held in Pensacola, in August 1559—a reminder that colonists attempted to build a settlement here four years before St. Augustine, "The Oldest City," was settled. Pensacola claims its place in history as "America's First Place City."

Gulf Breeze X-Files Gulf Breeze, which occupies the peninsula between Pensacola and Pensacola Beach, has the dubious distinction of being the world's UFO sighting capital. Most explain this away by the presence of air force bases and their wacky experiments. In any case, you may want to keep an eye to the sky while you are thereabouts.

Pensacola Naval Air Station Lighthouse

Off Rte. 292A on Blue Angel Parkway; 3822 Taylor Rd., Pensacola (stop at the visitor's gate to get directions to the lighthouse); (850) 455-5167. Open 9:30 a.m. to 4:45 p.m. daily from Mar through Oct; and 8:30 a.m. to 3:45 p.m. daily from Nov through Feb. Tours on Sat noon to 4; admission $5, $3 senior/military, under age 7 is $3.

Visitors must have shoes and be seven or older to climb the 172 steps of the lighthouse.

Perdido Key Gulf Islands National Seashore Day Use Area

(ages 4 to 12)

Route 292/Johnson Beach Road; (850) 934-2600; www.nps.gov/guis/planyourvisit/perdido-key.htm. Open 8 a.m. to sunset daily. Park entrance is $8 per car, $3 per bike or hiker for a seven-day pass, good also at Fort Pickens National Park and Santa Rosa Day Use Area.

Beachgoers can park and take advantage of sugar-fine sands, clear aquamarine waters, well-maintained picnic shelters, and other facilities. You can continue to walk along the beach where the road ends—undisturbed by modern conveyances—for 6 miles. During the summer, you'll find food concessions and lifeguards.

Perdido Key State Park (all ages)

15301 Perdido Key Dr.; (850) 492-1595; www.floridastate parks.org/perdidokey/. Open 8 a.m. to sunset daily. Park entrance is $3 per car.

Less out of the way than the national seashore, this 247-acre beach park lies in the midst of the island's condominium community. There are picnic facilities but no lifeguards. Shops and water-sports concessions are nearby.

Smart Travel

- The Panhandle's extra-white sand extra-magnifies the sun's intensity. One-up your family's normal SPF and don't forget sunglasses for everyone. This stuff is like looking at the sun's glare reflected off snow drifts. It can fry your eyeballs.

- Walking in the Panhandle's brand of superfine sand puts a strain on the legs—1 mile of beach walking bears little resemblance to 1 mile on hard surfaces. Go easy and take plenty of water.

- Most beaches post flags to alert bathers about sea conditions. Purple means dangerous marine life, green means low hazard/calm condition, yellow means medium hazard/moderate surf or currents, red means high hazard/high surf or currents, and double red, with a no-swimming symbol, means the water is closed to the public. If a red or a double red flag is flying on the beach, do something else that day. The danger, even for strong swimmers, is real.

- Thorny, scrubby sandspurs arm coastal regions throughout Florida. Stay on pathways when walking to and from the beach, and make sure everyone wears shoes. To remove the prickly burrs from bare feet or shoe soles, lick your fingers before lightly grasping the pests. Check shoes before going inside. They like to grab on to carpeting and attack when least expected.

- Panama City Beach, Fort Walton Beach, and, to a lesser extent, Pensacola Beach are spring break magnets. College students pour in by the thousands. Resorts become all-night party spots, and streets fill with beer hounds. Not a pretty picture for the family. Avoid these towns at all costs during March and early April.

Sam's Fun City (all ages)

Just south of I-10 on Rte. 29; 6709 Pensacola Blvd., Pensacola; (850) 505-0800; www.sams funcity.com. Call or visit the Web site for hours and prices; there are many different rides and combinations.

Cartoon characters Dudley Do-Right, Underdog, and Rocky and Bullwinkle provide the theme for this park. Amusements include an eighteen-hole mountain minigolf course, a Ferris wheel, go-kart and antique-car tracks, amusement park rides, laser tag, a video arcade with simulators, and Surf City Water Park is open during the summer.

Santa Rosa National Seashore Day Use Area (ages 6 to 12)

Via de Luna; (850) 934-2600; www.nps.gov/archive/guis/extended/fla/Facilities/Picnic.htm. Open 8 a.m. to sunset daily. Park entrance is $8 per car, $3 per bike or hiker for a seven-day pass to all Florida Gulf Islands National Seashore accesses.

Past the business and resort district of Pensacola Beach, and then past its residential neighborhoods, you come to a desolate stretch of beach, a day-use segment of Gulf Islands National Seashore. Here, you can lose yourself among the dunes, have a beach-blanket picnic, and snooze on some of the world's softest sands. Facilities were totally destroyed in 1995 by Hurricane Opal but have been rebuilt.

T. T. Wentworth Jr. Florida State Museum (ages 3 to 9)

330 South Jefferson St., Pensacola; (850) 595-5990. Open 10 a.m. to 4 p.m. Mon through Sat. Admission is included in Pensacola Historic Village fees, above.

Here's where your Pensacola Historic Village tour begins. Outside, you'll see a colonial archaeological dig in progress. Inside, you can purchase tickets and pick up a tour map and other local information. A beautiful example of local Mediterranean-Revival style architecture, the museum once served as city hall. Its first floor is devoted to the slightly oddball collection of Mr. Wentworth. Among the artifacts are a petrified cat and the world's largest pair of shoes. Exhibits on the second floor rotate, except for a permanent Coca-Cola nostalgia collection. The Discovery Gallery on the third floor lets kids experience real-life situations on their scale. They can "pretend work" at a radio station, grocery store, post office, and city hall.

The Zoo (all ages)

5701 Gulf Breeze Parkway, Gulf Breeze; 10 miles east of Gulf Breeze on Hwy. 98; (850) 932-2229; www.thezoonorthwestflorida.org/; www.the-zoo.com. Open 9 a.m. to 5 p.m. (last admission 4 p.m.) daily. Admission is $11.50 plus tax for adults, $10.50 for seniors, and $8.25 for children ages 3 to 11. Under 3 free.

In wide open spaces, 900 animals—everything from pygmy hippos to black rhinos—forage and go about life. You can see them all aboard the Safari Line minitrain ($3 plus tax) or take part in feeding giraffes. Other attractions include a petting farm of domestic animals, a nursery and incubator room, wildlife demonstrations on weekends, food concessions, and a great wildlife gift shop.

Where to Eat

Flounder's Chowder House. 800 Quietwater Beach Rd., Pensacola Beach; (850) 932-2003; www.flounderschowderhouse .com. You can't miss the landlocked thirty-ton shrimp boat. Open daily for lunch and dinner. $$

Peg Leg Pete's Oyster Bar. 1010 Fort Pickens Rd., Pensacola Beach; (850) 932-4139. Little buccaneers receive their meals in a beach sand bucket. Oysters and affordable Cajun dishes. Daily lunch and dinner. $–$$

Where to Stay

Best place for families to stay is on Pensacola Beach.

Days Inn Pensacola Beach Resort. 16 Via de Luna Dr., Pensacola Beach; (850) 934-3300 or (800) 934-3001; www.pensacola beachresort.net. Offers a Gulf beach, two pools, and continental breakfast; pet friendly. $–$$$

Holiday Inn Express Pensacola Beach. 333 Fort Pickens Rd., Pensacola Beach; (805) 932-3536 or (800) HOLIDAY. Formerly the Dunes, this Gulf-front resort has a heated pool, continental breakfast, golf and recreational packages. $$–$$$$

For More Information

Pensacola Convention and Visitors Information Center. 1401 East Gregory St., Pensacola 32501; (850) 434-1234 or (800) 874-1234; www.visitpensacola.com.

Emerald Coast

About a half-hour east of Gulf Breeze on Hwy. 98.

East of the Navarre Beach bridge, the road leads to Fort Walton Beach and Destin, a stretch of seashore known as the Emerald Coast. It marks the onset of coastal Hwy. 98. What was one of Florida's most scenic drives is fast becoming a peek-a-boo game between emerald green water and the condos, hotels, and seaside cottages that line the shore.

Fort Walton Beach begins on the mainland and spills onto Okaloosa Island, where the gorgeous white beaches have attracted sun-seekers for decades. In years past, this resort town had become a tacky haven for students on spring break. However, it has spruced up its image with a more modern look that enhances its appeal and affordability for families. The attractions are small, a couple of hours' worth of entertainment, which works well for fitting in beach time—a must in this land of dunes and shimmering green water.

Besides fun-time diversions, the Fort Walton Beach area offers some nice, small learning experiences that won't tax the kids' attention spans.

Just a bridge away from Fort Walton Beach's east end, Destin is a newer version of a seaside resort. Its amusement parks are on a grander scale, and the town in general is better thought out. It has a reputation as the World's Luckiest Fishing Village and

Seafood **Satiation**

The **Destin Seafood Festival** takes place each year during the first week of October, and 30,000 people turn up to partake of its goodies. About twenty restaurants sell samples of their best dishes from booths, and festivalgoers can nosh while they tour arts and crafts displays or listen to bands. For the younger set, from toddlers to teens, there's Tadpole Town, with rides and a kids' activity tent. Festival admission is free.

maintains an extensive fleet of fishing charters, tournaments, and seafood restaurants to prove it.

Amberjack, triggerfish, snapper, and grunts are common catches. Billfishing for sailfish and marlin is good from summer through fall. The town promotes its good fortune with shark, king mackerel, billfish, and cobia tournaments throughout the year. Destin/Ft. Walton Beach/Emerald Coast Visitors Center (800-322-3319).

Air Force Armament Museum (ages 6 to 12)

100 Museum Dr., Eglin Air Force Base; (850) 651-1808; www.afarmamentmuseum.com/. Open 9:30 a.m. to 4:30 p.m. daily; closed federal holidays. Admission is free.

Warplane hounds can whet their appetites on indoor and outdoor aircraft, and missile, bomb, and weapon exhibits. The park outside is literally cluttered with monster fighter craft (including one called "Warthog") and their artillery. There's also a picnic grounds. Inside, a thirty-two-minute movie explains the history of the Eglin base and its role in the development of armament, and two cockpits give kids a hands-on experience.

American Spirit Party Boat Fishing

194 Hwy 98 East, just east of the Destin Bridge; (850) 837-1293; americanspiritpartyboat fishing.com. Fare is $45 per person for a half-day excursion (plus tax); half price for kids ages 8 to 12.

Some of the best fishing party boats on the scene. The crew is helpful with reeling in and cleaning your catch.

Beasley County Park

East of Fort Walton Beach on Hwy. 98 East.

One of the nicest Fort Walton Beach public access points, it frames a bed of Okaloosa's famous fluffy sands between huge dunes and that indescribable green sea. It is well maintained with a Florida-style shelter, picnic facilities, and lifeguards.

Big Kahuna's (all ages)

1007 Hwy 98 East, Destin; (850) 837-4061. Seasonal hours—during summer, it opens at 10 a.m. and closes according to demand; it's closed during winter. Call park in advance before you go, or visit its Web site, www.bigkahunas.com. Water park admission is $36.99 for those 48 inches or taller; $29.99 for seniors and those under 48 inches tall and 3 years or older; 2 and younger are free. Golf, go-kart, and adrenaline ride fees range from $6.29 to $54.99 for combinations.

The grandest of Destin's kid parks, it brags up its water park for "the world's longest tube river," and the Bombs Away Bay with Mayan ruins and a real B-25 bomber. On the dry side, it has carnival games, fifty-four holes of miniature golf, go-karts, kiddie land, a Vertical Accelerator that drops ten stories and two other "adrenaline attractions," an ice-cream parlor, and other junk-food concessions. Activities are limited in the winter months.

The Emerald Coast Science Center (ages 3 to 10)

139 Brooks St., off Hwy. 98 west of the bridge to Okaloosa Island, Fort Walton Beach; (850) 664-1261; www.ecscience.org. Sept to May open 9 a.m. to 2 p.m. Mon through Fri; 11 a.m. to 4 p.m. Sat and Sun. June to Aug open 9 a.m. to 4 p.m. Mon through Fri; 11 a.m. to 4 p.m. Sat and Sun. Admission is $5.00 for adults, $4.00 for seniors and kids 13 to 17, and $3.50 for children ages 3 to 12.

Make a 4-foot bubble, play on the computer, and experience a wind tunnel among the 250 interactive displays. There are critters, like geckos and snakes, and science experimentation that intrigues all ages.

Gulfarium (all ages)

1010 Hwy 98 East, Fort Walton Beach; (850) 244-5169; www.gulfarium.com. Opens at 9 a.m.; shows begin at 10 a.m., noon, 2 and 4 p.m., and a summer 6 p.m. show. Admission is $19.25 for adults, $16.75 for seniors, and $11.50 for children ages 3 to 10. **Free** for ages 2 and under (tax not included). Military is $1 off those prices.

At Fort Walton Beach's premier attraction, dolphins and seals perform acts and scuba divers demonstrate. The state's second oldest such facility, it also does rehabilitation and educational work. Gulfarium has a beach setting, which makes it feel more natural to see dolphins leaping into the air.

Henderson Beach State Park

17000 Emerald Coast Parkway, Destin; (850) 837-7550; www.floridastateparks.org/henderson beach/default.cfm. Open 8 a.m. to sunset daily. Park entrance is $6 per vehicle, $3 for single occupant.

Destin's premier beach, it spans a beautiful dunesy stretch east of town, away from the crowds. The park recently added sixty campsites to its facilities.

Indian Temple Mound Museum (ages 4 to 10)

139 Miracle Strip Parkway (Hwy. 98), just west of the bridge to Okaloosa Island, Fort Walton Beach; (850) 833-9595; www.fwb.org/museum. Open Mon to Sat 10 a.m. to 4:30 p.m. Admission is $5.00 for adults, $4.50 for seniors and military, and $3.00 for children ages 4 to 17.

The centerpiece of the attraction, an 800-year-old, 17-foot-tall mound, took 100,000 cubic feet of soil to build—an estimated 500,000 basketsful carried by natives to the site. The mound was used for worship and held the home of the tribe's political and religious leader. The museum showcases the largest collection of native Indian ceramic artifacts in the United States. Admission includes entry to the Camp Walton Schoolhouse and the Garnier Post Office Museum.

James W. Lee Park

Scenic Hwy. 98.

It lets you park for **free** (but the lot fills quickly on sunny days) and has a popular seafood restaurant and picnic shelters.

On a **Budget**

- **Capitol Complex,** Tallahassee, free admission
- **Museum of Florida History,** Tallahassee, free admission
- **Mission San Luis Archaeological and Historic Site,** Tallahassee, free admission
- **National Museum of Naval Aviation,** Pensacola, free admission to most parts
- **Naval Live Oaks,** Gulf Breeze, free admission
- **Air Force Armament Museum,** Fort Walton Beach, free admission
- **Alvin's Island-Magic Mountain Store,** Panama City Beach, free admission
- **Junior Museum of Bay County,** Panama City, free admission

Kokomo Snorkeling Headquarters

400 Harbor Blvd., behind Marina Cafe, Destin; (850) 837-9029; www.kokomosnorkeling .com. Fares are $26 for adults, $22 for children 12 and under, and $15 for nonsnorkelers for a three-hour trip.

Snorkeling excursions take you to live shell and fish finds in clear waters. Open Apr through Oct. Reservations suggested.

Okaloosa Island Park

Hwy. 98, Fort Walton Beach.

Boardwalk complex offers access to the beach's amazingly white sands and the Okaloosa Fishing Pier, as well as shopping and dining.

The Track Family Recreation Center (all ages)

1125 Hwy 98, Destin; (850) 654-4668; www.funatthetrack.com. Open in the summer from 9 a.m. to midnight. Off-season hours vary. Closing hours may vary according to attendance. Admission is charged per activity.

Go-karts, miniature golf, bungee jumping, kiddie rides, video arcade.

Where to Eat

A.J.'s Seafood and Oyster Bar. 116 Hwy 98 East, just east of the Destin Bridge, Destin; (850) 837-1913; www.ajs-destin.com/. Serves the best of local seafood daily for lunch and dinner. $$–$$$

Fudpucker's. 20001-A Emerald Coast Hwy, Destin; (850) 654-4200; www.fudpuckers .com/destin.htm. Recently expanded with ample outside decks. Shipwreck motif, casual, with a comprehensive menu of faddish munchies, burgers, and seafood. Lunch and dinner daily. Menu for "little puckers." Gator show (free) on the hour from 8 a.m. to 8 p.m. $$

Where to Stay

Marina Bay Resort. 80 Miracle Strip Parkway, Fort Walton Beach; (850) 244-5132; www.marinabayfla.com. On Intracoastal Waterway. Boat dock. Amenities include full kitchen, heated pool, sauna, and bicycles. $–$$$

SunDestin Beach Resort. 1040 Hwy 98 East, Destin; (850) 837-7093 or (800) 336-4853; www.sundestinresort.com/. One- to three-bedroom modern apartments with indoor and outdoor pools, health club, shuffleboard, and kids' recreational program in season. $$–$$$$

For More Information

Emerald Coast Convention and Visitors Bureau. 1540 Miracle Strip Parkway, Fort Walton Beach 32549; (850) 651-7131 or (800) 322-3319; www.destin-fwb.com.

South Walton County

South Walton County begins on Hwy. 98 East where Destin leaves off.

Destin encroaches upon what is known as South Walton County, a natural, well-planned stretch of eighteen quaint to upscale beach communities. Scenic Rte. C-30A takes a back-road look at the quiet, away-from-it-all neighborhood off Hwy. 98. At various tucks in the road, beach communities have gathered, each exerting its own character. Grayton Beach, the first beach community between Pensacola and Apalachicola to develop, ca. 1920, is most appealing. Get there via Rte. 283. Historically it attracted surfers, artisans, and free spirits. More recently, yuppies have discovered the town. As a result, Grayton Beach is experiencing a nudge in growth off its traditional path of renovated historic cottages and artsy, humble beach abodes.

An overnight success begun in the early 1980s, Seaside was conceived as the embodiment of beach-town memories—a place where people rocked on front porches and children played carefree in the surf. It grew quickly as an award-winning community model in shades of pastel and Florida-style Victorian chic. One of the Panhandle's most upscale resort options, it embraces families and encourages old-fashioned values, despite its new veneer. Rosemary Beach is east of Seaside, built by the same developer and with the same concept of a self-sustaining community, but is more upscale.

Blue Sky Kayak (ages 5 to 12)

Matt Labo; (850) 368-3155; www.blueskykayak.com. Two-hour tours are $55 for adults and $30 for children under 10.

Families will enjoy the Western Lake Discovery Expedition, an easy guided paddle in shallow waters. Follow in the footsteps of Indians, early settlers, Spanish conquistadors, and others as you look for bobcat, deer, birds, and other wildlife. Their tracks may be spotted on a short stop in their natural habitat.

Eden Gardens State Park (ages 8 to 13)

1 mile north of Hwy. 98 on Rte. 395; Point Washington; (850) 231-4214; www.floridastate parks.org/edengardens/. Gardens are open 8 a.m. to sundown. Guided mansion tours are offered on the hour from 10 a.m. to 3 p.m. Thurs through Mon. Admission to the park is $4 per vehicle. Mansion tour is $3 for adults, $1.50 for children ages 12 and younger.

A remnant of the region's lumbering era, this neoclassic plantation-style manor is the centerpiece for gracious gardens of ancient moss-dripping live oaks and blossoming camellias and azaleas. Peak blooming period is mid-March. Bring a picnic lunch, tour the house, and revel in the peace and Old South beauty.

Grayton Beach State Park (all ages)

Route C-30A, 357 Main Park Rd., Santa Rosa Beach; (850) 231-4210; www.floridastateparks .org/graytonbeach. Open 8 a.m. to sunset daily. Park entrance is $5 per vehicle of eight persons or fewer, $1 per extra passenger, cyclist, or pedestrian.

One reason Grayton Beach has been "discovered" is the high national beach rating accorded this park by Dr. Stephen Leatherman, a coastal geographer more commonly known as Dr. Beach. Here, snow white sand dips into spring-clear, aqua waters and builds mounds of grass-tufted dunes. Not far off the beach, forests of pines and fresh- and salt-water lakes make you feel like you've suddenly arrived in the mountains. The juxtaposition of the two contrasting terrains provides a pleasant disarray in your sense of place. There's lake and Gulf fishing, with a boat ramp onto the brackish lake. A nature trail tours inland areas. Camping is allowed in thirty-seven wooded sites that have grills, picnic tables, water, and electricity. The park also offers rental cabins. (Reservations are recommended, 800-326-3521.)

Sandestin Golf and Beach Resort (all ages)

9300 Emerald Coast Parkway West, Sandestin; reservations (800) 622-1038 or information (866) 931-3678; www.sandestin.com.

If you're looking for a full-service family resort in this vicinity, look no further than Sandestin. Within this 2,400-acre community, you'll find accommodations from hotel rooms to family villas, a beach, seventy-three holes of golf, tennis, bike rentals, Kid Zone summer programs, a pirate's playground, a nature park, and a marina that rents boats and organizes fishing charters. For older kids, the sailing school is super. $$$

Seaside Kids Programs

Each summer, Camp Seaside (850-231-2246) keeps the children of resort guests productively occupied with recreational and crafts projects. The resort also sponsors special enrichment programs throughout the year, such as a children's architectural camp. Ruskin Place, the community's artist colony, offers workshops for both children and adults. One shop lets them paint their own pottery pieces. Storytelling takes place at the town's outdoor amphitheater.

Topsail Hill State Park (ages 6 to 13)

7525 West Scenic Hwy 30A, Santa Rosa Beach; (850) 267-0299; www.floridastateparks.org/
TopsailHill. Open 8 a.m. to sunset. Admission is $3 per vehicle of eight persons or fewer,
$1 per extra passenger, cyclist, or pedestrian.

Its undeveloped beachfront serves as a nature conservatory and is touted as the most
pristine, primitive coastal stretch in Florida. Unregimented sand trails take you through
cypress swamp, pine forest, sand scrub, and heaving dunes beach with few souls in sight.
An RV resort has been added in recent years, and bungalows are available for rent.

Where to Eat

Bud & Alley's. 2236 Rte. 30A, Seaside;
(850) 231-5900. The place to go for a family
splurge. Creative, cutting-edge dishes, kids'
menu, seaside atmosphere. Open daily for
lunch and dinner March through October;
Closed two weeks each December. $$$

Gilligan's. 530 Hwy 98E, Destin; (850) 650-
4400. Not his island, but casual dining for
lunch and dinner on a deck overlooking water
and beach. Kids' menu. $–$$$

Goatfeathers. 3865 Rte. 30A, Santa Rosa
Beach; (850) 267-3342. Family favorite with
seafood sandwiches and po'boys, Louisiana
specialties, and fun finger foods. Lunch and
dinner seven days a week. $$$

Pompano Joe's Seafood House. Miramar
Beach; 2237 Old Hwy 98, Destin; (850) 837-
2224. On the beach and replete with colorful
seaside character and great food. Lunch and
dinner daily. $$$

Where to Stay

Rosemary Beach Cottages. Rosemary
Beach; (888) 855-1551; www.rosemarybeach
.com. At this very upscale version of Seaside
you may rent everything from (a very few)
hotel rooms to cottages to large and sumptu-
ous homes. Be prepared to walk a lot and
climb stairs at times, as the emphasis here is
on recreating a tight urban setting with multi-
story buildings. $$$–$$$$

**Sandestin Beach Hilton Sandestin
Beach Golf Resort & Spa.** 4000 Sandestin
Blvd. South, Destin, Florida; (850) 267-9500
or (800) 367-1271. Minimum age to check in
is 25. Four hundred of the 600 suites have
bunk beds for the kids. Kitchenettes, a well-
planned kids program, and use of Sandestin
Resort facilities. $$$

Seaside Cottages. Seaside ; (866) 966-
2565; www.cottagerentalagency.com. More
than 270 cottages—from one- to six-bedroom,
fully furnished and character replete—are
perfect for family seaside vacations. Swimming pools, tennis courts, playground,
croquet, shuffleboard, recreational rentals.
Three-day minimum in summer and over holidays in some cottages. (Prices are per unit.)
$$$–$$$$

For More Information

**South Walton Tourist Development
Council.** P.O. Box 1248, Santa Rosa Beach
32459; (850) 267-1216; www.beachesof
southwalton.com.

Panama City Beach and Panama City

About half a mile east of Seaside on Highway 98.

The Disney World of the Panhandle, Panama City Beach brims with attractions and activities tailored to families. It wins awards for its good value, but avoid it at spring break.

Most of the community's attractions lie on Hwy. 98 (Panama City Beach Parkway) and Alternate 98 (Front Beach Road/Thomas Drive). That makes them the most-traveled routes, ones you want to avoid in the middle of the day during peak spring break and summer periods. The gorgeous beach and Gulf waters focus vacationer attention on water sports, from diving and snorkeling to Jet-Skiing and fishing.

Alvin's Island-Magic Mountain Store (ages 2 to 6)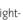

12010 Front Beach Rd., Panama City Beach; (850) 234-3048 or (888) 4-ALVINS; www.alvins island.com. Open 8 a.m. to midnight daily.

Across the side street from the amusement parks, it is part souvenir mart, part free sight-seeing attraction, with aquariums, alligator-feeding shows, and tropical birds to entertain the kids while you pick up inexpensive T-shirts, shells, toys, and Florida souvenirs. By the way, there are six Alvin's in Panama City Beach alone, dozens elsewhere throughout Florida. This one happens to be a hop away from the rides.

Gulf World Marine Park (ages 4 to 12)

15412 Front Beach Rd., Panama City Beach; (850) 234-5271; www.gulfworldmarinepark .com. Open 9 a.m. to 5 p.m. daily (shortened hours in winter). Admission is $24 for adults, $15 for children ages 5 to 11; 4 and under free. Dolphin Encounter, $110 to $150, depending on the season.

Besides the usual marine-park attractions, it offers scuba demonstrations and educational dolphin and sea lion shows. Kids can touch a stingray and watch a shark feeding. The attraction also has tropical gardens graced by flamingos, parrots, and a loggerhead turtle and shark channel, plus a dolphin encounter program.

Junior Museum of Bay County (ages 4 to 12)

1731 Jenks Ave., Panama City; (850) 769-6128; www.jrmuseum.org. Open 10 a.m. to 5 p.m. Mon through Fri and 10 a.m. to 4 p.m. Sat. Suggested donations are $5 per person, 1 year old and under free.

Nature trails, a train engine, a pioneer village, and live chickens and ducks make learning fun. Indoor exhibits teach about the body, nature, and other scientific elements with games and interactivities.

Museum of Man in the Sea (ages 6 to 12)

17314 Panama City Beach Parkway, Panama City Beach; (850) 235-4101; www.maninthesea
.org. Open 10 a.m. to 4 p.m. daily. Admission is $5.00 for adults, $2.50 for children ages 6
to 16.

This unusual museum underscores the area's reputation for great diving. It traces the
history of underwater adventure from its humble beginnings and diving bells to modern
times and recreational scuba equipment. Kids gravitate to the exhibits of treasures from
Florida shipwrecks.

Ripley's Believe It Or Not! Museum (all ages)

9907 Front Beach Rd., Panama City Beach; (850) 230-6113; www.ripleyspanamacitybeach
.com. Opens at 10 a.m. daily. Closes at 11 p.m. Mon through Fri and midnight Sat and Sun;
last tickets sold one hour before closing. Museum admission is $15.99 for adults, $12.99
for children ages 6 to 12; under 6 free. Combo tickets available.

This brand-new museum, built to resemble a luxury liner run aground, houses hundreds
of strange and unusual exhibits. The bizarre gives way to the unique in a stretch limo
plated with gold coins worth $1.3 million. For an additional fee, you can take a ride in a
moving theater.

Sea Dragon Pirate Cruise (all ages)

5325 North Lagoon Dr., Panama City Beach; (850) 234-7400 or (866) 964-6461; www.pirate
cruise.net. Fares are $21 for adults 15 and older, $19 for seniors, $17 for children ages 3 to
14, $11 for children ages 1 and 2; babies free. From 10 a.m. daily, weather permitting.
Call for schedule.

Heave-ho mateys for a two-hour cruise on a pirate ship within cannon range of Shell
Island. Pirate hats are the headgear of the day for little privateers hunting for treasure.

Shipwreck Island (ages 3 to 12)

12201 Middle Beach Rd., Panama City Beach; (850) 234-0368; www.shipwreckisland.com.
Open generally 10:30 a.m. to 5:00 p.m., but the schedule varies. Closed after Labor Day
until Apr. Admission is $32 for persons taller than 50 inches, $27 for persons between 35
and 50 inches tall, $21 for seniors. Free for those under 35 inches tall.

This attraction offers rides the likes of Tadpole Hole, Elephant Slide (all for tot-types), and
the thrilling Raging Rapids, Pirate's Plunge, and the six-story White Knuckle River tube
ride. Lifeguards supervise. No food or coolers can be brought into the park.

St. Andrews State Park/Shell Island (all ages)

East end of Thomas Drive, 4607 State Park Lane, Panama City Beach; (850) 233-5140; www
.floridastateparks.org/StAndrews. Park entrance is $8 per vehicle with up to eight passen-
gers, $1 for a single passenger, and for extra passengers, bicyclists, and pedestrians. The
shuttle to Shell Island costs $9.50 for adults, $5.50 for children ages 6 to 12. Snorkel equipment rentals available. Shuttle is closed during the off-season and runs every hour or half
hour, 10 a.m. to 4 p.m., Mar to Oct.

When you're ready to get away from the Ferris wheels and racetracks, this is your place. Set up camp and bask on the glorious white beach, or follow nature trails into pine forest and have a picnic. Fishing enthusiasts can cast from its gulfside pier, bayside pier, or from the rock jetty at the pass between the park and Shell Island.

Zoo World (ages 2 to 10)

9008 Front Beach Rd., Panama City Beach; (850) 230-1243 or (850) 230-4839; www.zoo worldpcb.net. Open 9:30 a.m. to 5:30 p.m. Mon through Sat and 11 a.m. to 5:30 p.m. Sun. Admission is $15 for adults, $12 for children ages 4 to 11 (plus tax); 3 and under, free. Military and seniors, ask about a lower rate.

Endangered animals and other rare creatures are among the inhabitants here. A petting zoo and infant care facility are prime attractions. You can buy a bucket of feed and even pet a giraffe. Sadly, the very popular Tonda, the orangutan, died in March 2009.

Where to Eat

Capt. Anderson's Restaurant. 5551 North Lagoon Dr., Panama City Beach; (850) 234-2225 or (888) US-TOP-50; www.captander sons.com. A Panama City Beach institution, it specializes in seafood and steaks, prepared by classic methodology and dependably well executed. Expect a wait. Open daily for dinner except Sun. Closed Nov through Jan. $$–$$$$

Pineapple Willy's Beachside Restaurant and Sports Bar. 9875 South Thomas Dr., Panama City Beach; (850) 235-0928 (recorded message) or 235-1225; www.pwillys.com. Outdoor deck and indoor dining room seating overlook the beach. Specialty is Jack Daniel's barbecue ribs served in a plastic souvenir bucket. Sandwiches, salads, seafood, and kids' menu. Lunch and dinner daily. $–$$$

Treasure Ship. 3605 Thomas Dr., Panama City Beach; (850) 234-8881; www.thetreasure ship.com. What could be more exciting than dinner on a treasure ship? This ship-shaped restaurant overlooks bay waters. The staff, dressed like pirates, serve seafood and steaks. The main dining room serves dinner only, but the waterfront Hook's Grille and Grog is open for lunch and dinner. $–$$$

Uncle Ernie's Bayfront Grill and Brew House. 1151 Bayview Ave., Panama City; (850) 763-8427; www.uncleerniesbayfrontgrill .com. Dine overlooking St. Andrews Bay in a late-1800s restored home and enjoy some of the best seafood, salads, and sandwiches around. Open daily for lunch and dinner. $$–$$$

Where to Stay

The Boardwalk Beach Resort. 9400 South Thomas Dr., Panama City Beach; (850) 234-3484 or (800) 224-GULF; www.board walkbeachresort.com. Actually two hotels in one, with 320 rooms in a variety of styles and ranges, interconnected by a beachfront boardwalk. Restaurants (kids eat free), beach bars, kids' club, and playgrounds. $–$$$$

Edgewater Beach Resort. 11212 Front Beach Rd., Panama City Beach; (800) 874-8686; www.edgewaterbeachresort.com. A step above most other resorts on the beach, this condominium resort features well-equipped luxury one- to three-bedroom accommodations, a fetching lagoon pool area, a restaurant, tennis, golf, and organized kids' activities. $–$$$$

Flamingo Motel. 15525 Front Beach Rd., Panama City Beach; (850) 234-2232; www

Other Panama City Beach
Amusement Parks and Attractions

Super Speed Fun Park (ages 4 to 12) 9523 Front Beach Rd.; (850) 234-1588. A haunted house and 3-D black-light minigolf add extra fun to the go-kart and bumper boat rides. Open daily 10 a.m. to midnight (summer); price depends on activity but starts at $5.63 (plus tax).

Airboat Adventures (ages 4 to 12) Beside West Bay Bridge, Hwy. 79, 14852 Bayview Circle; (850) 230-3822; www.swampvette.com. Look for wildlife in a boat powered by a huge fan. Half-hour ride $18.95 adults, $11.95 children.

Barnacle Bay (ages 4 to 12) 11209 Front Beach Rd.; (850) 234-7792. Generally open 10 a.m. to midnight in spring/summer, 10 a.m. to 8 p.m. in winter. Charge for eighteen holes is $8.50 for golfers ages 8 and older and $7.00 for children ages 4 to 7 (plus tax). Miniature golf.

Coconut Creek Mini Golf and Gran Maze (ages 4 to 12) 9807 Front Beach Rd.; (850) 234-2625. Opens daily at 9 a.m. Admission is $16.00 for unlimited use of facilities, $9.50 for eighteen holes of golf or maze play.

Rock It Lanes (ages 7 to 12) 513 Beckrich Rd.; (850) 249-2695; www.rockit lanes.com. Open 10 a.m. to 2 a.m. Mon through Sat and noon to 2 a.m. Sun. $5 skating rink; call for information on bowling, billiards, and a mega arcade with 130 games.

Capt. Anderson's Marina (ages 4 to 12) 5550 North Lagoon Dr.; (850) 234-3435; www.captainandersonsmarina.com. Open daily 9 a.m. to noon and 1 to 4 p.m. $18 adults, $10 children 2 to 11. Watch dolphins and other sea life on a glass-bottom boat cruise to Shell Island where you can add to your shell collection.

.flamingomotel.com. Family oriented, lush, and beachfront. Rooms and efficiencies sleep up to eight. Refrigerators in all rooms, full kitchens in others. Two swimming pools and hot tub. Ask about special family rates. $–$$

Marriott Bay Point Resort Village. 4200 Marriott Dr. off Thomas Drive, Panama City Beach; (850) 236-6000 or (800) 874-7105. A destination golf resort away from the beach, it offers full services, including kids' program, biking, exercise room, marina, and pools. $$–$$$$

For More Information

Panama City Beach Convention and Visitors Bureau. 17001 Panama City Beach Parkway (mailing address: P.O. Box 9473, Panama City Beach 32417), Panama City Beach; (850) 234-6575 or (800) PC-BEACH; www.panamacitybeachfl.com.

Apalachicola Area

Continue along Hwy. 98 for about an hour's drive.

East of Panama City, the Panhandle pace relaxes. Nature and hometowns dictate a tempo that seems worlds away from the airbrushed T-shirt and body piercing shops to the west. Mexico Beach presents a laid-back strip of sand not yet infected by high-rises or high prices. The distinctive odor of pulp mills greets you as you cross the bridge to Port St. Joe, but past that, the gulfside town offers superb scalloping, fishing, and diving, plus a historic site or two.

Continue along Rte. C-30 east of Port St. Joe about 40 miles to find a secluded sliver of Gulf Coast shoreline, a land of minimal development and beach wilderness known as Cape San Blas, and its offshore loner island, St. Vincent. Cape San Blas juts from Panhandle Gulf shores like the prong of a sprung safety pin. Long and lanky, the peninsula, with its tenuous grasp to the mainland, is more like an island in its isolation.

Apalachicola, which shares its name with a river and a species of local oyster, is one of Florida's prettiest old towns. Developed in the early 1800s as a cotton port, its waterfront warehouses and other historic buildings have been restored to preserve fifty-some sites—more pre–Civil War structures than anywhere else in Florida. Many of the old buildings hold galleries and charming boutiques that beg to be browsed. Stop in at the local chamber of commerce for a historic-district walking tour.

A trip across the 4-mile-long Bryant Patton Bridge to St. George Island is a must. The bridge crosses Apalachicola Bay at Eastpoint. Watch for the signs. Only recently discovered as a summer beach refuge and fishing hot spot, St. George Island offers overnighters an inn, a motel, state park camping, and house rentals. This is a good place to journey for lunch, where something with oysters is *de rigueur*.

East of Apalachicola in Carrabelle, you'll see the world's smallest police station on Hwy. 98.

The Constitution Convention State Museum (ages 6 to 12)

200 Allen Memorial Way, Port St. Joe; off Hwy. 98 east of Port St. Joe; (850) 229-8029. Tours are given 9 a.m. to noon and 1 to 5 p.m. Thurs through Mon. Admission is $1 for visitors age 7 or older.

Turn off the beach road and look for the small building at the north end of the parkway. Talking mannequins reenact Florida's first state Constitution Convention and the history of a long-gone town named St. Joseph, which was decimated by hurricane and yellow fever in the mid-1800s.

John Gorrie State Museum (ages 8 to 12)

1 block off Hwy. 98 on Sixth Street, Apalachicola; (850) 653-9347; www.floridastateparks .org/johngorriemuseum. Open 9 a.m. to 5 p.m. Thurs through Mon. Admission is $2 for visitors ages 7 and older.

Florida **Trivia**

Amazing Scallop Facts What has one hundred blue eyes and can swim sideways? A Florida sea scallop. Once common throughout the state, its populations have suffered from pollution and other factors. Today, recreational scalloping is allowed only north of the Suwannee River between July 1 and September 10. Limits apply. Commercial scalloping has been banned statewide. Most popular scalloping locales are around Port St. Joe near Apalachicola and at Steinhatchee on the Nature Coast.

This museum pays tribute to Apalachicola's most important historical figure, a nineteenth-century physician who, in trying to develop a method for making yellow fever sufferers more comfortable, invented a forerunner of today's ice-making machine and air conditioner.

Salinas Park (ages 2 to 10)
On Rte. C-30E, near the intersection of Rte. C-30, Cape San Blas.

This roadside park embraces a beautiful white beach, shady picnic areas, a playground, and a dunes-top gazebo. When the weather is warm, the biting insects are horrendous, so come prepared. Also beware of sandspurs when you step off the boardwalk.

St. George Island State Park (all ages)
**1900 East Gulf Beach Dr., St. George Island; (850) 927-2111; www.floridastateparks.org/
stgeorgeisland. Open 8 a.m. to sunset daily. Park entrance is $6 per vehicle with up to
eight passengers, $3 for a single passenger, and $1 per extra passenger, bicyclist, and
pedestrian. East end access is $6 for adults, and free for children under 12.**

St. George Island is one long stretch of sand, reached by a 4-mile bridge from Eastpoint, on Hwy. 98 on the mainland. The best beach lies beyond state park gates, where the dunes tower and the birds come to stay warm and nest. Go there to camp, canoe, and hike inland trails along rush-fringed marshes and freshwater ponds.

St. Joseph Peninsula State Park (ages 3 to 12)
**8899 Cape San Blas Rd., Port St. Joe; north of Cape San Blas; (850) 227-1327; www.florida
stateparks.org/STJOSEPH. Open 8 a.m. to sunset daily. Park entrance is $6 per vehicle of
eight persons or fewer, $1 per extra passenger, cyclist, or pedestrian.**

The ultimate beach lies at the end of the road, where civilization meets utter wilderness, at the tip of the cape. Tall dunes sequester the beach from the road and leave you in a still world of ghost crabs and shorebirds. Across the road, a boat ramp and a picnic shelter bring you back in touch with reality. Camp and cabin sites, ADA-compliant campsites, canoe and nature trails, and a 1,650-acre wilderness preserve occupy the park's 2,500 acres. It's a good place to see migratory birds and monarch butterflies.

St. Vincent National Wildlife Refuge (ages 8 to 12)

For permits and information contact the refuge manager at P.O. Box 447, Apalachicola 32329; (850) 653-8808; www.fws.gov/saintvincent. Visitor center at 479 Market St., Apalachicola is open 10 a.m. to 3 p.m. Mon through Thurs.

One of the area's most acclaimed destinations is accessible by charter or private boat only. (Call the Apalachicola Bay Chamber of Commerce, 850-653-9419, for information.) Once a private hunting preserve, it holds a diverse selection of native and exotic wildlife: Asian sambar deer, white-tailed deer, red wolves, and bald eagles. The island's small lakes, ponds, and creeks are open for fishing May through September. Freshwater fish include bream, shellcracker, speckled perch, catfish, and bass. To manage the populations of deer and feral hogs, controlled annual hunts are held. Camping is allowed in conjunction with the hunts. All participants must be approved by the refuge manager.

Where to Eat

Boss Oyster Restaurant. 123 Water St., Apalachicola; (850) 653-9364; www.apalachicolariverinn.com/boss.html. Oysters right from the bay prepared seventeen different ways, plus other seafood specialties (including seafood pizza) in a casual atmosphere. $$–$$$

Gibson Inn's Café MOMI. 51 Ave. C, Apalachicola; (850) 653-2191; www.gibsoninn .com. This is the most formal Apalachicola has to offer, but it's fine for kids, especially for lunch. Seafood is done Florida and Cajun style. $$$

Sisters Restaurant. 236 Reid Ave., Port St. Joe; (850) 229-7121. Lunch on home-cooked specials, salads, and sandwiches at this quaint restaurant. Open daily 11 a.m. to 2 p.m. $–$$

A Woodyard **Adventure**

You don't need to be a camper to know there's a reason raccoons have a striped tail and a mask. As robbers of the animal world, they steal everything they can get their little "hands" on. At the same time they're so cute and inquisitive, that even when annoyed, you can't help but laugh at their antics. As campers we've had them keep us awake rummaging through metal garbage cans, actually pry open a cooler, and run inside the tent to take off with a loaf of bread. But the most memorable incident Scott and I remember took place at St. Joseph's Peninsula State Park. This chubby little beast in the gray-brown fur coat sat up in a tree to watch us toast marshmallows. Of course Scott couldn't resist giving him one. Unable to wash it, of course the mushy insides stuck to his fingers. His solution? He just reached for a towel I'd strung up to dry, and wiped his hands clean.

Where to Stay

Rental homes and rustic cabins are your primary option on Cape San Blas and St. George Island. Elsewhere you'll find inns and B&Bs.

Gibson Inn. 51 Ave. C, Apalachicola; (850) 653-2191; www.gibsoninn.com. Built in 1907 and restored in 1983; each of its thirty-one rooms is individually furnished Victorian style. $–$$

Old Saltworks Cabins. Rte. 30E, Cape San Blas; 1085 Cape San Blas Rd., Port St. Joe; (850) 229-6097. One of several cabin resorts on Cape San Blas, it offers a taste of history and entertainment for the kids. It spreads from Gulf to bay with pleasantly modern cabins, a historic museum that remembers the site's former life as a Civil War salt plant, and Fort Crooked Tree, where kids can intermingle their imaginations with mannequins in Civil War dress. A few one-day cabins, $, and week rates (most cabins) $$$$

For More Information

Apalachicola Bay Chamber of Commerce. 122 Commerce St., Apalachicola 32320; (850) 653-9419; www.apalachicolabay.org.

Gulf County Chamber of Commerce. P.O. Box 964, Port St. Joe 32457; (850) 227-1223; www.gulfcountybusiness.com.

The Big Bend

Continuing along Hwy. 98.

This marshy stretch of shoreline holds a subtle intrigue. Its lack of spectacular sand beaches leaves it forgotten by most tourists other than those looking for plentiful wildlife, fishing towns, and water sports. Some of Florida's earliest Indian and European colonial settlements took advantage of the strategic location at this crossroads between peninsula and panhandle.

This drive skirts a rare stretch of wilderness: the immense, more than half-million-acre Apalachicola National Forest, Wakulla Springs State Park, St. Marks National Wildlife Refuge, and the Aucilla Wildlife Management Area.

Gulf Specimen Marine Laboratories Aquarium (ages 4 to 12)

222 Clark Dr. at Palm Street south of Hwy. 98 (P.O. Box 237, Panacea 32346), Panacea; (850) 984-5297; www.gulfspecimen.org. Open 9 a.m. to 5 p.m. Mon through Fri, 10 a.m. to 4 p.m. Sat, noon to 4 p.m. Sun. Admission is $7:50 for adults, $6 seniors, and $5 for children 3 to 11. Under 3, free.

Jack Rudloe, author of *Living Dock at Panacea* and other Florida-related naturalist books (and the inspiration for the Doc Ford character in the Florida mysteries by Randy Wayne White), operates this nonprofit organization, which stocks schools with sea-life specimens and conducts research. You can visit the lab—unsophisticated but full of great surprises, such as an electric fish. A touch tank and aquariums fill several rooms and hold sharks, stingrays, moray eels, and other unusual creatures that are native to Florida waters.

Florida **Trivia**

Oyster Facts in a Shell On the average, an annual commercial harvest of Apalachicola Bay oysters produces enough meat to cover a football field three deep. Franklin County produces 90 percent of Florida's oysters and 10 percent of the nation's supply. Oyster lovers are still advised to eat raw oysters only in months with an "R" in the name. (In other words, avoid those caught in the warm summer months when the ocean algae bloom.) The young, the old, and those with certain health problems should avoid eating raw oysters altogether.

San Marcos de Apalache Historic Site (ages 7 to 12)
South end of Rte. 363; 148 Old Fort Rd., St. Marks; (850) 922-6007; www.floridastateparks .org/sanmarcos. Open 9 a.m. to 5 p.m. Thurs through Mon. Admission to the museum is $2 for visitors ages 6 and older. Entrance to the grounds is **free.**

St. Marks began its life as an important center, first for the Apalachee Indians and later, ca. 1679, for Spanish explorers, who named it San Marcos de Apalache. Today the remains of the Spanish fort and a museum bear witness to the early importance of the strategically placed town, now a humble fishing village.

St. Marks National Wildlife Refuge (ages 5 to 12)
Off Hwy. 98; 1255 Lighthouse Rd., St. Marks; (850) 925-6121; www.fws.gov/saintmarks. Visitor center open 8 a.m. to 4 p.m. Mon through Fri and 10 a.m. to 5 p.m. weekends. Park entrance is $5 per car.

A historic lighthouse and monarch butterflies draw most visitors to this vast 65,000 acres of marsh and woodlands. The butterflies arrive in thick, colorful swarms every fall, making trees seem to blossom in orange and black. The best place to find the butterflies is at the refuge's lighthouse on the bay. St. Marks also offers biking, hiking, and canoeing opportunities.

Wakulla Springs State Park (ages 3 to 12)
North of Hwy. 98, west of St. Marks; 550 Wakulla Park Dr., Wakulla Springs; (850) 926-0700; www.floridastateparks.org/wakullasprings. Open 8 a.m. to sunset daily. Park entrance is $6 per vehicle of eight persons or fewer, $1 per extra passenger, cyclist, or pedestrian. Boat tour fares are $6 for adults and $4 for children ages 12 and under for a forty-five-minute tour.

Swim in one of the world's deepest and largest freshwater springs. Take a glass-bottom boat or jungle cruise into the realm of alligators and anhingas. One of the park's highlights is its 1937 marble-floored Wakulla Springs Lodge, where you can get a room, an ice-cream cone, some lunch, or a T-shirt.

The Wilderness Way (ages 7 to 12)

3152 Shadeville Rd., Wakulla; (850) 877-7200; www.thewildernessway.net. Recently relocated from Tallahassee, 12 miles to the north, Open Tues to Sat, 9 a.m. to 6 p.m., Sun 10 a.m. to 5 p.m.

For a guided introduction into the region's wilderness, join a paddling or hiking trip with the history and wildlife experts at the Wilderness Way. Canoeing and kayaking clinics; bird-watching; paddling trips on the St. Marks, Wacissa, Aucilla, or Wakulla Rivers; and specialty trips are also available.

Where to Eat

Wakulla Springs Lodge. Wakulla Springs State Park, 550 Wakulla Park Dr., Wakulla Springs; (850) 224-5950. A grand lodge built in 1937 and overlooking the spring, it's a great place for a Southern-style breakfast, lunch, or dinner any day of the week. Kids' menu and soda fountain. $$

Where to Stay

Wakulla Springs Lodge. Wakulla Springs State Park, 550 Wakulla Park Dr., Wakulla Springs; (850) 224-5950. A historic lodge set on the banks of a sparkling, wildlife-rich spring. $$

Weekend Jaunt: Northern Springlands

Head east off Hwy. 98/19 to visit the largest grouping of natural springs in the world. For information, an interactive map, a printable/viewable copy of their Visitor Guide, and phone numbers of area chambers of commerce and visitor centers check the Web site at www.originalflorida.org.

Wakulla Springs heads Florida's springlands, a concentration of more than one hundred inland limestone springs that spreads to the south as far as Orlando. Before beaches became a magnet, these windowpane springs and their resultant health resorts attracted Florida's earliest tourists. Today the springs are a mecca for snorkelers and scuba enthusiasts, though entering the underground water-filled cavern system is for trained professionals only. The roads that head east off Hwy. 98/19 lead to these springs, as well as to their state parks and a wealth of wildlife, oak canopies, diving caves, and canoeing outposts. Many of the springs are part of the Suwannee River basin. Most of the attraction is natural, but you may enjoy exploring some of the quiet old towns, such as High Springs, where you can stroll through antiques shops, arts and crafts boutiques, a museum, and historic bed-and-breakfast inns in vintage buildings.

Florida Trivia

Fluttering By The Panhandle is a major hatching locale for monarchs as they make their annual 5,000-mile journey from northern Canada to Mexico. It takes five generations of butterflies to complete the trip. From late October through November, the region dances with the orange and black flutter of swarming wings. Prime monarch rest stops include St. Marks National Wildlife Refuge and St. Joseph Peninsula State Park.

Ichetucknee Springs State Park (ages 6 to 12)

12087 S.W. U.S. Hwy 27, Fort White; (386) 497-4690; www.floridastateparks.org/ichetucknee springs. Two entrances are located off Hwy. 27 between Fort White and Branford, with tram transportation between the two entrances (admission at the north entrance may be limited in peak summer season). Open 8 a.m. to sunset daily. Park entrance is $6 per vehicle of eight persons or fewer, $3 for a single passenger. Additional fees for canoeing and tubing apply.

The "river" is about 20 feet wide in places, and in peak times you could walk down over the tops of inner tubes. Weekdays are better; we've gone down it totally alone (and we had to hoof it back too, the tram shuttle only runs when there is enough business.) The preferred activity in the 72-degree waters of this designated National Natural Landmark is inner-tubing, bring your own or rent them. Canoeing, swimming, snorkeling, hiking, and camping are also pursued. Use is limited to 2,000 visitors a day to protect the natural environs. Canoe, raft, and tube rentals are available inside and outside the park.

O'Leno State Park (ages 7 to 12)

6 miles north of High Springs on Hwy. 441, High Springs; (386) 454-1853; www.floridastate parks.org/oleno. Open 8 a.m. to sunset daily. Park entrance is $5 per vehicle of eight persons or fewer, $1 per extra passenger, cyclist, or pedestrian.

Hikers especially love it here! Its 15 miles of nature trails explore an old limestone quarry, underground river, and natural bridge.

Stephen Foster Folk Culture Center State Park (ages 6 to 12)

Hwy. 41 North Park, White Springs; (386) 397-4331; www.floridastateparks.org/stephen foster. Open 8 a.m. to sunset daily; carillon tower, craft shops, and museum open 9 a.m. to 5 p.m. Park entrance is $5 per vehicle of eight persons or fewer, $1 per extra passenger, cyclist, or pedestrian.

Stephen Foster, who wrote "Old Folks at Home," included the Suwannee River because it had the right number of syllables. He never saw the river and so missed out on one of Florida's wonders. In addition to its history museum and memorial to Florida's favorite composer, this popular attraction lets you experience "way down upon the Suwannee River." At Craft Square, demonstrators practice old-time craftsmanship and artisans sell

Way Down upon the Suwannee River

The historic Suwannee River originates in Georgia's Okefenokee Swamp and runs along eleven Florida counties for 235 miles. It holds more than seventy springs and was a center of ancient Timucuan Indian civilization. Composer Stephen Foster, who wrote "Old Folks at Home," Florida's state song, never even saw the Suwannee River, nor did he step foot in Florida.

their wares while a carillon tower chimes the well-loved tunes of Stephen Foster. The gift shop sells old-fashioned toys and stick candy. First Saturdays feature a daytime arts festival and a coffeehouse at 7 p.m. with music, stories, etc. Campsites and picnicking facilities are also available.

Other Folk Culture Center events include:

• Stephen Foster Day, January

• Antique Tractor and Gas Engine Show, April

• Florida Folk Festival, May

• Quilt Show and Sale, October

• Rural Folklife Days, November

• Christmas Festival of Lights, December

Suwannee Canoe Outpost (all ages)

Inside the Spirit of the Suwannee Music Park on Hwy. 129; 2461 Ninety-fifth Dr., Live Oak; (386) 364-4991 or (800) 428-4147; www.canoeoutpost.com. Canoe or kayak rentals are $12 to $34 per adult for day trips, depending upon the trip's duration. Children ages 3 to 12 pay half price.

Canoe/kayak rentals and shuttle outside the park for day and overnight trips.

Florida Trivia

Springs Trivia Florida counts more than 300 natural springs. They are a product of Florida's honeycombed limestone foundation and hydrostatic pressure. About thirty of Florida's springs qualify as first magnitude, meaning they have an average flow of greater than one hundred cubic feet per second. Most of the northland springs maintain a cool 72 degrees year-round.

Panhandle Climes

The four seasons perform more dramatically in the Panhandle than elsewhere in Florida. Temperatures range from an average of 83 degrees in summer to 50 degrees in winter. Snow does occasionally fall at these latitudes. If visiting in late fall, winter, or early spring, pack to dress in layers. Summer and early fall, temperatures stay warm day and night.

The Panhandle sees its share of tropical storm and hurricane warnings June through October. Plenty of advance warning allows time to evacuate.

The Suwannee County Historical Museum (ages 8 to 12)

208 North Ohio Ave., Live Oak; (386) 362-1776; www.museumsusa.org/museums/ info/1160505. Open 9 a.m. to 3 p.m. Tues through Sat. Donations requested.

The museum glorifies the Cracker way of life at its railway station home. New exhibits focus on railroad history and a Timucuan Indian village restoration, plus an extensive telephone history display. The museum also includes a moonshine distillery (no longer working) and a pioneer family kitchen.

Suwannee River State Park (ages 6 to 12)

15 miles west of Live Oak off Hwy. 90; 20185 County Road 132, Live Oak; (386) 362-2746; www.floridastateparks.org/suwanneeriver. Open 8 a.m. to sunset daily. Park entrance is $5 per vehicle of eight passengers or fewer, $1 for a single passenger. Canoe rental for $15 half day or $25 full day.

If you're hooked on canoeing, this is the place to head in these parts. The canoe trail that goes through the park actually begins in the Okeefenokee Swamp in Georgia. Take a short hike along a cliff overlooking the historic Suwanee River to Balance Rock, or go for a dip in a secluded sinkhole. There's also picnicking, a boat ramp, a playground, campsites, and cabin rentals.

The Nature Coast: Cedar Key

Follow Hwy. 98 and take designated side roads. To get to Cedar Key, head south on Rte. 345 out of Chiefland, then west on Rte. 24.

What's south of Florida's Big Bend has been termed "The Nature Coast" in recognition of its flourishing wildlife. Hwy. 98 skirts this area, but you really must side-trip off to see what's so real about Florida in these parts. West of the main highway, the Gulf coastland exudes a quiet, marshy temperament more conducive to thriving fishing villages than resort enclaves. Towns with names such as Keaton Beach and Horseshoe Beach retain the atmosphere of eras past, while Steinhatchee has evolved into a low-key resort devoted to fishing and canoeing. Don't forget to sample the oysters, scallops, blue crabs, and other local delectables.

The best the coast has to offer is Cedar Key, one of Florida's earliest flourishing towns. Pencil manufacturing and lumbering enabled it to prosper in the mid-1800s. In the later 1900s it dwindled to a quiet home for oystermen and sport fishermen, but in recent years Cedar Key has boomed with condos, hotels, restaurants, and an enlarged marina to accommodate all the boaters who make this their mecca. Architecture, even new construction, is very much old Cracker Florida in style. The town sits on two of a cluster of out-of-the-way islands, many of which have been designated as part of Cedar Keys National Wildlife Refuge.

At this unpretentious preserved relic of yesteryear, take a self-guided tour around the historic district; you can get a map from the local chamber of commerce. Cedar Key's waterfront along Dock Street holds what's best loved about the quaint little town—art galleries, artisan shops, and seafood restaurants.

Cedar Key Historical Society Museum (ages 5 to 12)

Second Street at Rte. 24; 609 Second St.; (352) 543-5549. Open 1 to 4 p.m. Sun through Fri, and 11 a.m. to 5 p.m. Sat. Admission is $1 for adults and 50 cents for children.

A small, homey facility in a circa-1870 building, it tells the story—with artifacts, photos, and newspaper clippings—of Cedar Key's past, throughout its various occupations of turtling, sponging, fishing, and pencil-making.

The Cedar Key Museum State Park (ages 8 to 12)

Hodges Avenue and Whitman Drive; 12231 Southwest 166 Court; (352) 543-5350; www .floridastateparks.org/cedarkeymuseum. Open 10 a.m. to 5 p.m. Thurs through Mon. Admission is $2 for those 6 and older; 5 and under, free.

Tucked away in a residential section, the modern museum documents island bygones, from its earliest inhabitants through its various phases of war, lumbering, fiber manufacturing, shipbuilding, and fishing. Its shell collection, donated by an early settler, is a highlight.

Top Family Resorts

1. **Old Saltworks Cabins,** Cape San Blas

2. **Seaside Resort,** Seaside

3. **Sandestin Resort,** Sandestin

4. **St. Joseph Peninsula State Park,** Cape San Blas

Top Family **Beaches and Parks**

1. **Fort Pickens National Park,** Pensacola Beach

2. **Wakulla Springs State Park,** Wakulla Springs

3. **Grayton Beach State Recreation Area,** Grayton Beach

4. **St. Joseph Peninsula State Park,** Cape San Blas

5. **St. George Island State Park,** St. George Island

Cedar Key Seafood Festival; Cedar Key Sidewalk Arts Festival (ages 9 to 12)

(352) 543-5600; www.cedarkey.org.

These two events take place along Second Avenue between Rte. 24 and the downtown city park, and tens of thousands of visitors join town residents each year to celebrate both. The Cedar Key Seafood Festival takes place annually during the third week of October, attracting 30,000 to 40,000 people. In addition to the food, it features arts and crafts, food concessions in the park, and all manner of seafood, from smoked mullet to crab cakes and fresh clams. The arts festival is smaller and occurs in April. Along with the artists exhibiting their wares, there's food, entertainment, live bands, and lots of fun for kids.

Manatee Springs State Park (ages 6 to 12)

End of Rte. 320 off Hwy. 98, 6 miles west of Chiefland; 11650 Northwest 115th St., Chiefland; (352) 493-6072; www.floridastateparks.org/manateesprings. Open 8 a.m. to sunset daily. Park entrance is $6 per vehicle of eight persons or fewer, $1 per extra passenger, cyclist, or pedestrian.

Named for the lovable Florida critter that favors it, the park encompasses a springhead that pumps out an average 100 million gallons of crystalline water daily. Activities include swimming in spring-cooled water, canoeing, kayaking, picnicking, fishing, biking, camping, and hiking the boardwalk through ancient cypress wetlands and into the Suwannee River.

Out-Islands

For transportation to the outer keys, contact Island Hopper at the City Marina Basin; (352) 543-5904; www.cedarkeyislandhopper.com. This pontoon boat makes daily excursions (call for schedule) and also rents boats. Two-hour tours of the outer islands are $21 for adults and $15 for children under age 12. Island drop-offs and pickups are $15 for adults, $10 for children under 12, and you set the pickup time. Boat rentals range from $90 for a four-person boat for four hours to $295 for a nine-person boat for eight hours.

Cedar Key itself has an artificial but pleasant city beach while the outer islands have a mixture of beach, mangroves, and upland hardwoods. Seahorse Key is the most interesting island, with its 52-foot ridge (Florida's highest coastal elevation), sand beach, and defunct

More Things to See and Do
in Northwest Florida

- **Apalachicola River Tours,** Apalachicola; (850) 653-2593
- **Forest Capital State Museum,** Perry; (850) 584-3227
- **Governor's Mansion,** Tallahassee; (850) 488-4661
- **Old City Cemetery,** Tallahassee
- **PJC Planetarium and Theatre,** Pensacola; (850) 484-1150
- **Tallahassee Antique Car Museum,** Tallahassee; (850) 894-9656

lighthouse now used by the University of Florida. The island is an important nesting area for pelicans, egrets, ibises, herons, and ospreys. There is no landing on Seahorse Key at all these days. Snake Key has a nice beach. It once held a quarantine hospital. Atsena Otie, nearest to Cedar Key, held the original town of Cedar Key. Remnants of its early settlements remain. While you may land on the beaches at Snake and Atsena Otie, you are not permitted to go inland (and it's not a great idea anyway; there is good reason for the name "snake"). Visit on the first weekend in May, and you will see one hundred or more small sailboats—including one owned by one of the book authors—parked at the Island Place in the harbor, lined up on Atsena Otie Key, or just flitting back and forth across the shallow waters.

Where to Eat

Akins Bar-B-Q & Grill. 1160 S. Main St. (Hwy 129), Bell; (352) 463-6859. Midway between Cedar Key and Gainesville. The tops in ribs, baked beans, and potato salad. Breakfast, lunch, and dinner daily. $

Coconuts of Cedar Key. 330 Dock St. (very west end); 352-543-6390; www.coconutsofcedarkey.com. Occupies the same funky wood structure that used to house the Captain's Table. There's an outside deck upon which to sit and admire the scenery, and an inside restaurant. Food is casual beachy. $

Fiddler's Restaurant. Hwy. 51 North, Steinhatchee; (352) 498-7427. Order seafood, and you won't find it any fresher than here in the scalloping-fishing capital of the coast. Expect forthright service and genuine sweet tea (according to a sweet-tea critic I know). Kids' menu. $$–$$$

Where to Stay

Beach Front Motel. 873 West First St. (P.O. Box 38, Cedar Key 32625), Cedar Key; (352) 543-5113; www.beachfrontmotelcedarkey.com. Unpretentious with swimming pool, rooms, and efficiencies. Kids under age 6 stay **free.** $$

Cedar Key Bed and Breakfast. 810 Third St., Cedar Key; (352) 543-9000 or (877) 543-5051; www.cedarkeybandb.com. Built in 1880 by the Eagle Cedar Mill as a guesthouse for its employees, it is a quiet spot, shaded by massive oaks, within walking distance of Cedar Key's most interesting places to visit. Though the owners discourage bringing babies and toddlers, well-mannered teens will enjoy its peaceful, gracious charm and a hearty, hot breakfast in the sunny porch dining room. $$–$$$

The Island Place. First and C Streets (P.O. Box 687, Cedar Key 32625), Cedar Key; (352) 543-5307; www.islandplace-ck.com. One of Cedar Key's modern lodging options, it offers thirty waterfront condominiums with one or two bedrooms. Kids under age 6 stay **free.** $$–$$$

Mermaid's Landing. 12685 Rte. 24, Cedar Key; (877) 543-5949; www.mermaidslanding .com. A touch of Old Florida in nine one- to four-room cottages with painted wood floors and pine paneling. Watch the sunset, feed the birds, or kayak on the shallow bay. $–$$

Steinhatchee Landing. Hwy. 51 North, Steinhatchee; (352) 498-3513 or (800) 584-1709. Vernacular-style luxury Florida cottages and homes off the beaten path in a fishing village setting. For families: swimming pool, playground, petting zoo, and canoes rented for a nominal fee. $$$–$$$$

For More Information

Cedar Key Area Chamber of Commerce. P.O. Box 610, Cedar Key 32625; (352) 543-5600; www.cedarkey.org.

Columbia County Tourist Development Council/Florida Welcome Center. 263 Northwest Lake City Ave., Lake City 32055; (386) 758-1397 or 758-1312; www.springs-r-us.com.

Annual Events

Civil War Reenactment. Eden State Gardens, Point Washington; (850) 231-4214. In late January, the gardens host a reenactment of the Seventh Vermont Volunteer Infantry, Company "A" Encampment.

Olustee Battle Festival and Reenactment. Lake City; (386) 752-2031 or (386) 758-0400; www.olusteefestival.com. Actors recall the Confederates' six-hour battle and victory over Union troops during the Civil War in the middle of February. The largest Civil War reenactment in the South. **Free.**

Springtime Tallahassee. Tallahassee; (850) 224-5012 or (800) 628-2866. Tallahassee's big annual event is an extravaganza of parades and fairs that runs for three weeks in April during prime azalea-blooming time. **Free.**

Seaside Easter Egg Hunt. Seaside; (850) 231-5424. An Easter Sunday visit from the Easter Bunny. **Free.**

Suwannee Bicycle Festival. Live Oak; (386) 397-2347; www.suwanneebike.org. Biking, canoeing, snorkeling, tubing, and kayaking in springs country, early May.

ArtsQuest. South Walton County; (850) 237-0885. A weeklong cultural fair that culminates with an art fair at Eden State Gardens early in May.

Billy Bowlegs Festival. Fort Walton Beach; (850) 244-8191 or (800) 322-3319. Starting early June, it's a week of pirate revelry, seafood, and entertainment. **Free.**

Destin Fishing Rodeo. Destin; (850) 837-6734 or (800) 322-3319. A month of fishing tournaments and events in October.

Indian Summer Seafood Festival. Panama City Beach; (800) PC-BEACH. A weekend of country music, seafood, exhibits, and fireworks in October.

Monarch Butterfly Festival. St. Marks National Wildlife Refuge; (850) 925-6121. A celebration of the annual monarch migration in October.

Spooky Springs. Wakulla Springs State Park; (850) 561-7217. Early in November, a night cruise, tricks, and treats.

Blue Angels Homecoming Air Show. Pensacola; (850) 434-1234 or (800) 874-1234. Daredevil stunt-flying by the world-famous team at their home station in July and November. **Free.**

Northeast
Florida

J   ust imagine! History was being made in Florida fifty years before the Pilgrims landed at Plymouth Rock—history of the most raucous, adventuresome sort! The city of St. Augustine, hub of the so-called First Coast, safeguards 400 years of history behind fortress walls and city gates. From St. Augustine north to Amelia Island's Fernandina Beach, from the sixteenth century to the twentieth, a colorful cast of historic characters included youth-seeking Juan Ponce de León, French conquistador Jean Ribault, privateer Francis Drake, French Huguenots, Spanish Minorcans, Civil War heroes, President Ulysses S. Grant, and railroad magnate Henry Flagler. Relics of the long years have been preserved despite Florida's architecture-devastating humidity, termites, and hurricanes.

Besides some of America's oldest structures, northeast Florida boasts a cache of untouted beaches and haunting wildlands of marsh, hardwood forest, and sandhill terrain. Big-city Jacksonville spills out to the Atlantic Ocean, along with the St. Johns River that runs through it. It is the coast's center of culture, commerce, and festivities, which cluster around downtown's riverfront.

The St. Johns, Florida's longest navigable inland waterway, with a length of 342 miles, has played a crucial role in the social history of Jacksonville and the towns along it to the south, from steamboat days to now.

Amelia Island and Fernandina Beach

Take the Rte. A1A exit off I-95 and head east for about twenty minutes.

What are your kids going to love most about Amelia Island? Its great beaches, no doubt. Yet even those who are blasé about history can't help but be intrigued by this island's past. A narrated tour of Amelia's cemeteries or a candlelit walk through an old fort will surely pique their interest. The historic district lies in the Italian Victorian port town of

NORTHEAST FLORIDA

Fernandina Beach. For a walking or driving tour of the area, pick up a copy of *Amelia Now*, available **free** in many stores.

Amelia Island Charter Boat Association (ages 5 to 13)

1 North Front St., Fernandina Harbour Marina, Fernandina Beach; (904) 261-2870; www .ameliaislandcharterboatassociation.com.

To arrange a fishing, sightseeing, sailing, or any type of water excursion, contact the association. Largemouth bass fishing is a specialty in local rivers.

Amelia Island Museum of History (ages 8 to 13)

233 South Third St., Fernandina Beach; (904) 261-7378; www.ameliamuseum.org. Open 10 a.m. to 4 p.m. Mon through Sat and 1 to 4 p.m. Sun. Admission is $7 for adults, $4 for students. Museum tours Mon through Sat at 11 a.m. and 2 p.m. and Sun at 2 p.m. Ghost tours Fri at 6 p.m.; $10 adults, $5 students. Special walking tours (reservations required) are $10 per person, groups of four or more.

Learn about the legends and deep history connected with Amelia Island: why some Timucua Indians didn't cut their hair, why the natives got along with the French but not the Spanish, and the haunting story of the island's namesake. The museum occupies the old county jailhouse and conducts living history tours of its 400 years' worth of artifacts. The ninety-minute tour may get long for younger children, but it is the only way to see the bulk of the exhibits downstairs. The museum also conducts specialty tours of the town's cemetery, lovely old churches, and other themed sights.

TopPicks for Family Fun in Northeast Florida

1. Going back in time at the Colonial Spanish Quarter Museum, St. Augustine

2. Listening to whale and manatee calls at the Museum of Science & History, Jacksonville

3. Talking to Yankee soldiers at Fort Clinch State Park, Fernandina Beach

4. Counting teeth at St. Augustine Alligator Farm and Zoological Park, St. Augustine

5. Going all-aboard at Jacksonville Zoo and Gardens, Jacksonville

6. Playing soggy pirate at Adventure Landing, Jacksonville Beach

7. Taking a sunset drive or walk along the hard-packed sands of Anastasia Island, St. Augustine

8. Exploring the children's gallery at Cummer Museum of Art and Gardens, Jacksonville

Who are the Minorcans?

In 1767 a Scottish physician named Dr. Andrew Turnbull brought 14,000 indentured servants and other recruits from Italy, Greece, and Minorca (a Spanish island) to build a brave new settlement around New Smyrna. His experiment failed, and most of the Minorcans fled to St. Augustine ten years later. Their influence is felt most potently in their unique datil pepper, which flavors local sauces, desserts, and pilaus with fire. The chile is grown only in St. Augustine and vicinity, from seeds passed from generation to generation.

Centre Street (ages 4 to 13)
Follow Rte. A1A as it becomes South Eighth Street to Centre Street.

At the heart of Fernandina Beach's 50-block historic district, nearly fifty of its structures predate the twentieth century. Classic buildings house shops great for browsing, antiques marts, restaurants specializing in the local white shrimp, and Florida's oldest surviving tavern. Frilly Victorian Italianate architecture embellishes the residential Silk Stocking District that emanates from Centre Street. Many vintage homes open their doors to guests as charming inns and bed-and-breakfasts, just as they did in the days of Ulysses S. Grant, when the town became Florida's first island resort.

Florida House Inn (all ages)
22 South Third St., Fernandina Beach; (904) 261-3300.

You may as well go gung-ho on this history thing and take the kids to eat in a historic setting, where dining is boardinghouse style. Built in 1857 as one of Florida's first hostelries, Florida House Inn still provides rooms with antebellum simplicity and meals with down-home Southern goodness. Breakfast, lunch, and dinner daily. $–$$$$

Fort Clinch State Park (all ages)
2601 Atlantic Ave., Fernandina Beach; (904) 277-7274. Entrance is on Atlantic Avenue, which is a continuation of Centre Street to the east. Open 8 a.m. to sunset (later for candlelight tours) daily. Park entrance is $6 per vehicle of eight persons or fewer, $2 per extra passenger, cyclist, or pedestrian. Fort is open 9 a.m. to 5 p.m.; admission is an additional $2 per person ages 6 and older; $3 each for weekend candlelight tours (by reservation only, May through Labor Day), which begin forty-five minutes after sunset and last about seventy-five minutes.

The town's proudest pre–Civil War relic stands at this state park. The well-preserved bastion is staffed with park rangers in Union dress, who relive the life of a Fort Clinch soldier. Kids are urged to ask them questions about their life in 1864. The view from the embankments is well worth the climb. Also demanding a visit within the 1,086-acre park are a 1,500-foot fishing pier, 4,000 feet of wide beach facing Georgia's Cumberland Island, picnic grounds, camping, towering dunes, and moss-shawled oaks. Candlelight tours (reservations required) inside the fort are held each Friday and Saturday night from early May through Labor Day to re-create how the soldiers saw it at night.

Island Falls Adventure Golf (ages 4 to 12)

1550 Sadler Rd., Fernandina Beach; (904) 261-7881. Open summers 10 a.m. to 11 p.m. daily; in winter (Oct through Feb), 2 to 10 p.m. Fri, 10 a.m. to 10 p.m. Sat, and 11 a.m. to 9 p.m. Sun. Admission is $6.78 for persons ages 13 and older, $5.85 for children ages 4 to 12, $2.00 for children 3 and under. Seniors and military, $6.31.

Streams and a waterfall provide a challenge at this eighteen-hole miniature golf course.

Isle of Eight Flags Shrimp Festival (all ages)

(904) 261-3248.

In early May, this big event celebrates Amelia's history of eight sovereign rulers (France, Spain, England, the "Patriots of Amelia Island," the Green Cross of Florida, Mexican rebels, the United States, and the Confederacy) as well as its seafood reputation, all to the tune of a pirate's lusty "yo-ho-ho." Sometimes the pirates even invade the harbor!

Kayak Amelia (ages 8 to 13)

13030 Heckscher Dr., Jacksonville; (904) 251-0016 or (888) 30-KAYAK; www.kayakamelia .com. Rates are $55 for a half-day guided trip; or rent equipment and pay $35 for a single kayak or $45 for a double kayak or canoe.

Experienced guides instruct novice kayakers and lead them on a guided nature and history tour of the island's creeks, rivers, marshes, and other backwaters.

Main Beach (all ages)

Route A1A (Fletcher Avenue) and Trout Street.

A more popular beach with families, it prohibits surfing. Families will find many other activities to keep them busy, however, including volleyball, a playground, miniature golf, and a game room.

Towering Timucuans?

Early explorers depicted the Timucuans as 7-foot giants who never cut their straight, black hair. In truth, the natives averaged slightly over 6 feet (still gigantic compared with the small-statured Spaniards), and widowed Timucua women did cut their hair. (They were not allowed to remarry until their hair grew back to its original length.) Men wore their hair in topknots to keep cool and thwart scalpers.

Northeastern Climes

The average annual temperature in the coast's northernmost reaches is 69.9 degrees; in winter, 67; in summer, 91. High season hits in summer in this part of Florida, when rates are higher, crowds more crowded, and hours extended at many attractions. Winter weather is normally pleasant, typically requiring long sleeves by day and more layers by night. Snow does fall in these latitudes, albeit rarely.

On the Water Adventures (all ages)
Egan's Creek Marina, Fernandina Beach; (904) 206-1762.

Birds, dolphins, and even wild horses may be seen on guided nature tours on this 26-foot ponga boat. Call to arrange times as brief as two hours to a full-day jaunt. Summer rates (subject to change) from one to six people start at $200 for two hours; a full day starts at $500.

Victorian Seaside Christmas (all ages)
Throughout Amelia Island; (904) 261-3248.

Downtown is where most of the action for the island's annual holiday festival takes place, beginning the Saturday after Thanksgiving and continuing through the holidays. Highlights include beach rides on a horse-drawn sleigh at the Ritz-Carlton, holiday parade and tree-lighting, children's tea with Santa, and a Civil War soldiers' Christmas reenactment.

Where to Eat

Look along Sadler Road for chain-style fast-food and family restaurants. For something with more atmosphere, refer to the other listings in this section.

Brett's Waterway Cafe. 1 South Front St., Fernandina Beach; (904) 261-2660. View of Cumberland Sound; shrimp, other seafood. Lunch and dinner daily. $$–$$$$

Where to Stay

Amelia Island Plantation. Rte. A1A, Amelia Island; (904) 261-6161 or (800) 874-6878; www.aipfl.com. Family-friendly, woodsy, and beachy destination resort with tram service, restaurants, kids' program, spa, nature center, and golf courses. $$–$$$$

Florida House. 22 South Third St., Fernandina Beach, Amelia Island; (904) 261-3300 or (800) 258-3301; www.floridahouseinn .com. One of the few local B&Bs that accepts children and pets, it is also historic (Florida's first guest accommodations, ca. 1857) and Southern-style friendly. $$–$$$$

Ritz-Carlton, Amelia Island. 4750 Amelia Island Parkway, Amelia Island; (904) 277-1100 or (800) 241-3333. Luxury beach resort with kids' programs Our Space, ages 13-19, and Ritz Kids, ages 5-12. $$$$

For More Information

Amelia Island Tourist Development Council. 961687 Gateway Blvd., Suite G, Amelia Island 32034; (800) 2AMELIA; fax (904) 261-2440; www.ameliaisland.org.

Fort George

Continue south of Amelia Island on Rte. A1A, also known as the Buccaneer Trail.

Huguenot Memorial Park (all ages)

10980 Heckscher Dr., Fort George, Jacksonville; (904) 251-3335. Open 8 a.m. to 8 p.m. in summer and 8 a.m. to 6 p.m. in winter. Admission is $1 per person 6 years of age and older, 8 a.m. to 10 a.m.; $3 per car after 10 a.m.

Situated at the mouth of the St. Johns River, this claw of sand is popular with swimmers, surfers, anglers, and campers.

Kingsley Plantation Historic Site (ages 5 to 13)

Fort George, Jacksonville (mailing address: 11676 Palmetto Ave., Jacksonville 32226); (904) 251-3537; www.nps.gov/timu. Open 9 a.m. to 5 p.m. daily. Admission is free or by donation.

The intriguing tale of one slave owner, his African wife, and his slaves unfolds. The long, haunting, unpaved drive to the plantation passes slave hut ruins and ends at the sea, where the manor and other outbuildings are preserved. Kids can learn from exhibits how tabby and cotton were made in plantation times. Ranger tours are offered at 2 p.m. daily.

Little Talbot Island State Park (all ages)

Route A1A/12157 Heckscher Dr., Jacksonville; (904) 251-2320. Open 8 a.m. to sunset daily. Park entrance is $5 per vehicle of eight persons or fewer, $2 per extra passenger, cyclist, or pedestrian.

Little Talbot Island's coastline is distinguished on one side by vegetated dunes and gorgeous, empty beach, while the other side is given over to salt marshlands. Bird-watchers find lots to enjoy. Anglers can cast in salt or freshwater. Make yourself at home in the picnic or camp area. Hiking trails follow the path of early missionaries, conquerors, and plantation owners. The beach at Big Talbot Island, to the north, is even less populated and edged by sand bluffs. It is part of the state park, but admission is only $1 for parking there (no facilities). Call Kayak Amelia at (888) 305-2925 for guided paddle tours and/or rentals.

Where to Eat

Small fish camps and their restaurants are about all you find along this remote strip, with the exception of the restaurant listed here.

Sandollar Restaurant. 9716 Heckscher Dr., Fort George, Jacksonville; (904) 251-2449. Perched at the mouth of the St. Johns near the ferry landing, with great views, seafood, and sandwiches. Lunch and dinner daily. $$–$$$

Mayport

Here the route splits in two directions. You can continue along Rte. A1A's coastal drive, or head into Jacksonville and take the town route back to the beaches.

Kathryn Abbey Hanna Park (all ages)

500 Wonderwood Dr., Jacksonville; off Rte. A1A; (904) 249-4700. Admission is $1 per person 8 to 10 a.m., then $3 per car from 10 a.m. to close.

A litany of beaches continues from Mayport southward. One of the local favorites, Hanna Park encompasses 450 acres devoted to wide, ocean-swept beach, heavily wooded nature trails (favored by mountain bikers), picnic areas, volleyball, kayak and other watersports rentals, and freshwater fishing. Campsites are available. Lifeguards supervise in summer. It's a terrific place for an all-day family picnic in the park.

Smart Travel

- Many of the best, most educational kids' toys are found in attraction gift shops, such as the one at Cummer Museum of Art and Gardens and the Museum of Science and History, where I bought Aaron Amber Insect-Nside—a slab of orange-yellow hard candy encasing a real (and edible!) cricket, asparagus fern, and larva. (Gross! Cool!) Steer them toward purchases that will entertain them in the car or on the plane.

- If you're traveling much of the state of Florida by road, try this to keep the kids involved. Create a map of the state marked with the outline of roads you'll be traveling and cities you'll be visiting. Have them color the stretch of road covered each time you reach a city along it.

- When traveling the interstate, detour the "are we almost there" chant by trying this: Tell your children the exit number where you'll be stopping next for an attraction, meal, or the night. They can then clock your progress by watching exit sign numbers. Involve a little math and ask them how many more exits you have to go.

- Another trick for keeping them occupied in the car: Keep a bag or box of car-only toys, games, puzzle books, picture books, coloring books, crayons, etc. Put it away between trips. That way it will be fresh and new each time you bring it out. Add a surprise for each trip.

- A picnic lunch at a rest stop or town park gives kids—and you—a chance to stretch.

Mayport Ferry, St. Johns River Ferry Service (all ages)

Route A1A; (904) 241-9969; www.stjohnsriverferry.com. **Ferry departs weekdays at 6, 6:20, and 7 a.m., and on the half hour and hour throughout the day until 10 p.m.; and on Sat and Sun at 6:20 and 7 a.m., and on the half hour and hour throughout the day until 10 p.m. The ride costs $3 for motorcycles, $5 for cars, and $1 per bicycle and pedestrian.**

The scenic quality of Rte. A1A reaches a nostalgic peak as it winds down to the mouth of the St. Johns River, which one must cross by car ferry. The ride takes only five minutes.

Where to Eat and Stay

See the Jacksonville Beach area listings for dining and lodging options.

Weekend Jaunt: Jacksonville

If you opt to take the route through town for some metropolitan input before continuing down the beaches, follow Rte. A1A from Fort George along the north bank of the St. Johns, where it turns into Heckscher Drive/Route 105, a scenic riverside drive marred by smokestacks.

Jacksonville is a big city (the fifteenth largest in the United States) and one of Florida's most industrial metropolitan areas. The smell of paper mills can be offensive, especially to children, when the wind's in the wrong direction. Still, it offers plenty of family entertainment and fun within its boundaries and along its beaches (see Jacksonville Beach listings). Downtown has undergone a renaissance along the St. Johns River, resulting in lively shopping, museums, and entertainment districts. The city is a bit difficult to navigate, especially confusing to a first-timer. For best results buy a city map and make a point to visit the old historic neighborhoods of San Marco and Riverside Avondale to get in touch with Jacksonville's soul.

Cummer Museum of Art and Gardens (ages 3 to 13)

829 Riverside Ave.; (904) 356-6857; www.cummer.org. **Open 10 a.m. to 9 p.m. Tues,** free **4 to 9 p.m.; 10 a.m. to 4 p.m. Wed through Fri; 10 a.m. to 5 p.m. Sat; and noon to 5 p.m. Sun; closed Mon. Admission is $10 for adults; $6 for seniors, military, and students with ID; children 5 and under are** free.

If you think art museums are too highbrow for small fry, try this one. In Art Connections they will enjoy getting involved in art by mingling with characters in a re-created masterpiece, painting by computer, or touching replicated elements from pieces in the collection. Besides its excellent hands-on section, Cummer has an impressive traditional gallery and beautiful riverside gardens where children can run.

Fort Caroline National Memorial (ages 5 to 13)

12713 Fort Caroline Rd.; (904) 641-7155; www.nps.gov/timu. **Call ahead for directions. Open 9 a.m. to 5 p.m. daily. Admission is** free.

On a **Budget**

- **Kingsley Plantation Historic Site,** Fort George, free admission

- **Huguenot Memorial Park,** Fort George, admission $1 per person 8 to 10 a.m.

- **Kathryn Abbey Hanna Park,** Mayport, admission $1 from 8 to 10 a.m.

- **Jacksonville Maritime Museum,** Jacksonville, free admission

- **Fort Caroline National Memorial,** Jacksonville, free admission

- **Castillo de San Marcos National Monument,** St. Augustine, admission free for guests ages fifteen and younger

French Huguenots originally settled this area in 1564, creating the first Protestant colony in North America. Northeast of town, a 680-acre park remembers their brave new world with a fort exhibit, a hammock nature trail, ranger-led walks, and a museum of nicely presented ecology and French and Timucuan exhibits, including a 6-foot owl totem that is the largest wood effigy recovered in North or South America. The site is headquarters for the 46,000-acre Timucuan Ecological and Historic Preserve, which also contains the nearby Ribault Monument and wilderness trails in its Theodore Roosevelt Area.

Jacksonville Jaguars (ages 5 to 13)
Alltel Stadium; 1 Stadium Place, on the east end of downtown; (904) 633-2000. Ticket prices start at $50.

The NFL team plays home games here September through December and is the source of extreme city pride.

Jacksonville Landing
2 Independent Dr.; off Hwy. 1; (904) 353-1188; www.jacksonvillelanding.com. Open 10 a.m. to 8 p.m. Mon through Thurs, 10 a.m. to 9 p.m. Fri and Sat, noon to 5:30 p.m. Sun.

Downtown Jacksonville is on the move. On the northern riverfront, Jacksonville Landing makes for a lively shopping, dining, and entertainment experience. Toy Factory (904-353-4874) is a really fun shop.

Jacksonville Maritime Museum (ages 7 to 13)
Southbank Riverwalk; 1015 Museum Circle; (904) 398-9011; www.jaxmaritimemuseum.org. Open 10:30 a.m. to 3:30 p.m. Mon through Fri, 1 to 5 p.m. Sat and Sun. Admission is free or by donation.

Local seafaring history spills from model, art, and photographic displays. Part of the museum is devoted to a 16-foot model of the aircraft carrier Saratoga and to Jacksonville-built World War II ships.

Jacksonville Zoo and Gardens (all ages)

370 Zoo Parkway; (904) 757-4462; www.jacksonville.org. Open 9 a.m. to 5 p.m. daily (extended hours on weekends through Labor Day). Admission is $13 for adults, $11 for seniors, $8 for children ages 3 to 12; children under 3, free. The train runs from 10 a.m. to 4:30 p.m. Mon through Fri, 9 a.m. to 5 p.m. Sat and Sun, weather permitting. Train admission is $4 for adults, $2 for children ages 3 to 12; under 3 free. Wildlife Carousel $2.

On Jacksonville's north side, the zoo enchants with a train ride, walk-through aviary, baby animal nursery, petting zoo, Chimpanorama, and African beasts roaming freely. Demonstrations and shows about alligators, other reptiles, and birds hold children's attention. New exhibits include Range of the Jaguar, Savanna bloom garden, Giraffe Overlook, and a play park with a splash pool.

Kids Kampus (ages 2 to 6)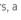

Next to Metropolitan Park on the Northbank.

This city park is incredible fun. Among the interactive gizmos and equipment, kids will find a toddler splash pool with geysers and sculptures, a sand area with mechanical diggers, a replicated Timucuan village, a wind machine, and kid-size streetscapes.

The Museum of Science & History (all ages)

1025 Museum Circle, Southbank; (904) 396-6674; fax (904) 396-5799; www.themosh.org. Open 10 a.m. to 5 p.m. Mon through Fri, 10 a.m. to 6 p.m. Sat, and 1 to 6 p.m. Sun. Admission (which includes the planetarium) is $9.00 for adults, $7.50 for seniors and military, $7.00 for children ages 3 to 12; under 3 free.

Here's a painless way to introduce learning into a vacation. Toddlers will have fun in the two-story, play-and-learn tree house in Kidspace. (How nice! They provide rubber aprons and a hand dryer for playing in the waterworks.) Everyone will be fascinated by the Atlantic Tails exhibit, where the kids can see the skeletons, listen to the voices, and track the migration patterns of whales, dolphins, and manatees. The Florida Naturalist Center showcases fish, turtles, baby alligators, and other live creatures. Tonga, a twenty-five-pound alligator snapping turtle lives in the courtyard. Hands-on stations demonstrate principles of vision, sound, electricity, and motion. History exhibits upstairs span the early settlement of the St. Johns River and northern Florida's Civil War days. The museum also hosts special programs, planetarium shows, and live animal demonstrations.

What's in a Name?

Well, Jacksonville by the original name Cowford probably didn't smell as sweet. It was first named for the narrow throat in the St. Johns River, where cattlemen could cross their herds. In 1822 the name was changed to honor Andrew Jackson.

Port of **Import**

During the 1991 Gulf War, Jacksonville was the busiest military port in the country, moving more supplies and personnel than any other port in the United States.

Southbank Riverwalk
Off Hwy. 1.

Facing Jacksonville Landing from across the river, this jaunty 1.2-mile boardwalk offers more excitement and cultural activity, including the Friendship Fountain and three museums listed below. Water taxis cross between the two areas (admission: $3 adults, $2 children one-way; kids under age 3 ride **free**). Public restrooms are provided at the marina.

Tree Hill—Jacksonville's Nature Center (all ages)
7152 Lone Star Rd.; off Arlington Road; (904) 724-4646; www.treehill.org. Open 8 a.m. to 4:30 p.m. Mon through Sat; tours Sat at 10 a.m. Admission is $2 for adults ages 18 and older, $1 for children.

The center interprets the environment of a hardwood forest via nature trails throughout forty acres and indoor local wildlife and rain forest exhibits. You can also explore butterfly, herb, and organic vegetable gardens and Turtle Town. Special family programs and guided tours take place monthly.

Where to Eat

Dave & Buster's. 7025 Salisbury Rd.; (904) 296-1525. A restaurant within a megaarcade—what could make kids happier? There are games and pastimes for everyone, and the food is much better than you'd expect from a video arcade—pizza, salads, pasta, steak, seafood (the grilled mahimahi is superb), sandwiches, plus kids' selections. Open daily for lunch and dinner. $$–$$$

River City Brewing Co. 835 Museum Circle; (904) 398-2299. Delicious eclectic, Asian, and tropically inclined food; kids' menu; dining indoors or outdoors along the river. Lunch and dinner Mon through Sat; brunch, Sun. Near Southbank attractions. $$–$$$

Where to Stay

Jacksonville hotels are designed primarily for business travelers. Most vacationers head to the beaches. Accommodations downtown are less expensive than on the beach. Best rates are on weekends.

Crowne Plaza Jacksonville Riverfront. 1201 Riverplace Blvd.; (904) 398-8800 or www.cpjacksonville.com The hotel rises above the rest on the St. Johns River, near all the riverfront action, and provides a grand black-marble lobby, 291 tastefully decorated rooms and suites, a swimming pool, and a restaurant. $–$$

For More Information

Jacksonville and the Beaches Convention and Visitors Bureau. 550 Water St., Suite 1000, Jacksonville 32202; (904) 798-9111 or (800) 733-2668; www.jaxcvb.com.

Jacksonville Beach

Follow Rte. A1A south from Mayport. From Jacksonville, go east on the Arlington Expressway and take Rte. 10 (Atlantic Boulevard) or continue along Hwy. 90 (Beach Boulevard). The beaches lie about 30 miles east of downtown and I-95. First Street South, 2 blocks off A1A, is the main oceanfront drag.

Jacksonville Beach sands are generally well populated, and teens will find a lot of the action they crave. Some parts are undesirable, with girlie shows and a run-down look. The beach community begins at Atlantic Beach and Neptune Beach to the north. Atlantic Beach is least rowdy and tacky.

Adventure Landing (all ages)

1944 Beach Blvd.; (904) 246-4386; www.adventurelanding.com. The water park portion is open seasonally. Other attractions are open 10 a.m. to 11 p.m. Mon through Thurs and Sun, 10 a.m. to midnight Fri and Sat. Admission to the water park is $27.99 for adults, $22.99 for children under 42 inches, and $15.99 for "Nite Splash." Free for children 3 and younger, and 10 percent discount to senior citizens and military people with identification. Tax is extra. Other rides and attractions are individually priced.

You could easily spend a day here, and it's a good place to do so when the weather's hot. The water park has a shipwreck-themed play area, the Hydro-Pipe, and a water coaster that actually goes uphill—well, for a short distance anyway. Not as intimidating as some water parks, its rides are tame to mildly wild, with lots for toddlers. It has a surf pool like many others do, but this one provides inner tubes, which makes it more fun. On the river inner-tube ride, you can ride with your young one on a double inner tube, another plus. Batting cages, go-karts, bumper boats, and two miniature golf courses provide dry outdoor activity. Inside the huge, air-conditioned arcade, kids of all ages find food and games—including laser tag—from which you'll have trouble tearing them away.

Atlantic Beach Town Center (ages 5 to 12)

Atlantic Boulevard, Atlantic Beach.

Here's a fun place to stroll through one-of-a-kind shops and along the beach, and have lunch or dinner. Stop at the Book Mark (299 Atlantic Blvd.; 904-241-9026), which has a children's room in addition to a great selection of Florida-related books.

Where to Eat

First Street Grille. 807 North First St.; (904) 246-6555. Casual but upscale dining on the beach, indoors or out. Seafood, burgers, and light bites. Lunch and dinner daily. $$–$$$

Sundog Diner. 207 Atlantic Blvd., Atlantic Beach; (904) 241-8221. This neighborhood kind of place has a diner façade outside and a retro look inside, complete with Dave Clark Five and Monkees tunes. The kids' menu is extensive, as is the regular menu—from meat loaf sandwich to seafood and sausage étouffée. Open daily for lunch and dinner. $–$$

Where to Stay

The beaches hold a steady stream of chain hotels and other accommodations.

One Ocean Resort Hotel & Spa. 1 Ocean Blvd., Atlantic Beach; (904) 249-7402 or (800) 874-6000; www.oneoceanresort.com. More stylish than most beach accommodations. Small pool and dining on-site. $–$$$

For More Information

Jacksonville and the Beaches Convention and Visitors Bureau. 550 Water St., Suite 1000, Jacksonville 32202; (904) 798-9111 or (800) 733-2668; www.jaxcvb.com.

St. Augustine

Follow Rte. A1A south out of Jacksonville Beach. Continue on it or split off onto coastal Rte. 203, which takes you along Ponte Vedra Beach's privileged resorts and homes, then reconnects with Rte. A1A. The trip from Jacksonville Beach to St. Augustine takes about a half hour.

Anyone who believes Florida has no history hasn't been to St. Augustine. Nor have they traveled its 144 blocks of sites listed on the National Register of Historic Places. St. Augustine's reputation as North America's oldest city plays a dominant theme in its realm of tourism, which tends toward the overdone. Despite its commercialism, the town's historic district provides a great way for kids to experience Florida's deep historical context and everyday life in the colonial era.

Anastasia State Park (all ages)

1340-A Rte. A1A South; (904) 461-2033; www.dep.state.fl.us/parks/District_3/Anastasia/ index.html. Open 8 a.m. to sunset daily. Park entrance is $8 per vehicle of eight persons or fewer, $2 per extra passenger, cyclist, or pedestrian.

At the historic district, Rte. A1A crosses the Bridge of Lions to the home of the beautiful hard-packed beaches that gave birth to the sport of beach paddle tennis. The best access is at the state recreation area, which encompasses 4 miles of sandy beach, offering volleyball, ocean swimming, surfing, sailboarding, fishing, and coastal camping. Go for a sunset drive on the beach, when you'll find it at its emptiest and loveliest—bathed in twilight, edged in dunes, and distanced from city life. During the day you can rent sailboards and take lessons from Anastasia Watersports (904-460-9111) or rent surf and boogie boards from Surf Station (904-471-WIND), or kick back and watch the shorebirds. There are oak-shaded picnic facilities near the beach.

Fort Facts

- Historians estimate that if Castillo de San Marcos were built today, using the same coquina rock and taking the same twenty-three years to complete, it would cost $79 million.

- The fort's soft, coquina rock walls stood strong because they could absorb cannon shot. One historian describes the outer wall as looking like a chocolate chip cookie.

Castillo de San Marcos National Monument (all ages)

1 South Castillo Dr.; (904) 829-6506; www.nps.gov/Casa. Open 8:45 a.m. to 4:45 p.m. daily. Admission is $7 for adults; children 15 and younger, free.

The colonial fort dominates the entrance to St. Augustine's celebrated historic district. In early times it was the entrance, and its walls completely encircled the town. Construction on the fort began in 1672 to replace previous wooden fortresses. Made of coquina rock, the massive fort kept enemies of Spanish, British, and American settlers at bay for 235 years. Like most forts, its strategic waterside location offers great views and picture-taking opportunities. Kids love the firing of the old cannons by period-uniformed soldiers.

Colonial Spanish Quarter Museum (ages 5 to 13)

53 St. George St.; (904) 825-6830; www.historicstaugustine.com. Open from 9 a.m. to 5:30 p.m. daily. Admission is $6.95 for adults, $5.95 for seniors, military free with ID, $4.25 for students ages 6 to 17. Historic package includes de Mesa-Sanchez House and Taberna del Gallo. $12.95 adult, $5.95 ages 6 to 17, sales tax included.

Costumed artisans, craftspeople, and street musicians keep alive the skills, arts, and crafts—blacksmithing, thread spinning, thatched roofing, hearth cooking, and more—of colonial days. Children can participate in some of the crafts or simply listen to costumed guides explain the history of the museum's ten homes and workshops. Learn about the lifestyles of eighteenth-century Spanish officers commissioned to this strange new land so far from home.

Dow Museum of Historic Houses (ages 8 to 13)

149 Cordova St.; (904) 823-9722; www.old-staug-village.com. Open 10 a.m. to 4:30 p.m. Mon through Sat and 11 a.m. to 4:30 p.m. Sun. Admission is $8.95 adult, $7.95 senior, $6.95 students with ID, under 5 free.

This new-old attraction contains eight historic buildings dating from 1790 to 1910 and archaeological sites dating from the sixteenth century. The oldest structure was once occupied by Napoleon Bonaparte's nephew, Prince Murat. Reenactors bring history alive.

Doorway Defense

Door frames in St. Augustine's colonial homes were built to accommodate the tallest family member, at 5 feet or less. When the tall Timucua Indians attacked, the diminutive doorways slowed them down, either by causing them to duck or by knocking them out.

Fiesta Falls (ages 4 to 13)

818 A1A Beach Blvd.; (904) 461-5571. Open 10 a.m. to 9:30 p.m. Mon through Fri and 9 a.m. to 10 p.m. Sat and Sun. Admission is $7.95 for adults, $6.95 for children ages 3 to 12 and for seniors.

Themed around old town's Spanish colonial motif, this eighteen-hole miniature golf course holds a Spanish galleon, waterfalls, and multileveled holes.

Fountain of Youth National Archaeological Park (ages 5 to 13)

11 Magnolia Ave.; (904) 829-3168 or (800) 356-8222. Open 9 a.m. to 5 p.m. daily. Admission is $8 for adults, $7 for seniors, $5 for children ages 6 to 12; under 6 free.

The first historic attraction you'll reach in this city of historic attractions, it claims to be Ponce de León's point of arrival in 1513 and St. Augustine's first colony. Stroll through excavations of the original colony, a planetarium, and life-size exhibits. You can even take a sip from Ponce de León's fountain and see how young it makes you feel.

Government House Museum (ages 8 to 13)

48 King St.; (904) 825-5033. Open 9 a.m. to 4:30 p.m. Mon through Fri, 10 a.m. to 4:30 p.m. Sat through Sun. Admission is $5 (plus tax) for adults, $3 seniors, $2 for children ages 6 to 18.

Browse exhibits detailing the city's cultural and architectural development.

Guana Tolomato Matanzas National Estuarine Research Reserve (ages 4 to 13)

North of St. Augustine at 2690 South Ponte Vedra Blvd., Ponte Vedra Beach; (904) 825-5071; www.gtmnerr.org. Visitor center open 9 a.m. to 4 p.m. daily. Closed on state holidays. Admission is $2 for adults 17 and up, $1 for children ages 10 to 17; under 10 free. Driving tour of nature trails is $3 per car extra.

Historians generally concur that Spanish explorer Juan Ponce de León probably made his first landing near the spot today preserved at Guana. Rte. A1A shoots through the middle of the park, which is lined with low shrubs and saw palmettos (*guana* is Spanish for "palm") for a visually soothing drive. Accesses allow you to park and enjoy the beach and other facilities. From the park's beach you can swim, surf, and fish. Other activities include nature study, fishing, and boating on the Guana and Tolomato Rivers, and hiking or biking on 9 miles of old service road.

Lighthouse Park

Across the street from the St. Augustine Lighthouse.

A good place for a picnic after you've climbed the lighthouse. You'll find a boat ramp, fishing pier, and restaurant.

Lightner Museum

75 King St.; (904) 824-2874; www.lightnermuseum.org. Open 9 a.m. to 5 p.m. daily. Admission is $10 for adults, $5 for children 12 to 18, free for children under age 12 when accompanied by an adult.

The museum is located at Henry Flagler's old Hotel Alcazar, one of his magnificent creations. The museum's three floors concentrate on America's Gilded Age of industrial prosperity with a "Brilliant Period" cut-glass display, antique furnishings, mechanical musical instruments, and Tiffany stained glass.

Marineland (all ages)

About 18 miles south of St. Augustine on Rte. A1A; 9600 Ocean Shore Blvd.; (904) 460-1275; www.marineland.net. Open 8:30 a.m. to 4:30 p.m. daily. General admission is $8.00 adult, $6.75 senior, $3.50 for children. Dolphin encounter prices vary from $65 to $400.

Diving, snorkeling, and dolphin encounters are the more unusual offerings at Marineland, which is Florida's—the world's!—first marine animal attraction (opened in 1938). Then there are the typical dolphin and seal shows, plus tropical fish aquariums.

Road Markers

Follow this tour from its beginning at northernmost Amelia Island and down the coast along Rte. A1A's meanderings. The road travels for a long stretch through pristine parklands. At Mayport, you can either continue along A1A or take a city detour into Jacksonville via Heckscher Drive, a panoramic riverside route. Routes 10 (atlantic Boulevard), 202 (J. Turner Butler Boulevard), and Hwy. 90 (Beach Boulevard) return you to the beaches. Avoid all in rush-hour traffic. Hwy. 1 and I-95, incidentally, run parallel to Rte. A1A and more directly north-south. If you have the time, you should stick to the coastal road with its delightful quirks—including an old-fashioned car ferry across the mouth of the St. Johns.

Within Jacksonville, Hwys. 1 or 17 and I-95 get you downtown efficiently, when it isn't rush hour, that is. I-295 skirts the downtown. I-10 intersects with both and heads west. Hwy. 301, at the western edge of town, goes south to Starke and Gainesville through rural heartland territory. North of Jacksonville, Rte. A1A connects to I-95.

Nights of Lights Festival (ages 4 to 13)

(904) 829-1711 or (800) OLD-CITY; www.getaway4florida.com.

St. Augustine's history most dramatically comes to life during period reenactments in the Old City from the third week of November through January 31. At Christmastime, the pageantry of night-guard detail lights the streets during Grand Illumination and Night Watch. Torch processions and fife-and-drum bands recall eighteenth-century tradition early in the season. Historic and holiday events continue throughout the month of December and into January.

The Oldest (Gonzalez-Alvarez) House (ages 6 to 13)

14 St. Francis St.; (904) 824-2872. Open 9 a.m. to 4:30 p.m. daily. Admission is $8 for adults, $7 for seniors, and $4 for children ages 6 to 18. Tickets also good for admission to the museum gardens and a historical museum.

The kids can experience how families lived in old St. Augustine. A home for more than 250 years, the house displays Spanish colonial, British Victorian, and American Territorial styles.

Oldest Wooden Schoolhouse (ages 5 to 9)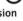

14 St. George St.; (904) 824-0192 or (888) 653-7245. Open 9 a.m. to 5 p.m. daily. Admission is $3.70 for adults, $2.50 for children ages 6 to 12; children under 6 free.

Students can appreciate how colonial kids learned their lessons and can receive a diploma of their own. An audio-animated schoolmaster and dunce explain elementary procedures in colonial days, pointing out the dungeon under the staircase, to which unruly students were sentenced. Explore the lovely gardens outdoors and ring the old school bell. The gift shop carries school-related items.

Ripley's Believe It or Not! (ages 6 to 13)

19 San Marco Ave.; (904) 824-1606; Open 9 a.m. to 7 p.m. Sun through Thurs, 9 a.m. to 8 p.m. Fri and Sat. Admission is $14.99 for adults, $13.00 for seniors, $7.99 for children 5 to 12; under 5 free.

Always fascinating for wide-eyed young ones, this first Ripley's is housed in a Moorish 1887 structure with exhibits that stretch the imagination to the limit. See the London Bridge re-created from 264,345 matchsticks, the Lord's Prayer carved into a grain of rice, a soda-can manatee, and a stuffed two-headed calf. Be careful when you make faces in the mirror; you never know who may be looking! Some of the stuff is a bit macabre for the very young and impressionable.

St. Augustine Alligator Farm and Zoological Park (all ages)

Southeast of the historic district on Rte. A1A; 999 Anastasia Blvd.; (904) 824-3337. Open 9 a.m. to 5 p.m. daily, to 6 p.m. in summer. Admission is $21.95 for adults, $10.95 for children ages 5 to 11; under 5 free.

Top Family Resorts

1. **Amelia Island Plantation,** Amelia Island

2. **Ritz-Carlton,** Amelia Island

3. **Marriott at Sawgrass Resort,** Ponte Vedra Beach

One of St. Augustine's most popular kid attractions concentrates on reptiles rather than reenactments. Like many places in St. Augustine, it is designated the oldest of its kind in America (opened 1893). It is as much about crocodiles as it is about gators. If you don't know the difference now, you will after your visit. The farm represents the world's only complete collection of crocodilians (which include alligators, crocodiles, caimans, and gharials—twenty-three species in all) from around the world. Monkeys, birds, and snakes also share the park. Entertaining wildlife shows educate your family about crocodilians and other reptiles—no gator wrestling here.

St. Augustine Lighthouse and Museum (ages 7 to 13)

Old Beach Road off Rte. A1A; 81 Lighthouse Ave.; (904) 829-0745; www.staugustinelight house.com. Open 9 a.m. to 6 p.m. daily (extended to 7 p.m. in summer). Admission to the museum and grounds is $7.50 for adults, $6.50 for seniors, and $5.50 for children ages 6 to 11; free for children ages 5 and younger. Admission to the museum and tower is $9 for adults, $8 for seniors, and $7 for ages 6 to 11, free for children ages 5 and younger. Children must be 44 inches tall to climb the tower.

Climb a 165-foot, 219-step lighthouse built in the late 1800s. Notice the cracks in its circular wall, a legacy of the earthquake that shook Charleston, South Carolina, in 1886. The visitor center holds maritime archaeological exhibits and flashes back to the history of the black-and-white-striped tower, which is the town's oldest brick structure.

St. Augustine Sightseeing Train (all ages)

170 San Marco Ave.; (904) 829-6545 or (800) 226-6545; www.redtrains.com. Tours run from 8:30 a.m. to 5 p.m. Admission is $16.99 for an adult three-day pass, $7.99 for children ages 6 to 12; under 6 free.

Save your feet and car brakes by hooking up with this tour (and stop circling the historic district endlessly in search of a parking spot). You can board from several locations. Tours are narrated, and the train lets you on and off at will. It's a good way to get an overview of the town's layout and history. With a good narrator, you can learn in great detail about St. Augustine's fabulous architecture, divided between the colonial era and the Flagler era— from the 1880s through the turn of the twentieth century, during which time the great railroad king Henry Flagler came to town to build hotels that looked like castles, magnificent churches, and a cache of other historical treasures.

Top Family Beaches **and Parks**

1. **Fort Clinch State Park,** Fernandina Beach

2. **Anastasia State Park,** St. Augustine

3. **Kathryn Abbey Hanna Park,** Mayport

4. **Washington Oaks State Gardens,** Palm Coast

St. Augustine's Restoration Area (ages 5 to 13)
Along St. George Street between South Street and Orange Street.

In St. Augustine's historic waterfront district, small, specialized museums and living-history rituals reveal the town's historic importance, while crafts shops, galleries, restaurants, and other stores sell goods and victuals of all manner behind vintage storefronts. Pedestrian-only St. George Street is the center of activity in the restoration area, which holds buildings dating back to 1566.

Tour St. Augustine (ages 6 to 13)
(904) 641-1009 or (800) 797-3778. Open 9 a.m. to 5 p.m. Mon through Sat. Walking tour at 8 p.m. every night. Admission for the walking tour is $12 for those 6 and older.

Kids into goose-bump tales? Take them on A Ghostly Experience. The haunted tour of St. Augustine provides ninety minutes of terror-tinged yarns and lore of the town's scariest places, including the dungeons of Castillo and the oldest (Huguenot) cemetery. The Historic Villages of St. Augustine is an interactive walk where kids can build a Timucuan canoe, grind corn into flour, and witness a blacksmith at work. Other theme tours are also available.

Victory III **Scenic Cruise** (all ages)
Municipal Marina; (904) 824-1806 or (800) 542-8316; www.scenic-cruise.com. Departs daily. Call for current seasonal schedule. Tickets cost $16.75 for adults, $13.75 for seniors (60+), $9.75 for children ages 13 to 18, and $7.75 for children 4 to 12.

For seabound adventure, take a scenic seventy-five-minute tour narrated by a local Minorcan-descended family. Snacks, beverages, beer, and wine are available on board.

Visitor Information Center (ages 4 to 13)
10 Castillo Dr.; across the street from Ripley's; (904) 825-1000. Center admission and movie are free.

Stop in for a free introduction to St. Augustine via diorama displays and video. Pick up your printed information with discount coupons here. The center shows a forty-five-minute dramatic movie presentation of St. Augustine's founding, titled *Struggle to Survive.* In the vicinity you'll find the Huguenot Cemetery (tours available; ask at the information center), the Gates to old St. Augustine, and Davenport Park, with a playground and restored old carousel, which you can ride for $1. Packages for the movie and other museums are available.

Washington Oaks State Gardens (all ages)

2 miles south of Marineland; 6400 North Ocean Shore Blvd., Palm Coast; (386) 446-6780. Open 8 a.m. to sunset daily. Park entrance is $5 per vehicle of eight persons or fewer, $1 per extra passenger, cyclist, or pedestrian.

This park takes you away into a land of mixed, crazy-quilt environments. Huge coquina boulders decorate the park's ocean beach, and peaceful ornamental gardens line its riverfront. It's a great place to sun, picnic, and explore along the nature trail. On weekends at 1:30 p.m. you can join in on interpretive walks of the gardens, trail, or beach.

Day Trip

From Rte. A1A, south of St. Augustine, take Routes 206, 207, and 100 southwest to Palatka, about a half hour away, to see some of Florida's astounding interior natural sights.

Ravine Gardens State Park (ages 6 to 13)

1600 Twigg St., Palatka; (386) 329-3721. Open 8 a.m. to sunset daily. Park entrance is $5 per vehicle of eight persons or fewer, $1 per extra passenger, cyclist, or pedestrian. The prime attraction in this river town is an unusual park. Its striking namesake feature becomes particularly picturesque in spring, when the azaleas and camellias bloom.

Mike Roess Gold Head Branch State Park (ages 5 to 13)

West of Palatka at 6239 Rte. 21, Keystone Heights; a side trip off Rte. 100 on Rte. 21; (352) 473-4701. Open 8 a.m. to sunset daily. Park entrance is $5 per vehicle of eight persons or fewer, $1 per extra passenger, cyclist, or pedestrian. Rolling sand hills, marshes, springs, lakes, mill ruins, and a deep ravine are contained within almost 2,400-acre confines. Take a cool dip in Lake Johnson, or toss in a line and try for some bass or speckled perch. Nature trails penetrate into the habitat of fox squirrels, gray foxes, scrub jays, and black bears. Lakefront cabins and a primitive campground accommodate overnighters.

More Things to See and Do
in Northeast Florida

- **Fort Matanzas National Monument,** St. Augustine; (904) 471-0116

- **G. Howard Bryan Museum of Southern History,** Jacksonville; (904) 388-3574

- **Jacksonville Museum of Modern Art,** Jacksonville; (904) 366-6911

- **Mission of Nombre de Dios,** St. Augustine; (904) 824-2809; www.mission andshrine.org

- **Old Jail and Florida Heritage Museum,** St. Augustine; (904) 829-3800; www .historictours.com

- **Peterbrooke Chocolatier,** Jacksonville; (904) 398-4812; www.peterbrooke .com

- **Spanish Military Hospital,** St. Augustine; (904) 827-0807

- **World Golf Hall of Fame,** St. Augustine; (904) 940-4123; www.worldgolfhall offame.org

Where to Eat

A1A Ale Works. 1 King St.; (904) 829-2977. A minibrewery, but fine and fun for kids as well as adults. Menu has a Cuban-Caribbean flair. Lunch and dinner daily. $$–$$$

Santa Maria Restaurant. 135 Avenida Menendez; on the dock at the marina; (904) 829-6578. You'll love the view. The kids will love the little trapdoors at many of the tables, handy for feeding the birds outside and the catfish below. The food is typical fried fish-house fare, and you're probably better off going for lunch. Just be sure to ask for a trap-door table. Lunch and dinner. Closed Wed during lunchtime. $$

Where to Stay

Aside from the accommodations below, St. Augustine offers everything from chain hotels and family-run motels to historic B&Bs, which, though charming, are not ideal for families.

Days Inn Historic. 1300 North Ponce de Leon Blvd.; (904) 824-3383 or (800) DAYS INN. Handily located near Old City attractions, with pool, restaurant, and 124 rooms. $$

Ponte Vedra Inn & Club. 200 Ponte Vedra Blvd., Ponte Vedra Beach; (904) 285-1111 or (800) 234-7842. Upscale lodging, a renowned spa, golfing, and kid-friendly amenities (swimming pools—including a wading pool—the beach, a playground, and a nursery) make this a top choice for family vacations. $$$–$$$$

Sawgrass Marriott Resort and Beach Club. 1000 PGA Tour Blvd., Ponte Vedra Beach; (904) 285-7777 or (800) 457-4653. Massive 508-room resort known for its world-class golfing (ninety-nine holes and home of the Players Championship at Sawgrass tournament) and kids' program. $$$–$$$$ (ask about summer family packages.)

For More Information

St. Augustine, Ponte Vedra, and the Beaches Visitors and Convention Bureau. 88 Riberia St., Suite 400, St. Augustine 32084; (904) 829-1711 or (800) OLD-CITY; www.visitoldcity.com.

Annual Events

Jacksonville Jazz Festival. Jacksonville; (904) 630-3686. Eight days of concerts and activities. Held in April. **Free.**

Beaches Festival Weekend. Jacksonville Beach; (904) 247-6236. The beaches "open" with a parade, sand-castle-building contest, and food vendors the last full weekend of April. **Free.**

Isle of Eight Flags Shrimp Festival. Fernandina Beach; (904) 261-3248 or (904) 261-0203. Seafood feasting in May with a pirate theme. **Free.**

Drake's Raid. St. Augustine; (800) OLD-CITY. A reenactment of Sir Francis Drake's sixteenth-century attack on the Spanish colony, early in June. **Free.**

Halloween Nights: Old Haunts in the Old City. St. Augustine; (800) OLD-CITY. October brings family activities, haunted tours, and festivities through the Historic District.

Nights of Lights. St. Augustine; (904) 829-1711 or (800) OLD-CITY. November through January, holiday festivities feature colonial reenactments. **Free.**

Victorian Seaside Christmas. Fernandina Beach; (904) 261-3248. Beginning Thanksgiving weekend, it lights up downtown and provides a variety of activities, including sleigh rides on the beach.

East Central
Florida

M uch of east central Florida was built with an eye toward travel—whether by train, race car, motorcycle, or spaceship. Still, the area balances space-age technology with untamed wilderness to present attractions and temperaments that are intriguingly diverse, from bald eagles to launch shuttles, citrus groves to drive-on beaches, surfboards to sea turtle nests.

This chapter covers the area from Flagler Beach and Daytona Beach to Stuart and Hobe Sound, with short detours inland.

TopPicks for Family Fun in East Central Florida

Ormond Beach and Environs

Located about a half hour south of St. Augustine Beach–Marineland along Rte. A1A or Hwy. 1.

First stop: Flagler Beach, named for Henry Flagler, Florida's choo-choo Sugar Daddy. Although Flagler was one of the earliest settlers of Ormond Beach, to the south, the town and its big brother, Daytona Beach, are more well known today for the automobile and its race-car pioneers.

To the south of the Flagler Beach area, the Halifax River widens the split between mainland and barrier island. Rte. A1A continues to take the coastal route into Ormond Beach.

Bulow Plantation Ruins State Historic Site (ages 5 to 13)

Follow signs west off Rte. A1A to Rte. 100 and turn south on Rte. 2001 (Old King's Road); (386) 517-2084; www.floridastateparks.org/bulowplantation. Open 9 a.m. to 5 p.m. Thurs through Mon. Admission is $4 per vehicle. Canoe rentals are available at $10 per hour or $40 per day.

This state site oddly juxtaposes elements of times past. On one hand, you'll explore ruins of a sugar mill and other plantation structures dating back to the early 1800s. It feels

EAST CENTRAL FLORIDA

Flagler Beach
Ormond Beach
Daytona Beach
Barberville
De Leon Springs
DeLand
New Smyrna Beach
Orange City
Lake Monroe
Sanford
Christmas
Titusville
Sharpes
Cocoa
Cape Canaveral
Cocoa Beach
Melbourne
Melbourne Beach
Sebastian
Vero Beach
Fort Pierce
Port St. Lucie
Jensen Beach
Stuart
Hobe Sound

Florida Turnpike

something like an Indiana Jones adventure. In an open-air interpretive center, you get a taste of Seminole Indian heritage and culture through artifact displays. While there, you can have a picnic and paddle a canoe along a 13-mile trail on Bulow Creek, through reclaimed oak and magnolia forest where sugarcane once fluttered.

The Casements (ages 7 to 13)

25 Riverside Dr. and Granada Boulevard (Route 40), Ormond Beach; (386) 676-3216; www .volusia.org/echotourism/cultural/casements.htm. Open 8:30 a.m. to 5 p.m. Mon through Fri and 8:30 a.m. to noon Sat. Guided tours 10 a.m. to 5 p.m., Mon through Fri and 10 to 11:30 a.m. Sat. Donations are requested.

The town's premier attraction, it was once the winter home of multimillionaire John D. Rockefeller. The circa-1912 palace today serves as a cultural center and museum that showcases historic Boy Scout memorabilia, Hungarian folklore, and Rockefeller artifacts.

Gamble Rogers Memorial State Recreation Area (all ages)

3100 South A1A, Flagler Beach; (386) 517-2086; www.floridastateparks.org/gamblerogers. Open 8 a.m. to sunset daily. Main park entrance is $5 per vehicle of eight persons or fewer, $1 per extra passenger, cyclist, or pedestrian; entrance for beach only is $4 per car.

Cradled between the Atlantic and the Intracoastal Waterway, it pleases nature observers with two waterfronts and 144 acres. Camp, picnic, swim, fish, and watch the shorebirds come to feed at low tide.

TopPicks for Family Fun in East Central Florida

1. Living the dream at John F. Kennedy Space Center

2. Shuttling into simulated space at Astronaut Hall of Fame/U.S. Space Camp Florida, Titusville

3. Feeling the thunder at Daytona International Speedway/Daytona USA, Daytona Beach

4. Staring at giant sloth bones and scary African masks at Museum of Arts and Sciences, Daytona Beach

5. Feeling like an ancient explorer at the pristine and quiet Merritt Island National Wildlife Refuge, Titusville

6. Shredding the waves at Sebastian Inlet

7. Cruising on the St. Johns River, Sanford

8. Manatee spotting at Blue Spring State Park, Orange City

9. Playing surrogate parent to a nest of sea turtle hatchlings at Hobe Sound National Wildlife Refuge, Hobe Sound

Smart Travel

- Pack plenty of books for the trip. Suggested topics: space travel, sea turtles, Navy frogmen, and citrus. During summer vacation, a few school workbooks keep the brain from lapsing.

- Sea lice are the bane of swimmers along the East Coast. Actually the larvae of thimble jellyfish, they get caught in swimsuits and emit an itchy venom that can drive you crazy. Watch for posted signs at beaches that warn of sea lice. Immediately after exiting the water, remove swimsuits and shower.

- Tar balls, remnants of old oil spills, are another common problem in these waters. Pack a tar solvent.

- Among the top injuries reported at Canaveral National Seashore are splinters from boardwalks. Be sure to keep the little ones shod to and from the beach, and remind them not to run their hands along the railing.

- When swimming around fishing piers, stay well clear to avoid being accidentally hooked.

Ormond Beach Performing Arts Center (ages 4 to 13)

399 North Hwy 1, Ormond Beach; (386) 676-3375; www.ormondbeach.org/pac. Tickets are reasonably priced.

Across the Intracoastal Waterway formed by the river, via Rte. 40, you'll find cultural and natural reasons to leave the alluring shoreline. Besides community theater and touring concert arts and drama productions, this center presents children's theater workshops and productions.

Tomoka State Park (ages 5 to 13)

2099 North Beach St., Ormond Beach; (386) 676-4050; www.floridastateparks.org/tomoka. The park is open 8 a.m. to sunset daily; the museum, 9:30 a.m. to 4:30 p.m. Park entrance is $5 per vehicle of eight persons or fewer, $1 per extra passenger, cyclist, or pedestrian.

Before there was Tomoka State Park, a Timucuan village and later a plantation, ca. 1766, occupied these 1,900 acres. Set between the lovely Tomoka and Halifax Rivers, it offers great canoeing and fishing, as well as camping, hiking, picnicking, and the Fred Dana Marsh Museum, where the works of an Ormond Beach sculptor and architect are gathered.

For More Information

Daytona Beach Area Convention and Visitors Bureau. 126 East Orange Ave., Daytona Beach 32114; (386) 255-0415 or (800) 545-0415; www.daytonabeach.com.

Ormond Beach Chamber of Commerce.
165 West Granada Blvd., Ormond Beach
32174; (386) 677-3454; www.ormondchamber
.com.

See Daytona Beach listings for nearby restaurants and hotels.

Weekend Jaunt: DeLand and Vicinity

From Ormond Beach, head for the contrasting beauty and culture of Florida's inlands along Rte. 40 to Barberville. Follow Hwy. 17 south to De Leon Springs, DeLand, and Orange City. South of Orange City, you can hop on I-4 west to reach Sanford and Lake Marion, then return to Daytona Beach via I-4 east.

Barberville's Pioneer Settlement for the Creative Arts
(ages 5 to 13)

West of Ormond Beach about 20 miles on Hwy. 40, located 2 blocks west of the intersection of Hwy. 17 and Rte. 40; 1776 Lightfoot Lane, Barberville; (386) 749-2959; www.pioneer settlement.org. Open 9 a.m. to 4 p.m. Mon through Sat. Admission with guided tours is $6 for adults, $4 for children ages 6 to 12.

The ten-acre wooded complex is dedicated to preserving traditional folk arts such as pottery, woodwork, and blacksmithing. The kids get a vision of life in early Florida and can visit a vintage railroad depot. In November, the attraction hosts a two-day Fall Country Jamboree, with artisans, crafters, music, and a corn boil.

Blue Spring State Park (all ages)

2100 West French Ave., Orange City; (386) 775-3663; www.floridastateparks.org/blue spring. Open 8 a.m. to sunset daily. Park entrance is $6 per vehicle with up to eight passengers, $1 for extra passengers, bicyclists, and pedestrians.

Manatees are the star attraction. They winter here, drawn by balmy 72-degree waters. So are families, who also enjoy the park's many recreational opportunities: fifty-one campsites, picnicking, swimming, scuba diving, and canoeing. Manatee educational programs are scheduled mid-November through mid-March.

The last weekend in January, the park cohosts the Blue Spring Manatee Festival. Besides entertainment and other festivities, the event offers the opportunity to see endangered-species exhibits. You can take a shuttle bus to the park to observe manatees when weather permits, attend an educational program, and tour the park's Thursby House, a historic home that is listed on the National Register of Historic Places.

Central Florida Zoological Park (all ages)

On the western shore of Lake Monroe, right off I-4's exit for S.R. 17/92; 3755 Hwy 17/92; (407) 323-4450; www.centralfloridazoo.org. Open 9 a.m. to 5 p.m. daily; closed

My Not Diving at **Blue Spring State Park**

Blue Spring is one of the popular SCUBA diving sites, with a fissure that extends down into the cavern system below. I once drove from Tampa—a considerable trek, then swam several hundred yards to the spring. I am a very experienced SCUBA diver but, that day in that place, looking down into the bowels of the spring, I decided to abort the dive and my partner and I left and went home to Tampa. This is as it should be. It does not matters how far you drive or how much effort or money you spend getting there, if you are not 100 percent ready to dive, you walk away. Or swim away. When it comes to SCUBA diving in Florida caverns, it pays to get older and not bolder.

Thanksgiving and Christmas Day. Admission is $10.95 for adults, $8.95 for seniors, $6.95 for children ages 3 to 12.

The park conducts a variety of seasonal programs designed to enlighten children about animal behaviors and endangerment. They range from Children's Storytime at the Zoo to Nature Niche, a weeklong study for six- to twelve-year-olds. Many of the zoo's animals are endangered species from around the world, including the red-ruffed lemur, clouded leopard, Aruba island rattlesnake, and Bali mynah bird.

De Leon Springs State Park (ages 5 to 13)
Ponce de Leon Boulevard and Burt Parks Road off Hwy. 17; 601 Ponce de Leon Blvd., De Leon Springs; (386) 985-4212; www.floridastateparks.org/deleonsprings. Open 8 a.m. to sunset daily. Park entrance is $6 per vehicle of eight persons or fewer, $1 per extra passenger, cyclist, or pedestrian.

South of Barberville, the site of an erstwhile sugar plantation later became a health resort and today is protected as a state park. Much of its modern-day reputation is stacked on the popularity of an on-site pancake house (see below). Work off a hearty meal there with a hike, a swim in the old spring-fed resort pool, or a canoe trip in the springs. One day in August, the park's A Day in Florida History features living-history presentations staged at camps for Timucuans, Spanish soldiers, Seminole Indians, and Civil War soldiers.

Hontoon Island State Park (ages 4 to 13)
2309 River Ridge Rd., DeLand; off Rte. 44 west of town; (386) 736-5309; www.floridastate parks.org/hontoonisland. Open 8 a.m. to sunset daily. Park entrance is free.

Surrounded by the St. Johns and Hontoon Dead Rivers, the park can be reached by private boat or a free passenger shuttle that operates from 8 a.m. until one hour before sunset. This is a nice place to spend a lazy day with a fishing pole in hand as the little ones swing on the playground. Six miles of trails accommodate bikers and hikers. Six rustic cabins and twelve campsites are available.

Lake Woodruff National Wildlife Refuge (ages 6 to 13)

2045 Mud Lake Rd., De Leon Springs; off Hwy. 17; (386) 985-4673; www.fws.gov/lakewood ruff. Open dawn to dusk daily. Admission is **free.**

Devoted naturalists head here to explore by foot or bike the nature trails, which penetrate pine and hardwood forest and ring dikes built around bird-feeding ponds.

Old Spanish Sugar Mill & Griddle House

De Leon Springs State Park, De Leon Springs; (386) 985-5644; www.planetdeland.com/ sugarmill. Serving 9 a.m. to 4 p.m. Mon through Fri and 8 a.m. to 4 p.m. Sat.

Make your own flapjacks on the griddle built into your table. Servers bring you pitchers of stone-ground, five-grain, and unbleached flour pancake batter, along with apples, bananas, chocolate chips, or any other condiments you request. The griddles raise the ambient temperature, so it's best to try this in cool weather. The restaurant, inside the gates at De Leon Springs State Park, opens daily for breakfast and lunch (when you can grill your own sandwiches). $

Rivership *Romance* (ages 4 to 13)

Monroe Harbour Marina; 433 North Palmetto Ave., Sanford; (407) 321-5091 or (800) 423-7401; www.rivershipromance.com. Admission for a three-hour tour is $38 for adults, $28 for children ages 3 to 12, but call or check the Web site for monthly specials and extra charges.

Perched on the edge of a bulge in the St. Johns River known as Lake Monroe, Sanford is the perfect place from which to embark on a narrated tour of the historic, wilderness-fraught waterway. (The town is also known as the Celery Capital of the World, but don't tell your kids that or they'll never want to go.) One of the most popular tours is aboard this replica of a 1940s steamer for lunch or dinner and dancing.

St. Johns River Cruises (ages 5 to 13)

At Blue Springs State Park, 2100 West French Ave., Orange City; (407) 330-1612; www.sj rivercruises.com. Cost for two hours is $22 for adults, $20 for seniors, $16 for children 3 to

Top Family Beaches and Parks

1. **Golden Sands County Park,** Vero Beach

2. **Fort Pierce Inlet State Park,** Fort Pierce

3. **Stuart Beach,** Stuart

4. **Playalinda Beach,** Canaveral National Seashore

5. **Daytona Beach,** Daytona Beach

Top Family **Resorts**

1. **Club Med Sandpiper,** Port St. Lucie

2. **Hutchinson Island Marriott,** Stuart

3. **Driftwood Resort,** Vero Beach

12; under 3 **free.** Ecotours depart 10 a.m. and 1 p.m. daily. Seasonal tours available 3:30 p.m. Jan through Apr.

Tours concentrate on the natural sights along local waterways during two-hour and full-day cruises. Spot manatees, alligators, deer, wild hogs, bald eagles, and other rare birds along the scenic route.

Where to Stay

DeLand Country Inn Bed & Breakfast. 228 West Howry Ave., DeLand; (386) 736-4244; www.delandcountryinn.com. Charming 1900 home with five bedrooms done in lace and fancy wallpaper sits right downtown, so you can porch sit and watch the world go by, or stroll through little DeLand, checking out antiques shops, parks, and the campus at Stetson University. It's kid- and pet-friendly; go for a swim in the screened pool, or play board games or basketball. Great breakfast, too. $–$$

Hontoon Landing Resort & Marina. 2317 River Ridge Rd., DeLand; (386) 734-2474 or (800) 248-2474; www.hontoon.com. Rooms, suites, and cottages overlooking the St. Johns River. Houseboat and pontoon rentals. $$

On a **Budget**

- **The Casements,** Ormond Beach, by donation
- **Lake Woodruff National Wildlife Refuge,** De Leon Springs, **free** admission
- **Sugar Mill Botanical Gardens,** Port Orange, **free** admission
- **New Smyrna Beach Sugar Mill Ruins,** New Smyrna Beach, **free** admission
- **Merritt Island National Wildlife Refuge,** Titusville, **free** admission
- **Fort Christmas,** Christmas, **free** admission
- **Jack Island Preserve,** Fort Pierce, **free** admission

For More Information

DeLand Area Chamber of Commerce.
336 North Woodland Blvd., DeLand 32720;
(386) 734-4331; www.delandchamber.org.

Daytona Beach

Anyone who has heard of Florida beaches has heard of Daytona Beach, for one reason or another. Its name sounds most often from the lips of college spring breakers and race-car fans.

Motor sports in Daytona Beach got their start on the hard-packed beaches, so it's not surprising that this is one of the few places in Florida that still allows cars to drive on most of its 23-mile-long beach. The beach is open to vehicles from sunrise to sunset November 1 through April 30 and from 8 a.m. to 7 p.m., May 1 through October 31. There is a $5 per day per vehicle user fee to drive on the beach February 1 through November 30, **free** the rest of the year. This contributes to its reputation as a party town, but it's just as much a family attraction. Along the beach, which stays well trafficked all day, you can rent all kinds of cool beach toys, including golf carts, four-wheelers, reclining bicycles, and boogie boards. Sun Splash Park, at 611 South Atlantic Ave., provides interactive fountains and other cool-down features.

To get to Daytona's other claims to fame, cross the Intracoastal Waterway at Hwy. 92. Find historic attractions in the downtown area by heading to the south of Hwy. 92 (International Speedway Boulevard) on Beach Street. Stroll lovely City Island Park or browse downtown stores, many of which occupy historic buildings. To get to the high-test attractions, head out on the highway, 92, that is.

Angell & Phelps Chocolate Factory (ages 4 to 10)　

154 South Beach St.; (386) 252-6531; www.angellandphelps.com. Open 9:30 a.m. to 5:30 p.m. Mon through Fri. Admission is free.

What kid, at whatever age, wouldn't love a trip to a chocolate factory? Take a **free** thirty-minute guided tour of this one and see how more than a hundred kinds of candies are made. The Angell & Phelps Restaurant and Wine Bar serves casual gourmet dishes such as soups and sandwiches, chili, and wraps.

Boardwalk Amusement Area and Main Street Pier (all ages)　

Ocean Avenue (off Rte. A1A); (386) 253-1212 for pier information. The pier is open 6 a.m. to 11 p.m. daily (hours extended in summer); its restaurant, 11 a.m. to 10 p.m. Admission to the fishing end of the pier, past the restaurant, is $5.00 for adults ($12.50 with pole rental), $3.50 for children ages 12 and under, $1.00 for spectators. Admission to Sky Lift is $6.00.

By day (at night it turns into a rowdier scene), take the kids to the Boardwalk, with its tents full of video games, rides, a castle-motif band shell, and, on the 1,000-foot-long pier, a gondola Sky Lift. It's like a fairgrounds on the beach! The beach around the pier has been declared pedestrian-only and is closed to vehicular traffic. From the pier, you can also charter fishing boats.

Daytona International Speedway and Daytona USA (ages 6 to 13)

1801 West International Speedway Blvd.; (386) 255-2700 (speedway) or (386) 947-6800 (Daytona USA); www.daytonausa.com. Track tours are conducted 9:30 a.m. to 5 p.m. daily when there's no racing. Daytona USA is open 10 a.m. to 6 p.m. daily (hours extended during racing events). Admission is $24 for adults, $19 for seniors and for children ages 6 to 12; under 6 free. May be closed for special events, so call or check the Web site.

Each March, thousands flock here for the energy and excitement of Daytona 500 NASCAR stock-car racing. Other major Speedweek events include the 400 NASCAR race in July, the 24-hour sports-car race in February, and the Daytona 200 for motorcycles in March. Year-round, you can travel backward by race car via a video wall showing early racing films, then take the thirty-minute narrated Speedway tour by tram. A highlight is a stop on the rim road behind turn four for a heightened overview of the grounds.

Opened in July 1996, Daytona USA further traces the history and hysteria of motor sports with interactive displays that allow visitors to assist at a pit stop, broadcast a race, design and test a stock car, and talk to their favorite drivers through video. Famous race cars, such as actor Paul Newman's Ford Mustang Cobra and each year's Daytona 500 winner, are on display. From a 55-foot theater screen, a film about the Daytona 500 race brings you as close to being there as you can get without fighting traffic. Buy your race-car souvenirs at the gift shop or at any one of several motor sports shops in the area.

Halifax Historical Museum (ages 6 to 13)

252 South Beach St.; (386) 255-6976; www.halifaxhistorical.org. Open 10 a.m. to 4 p.m. Tues through Sat. Admission is $5 for adults, $1 for children under age 12; Thurs afternoon by donation.

The museum resides in an old bank building and holds memorabilia from prehistoric Indian eras to the early days of beach car racing. You can see a wood-carved model of what the boardwalk area looked like in 1933.

Lighthouse Point County Park (all ages)

5000 South Atlantic Ave., Ponce Inlet; (386) 756-7488. Admission is $3.50 per car of eight passengers or fewer, $1.00 per extra passenger.

For a quieter beach scene, without the anxiety beach traffic can cause parents with toddlers, spend your sun time here. This end of the island is much quieter, and the fifty-five-acre beach is more natural, edged in small dunes. A jetty keeps waters calm.

Museum of Arts and Sciences (ages 7 to 13)

352 S Nova Rd.; (386) 255-0285; www.moas.org. Open 9 a.m. to 5 p.m. Tues through Sat and 11 a.m. to 5 p.m. Sun. Admission is $12.95 for adults, $10.95 for seniors, and $6.95 for children 6 to 17; under 6 free. The museum fee includes the planetarium show, but

planetarium tickets may be purchased separately at $4 for adults and $3 for children 6 to 17. Planetarium shows are scheduled at 3 p.m. Tues through Fri and 2 and 4 p.m. Sat and Sun.

This attraction will surprise you with its many layers of enrichment possibilities. Centered on the ninety-acre Tuscawilla Preserve, its approach to discovery is holistic. For the wee ones, there's a 13-foot-tall skeleton of a 130,000-year-old giant ground sloth and the skeleton of a huge armadillo ancestor, plus the museum's drawers and showcases full of other fossils. Older children will enjoy the **free** world's largest Cuban art collection, Indian artifacts, and exhibits from thirty different African cultures. Other components range from changing displays of fine art to hikes through a coastal hammock environment and shows in the planetarium.

Pirate's Island Adventure Golf (ages 4 to 13)

3420 South Atlantic Ave., Daytona Beach Shores; (386) 767-9397. Open 10 a.m. to 10 p.m. Sept through Feb and 9 a.m. to 11 p.m. Mar through Aug. Admission is $9.49 for adults, $7.49 for children ages 5 to 12.

Not far off the beach you'll find more miniature golf and small amusement parks than even the most ambitious parents could exhaust in a week's stay. This eighteen-hole course is a nice one.

Ponce de Leon Inlet Lighthouse (ages 6 to 13)

4931 South Peninsula Dr., Ponce Inlet; (386) 761-1821; www.ponceinlet.org. Open 10 a.m. to 6 p.m. daily, with extended summer hours. Admission is $5.00 for adults, $1.50 for children ages 11 and under.

Don't be fooled by all the amusement park and speed-demon attractions: There's history in Daytona Beach, too. The area's most popular vintage structure stands watch at the beach's south end. The lighthouse was built more than a hundred years ago. You can still climb its 203 spiraling steps to the top of a 175-foot red tower (the second tallest in the United States) and sigh at the sweeping panorama. A small colony with historic buildings surrounds the tower; one houses an antique French-cut lighthouse lens that kids like for its prism effect. After you've climbed the lighthouse, you can buy a certificate attesting to your accomplishment in the gift shop.

Shenandoah Stables (ages 7 to 13)

1759 Tomoka Farms Rd.; (386) 257-1444. Rides cost $25 per hour. Children under age 7 can ride with an adult for $5 extra.

It takes reservations for family rides along country trails and offers lessons on horses and ponies. Ask about the kids' summer riding program.

A Tiny Cruise Line (ages 5 to 13)

Halifax Harbor Marina, 425 South Beach St.; (386) 226-2343; www.visitdaytona.com/tiny cruise. Ticket prices for a one-hour excursion are $13.61 for adults, $8.21 for children ages 4 to 12; $20.42 and $12.20 for two hours. Tax is extra.

Boat tours on the Halifax River are themed variously for estate-gawking, wildlife-sighting, downtown history, and sunset and city lights.

Where to Eat

Lighthouse Landing. 4940 South Peninsula Dr., Ponce Inlet; (386) 761-9271; www.lighthouselandingrestaurant.com. The oldest restaurant on Florida's east coast. Waterside place, picnic tables, fish, and sandwiches indoors or out. Lunch and dinner daily. $–$$

Ocean Deck. 127 South Ocean Ave.; (386) 253-5224; www.oceandeck.com. The upper deck offers fine dining. Down below at beach level, things are more casual and family appropriate. Open daily for lunch and dinner, it serves a wide variety of sandwiches, seafood, salads, and appetizers. $$

Where to Stay

Plaza Resort. 600 North Atlantic Ave.; (386) 255-4471 or (800) 225-0329; www.plazaresort andspa.com. Formerly the Holiday Inn, this remake has upgraded the hotel and added a spa, but it's still affordable, with a beach location, swimming pool, and snack bar that families like. $$–$$$

Shores Resort and Spa. 2637 South Atlantic Ave., Daytona Beach Shores; (386) 767-7350 or (800) 525-7350; www.shores resort.com. One of Daytona's most luxurious accommodations; 214 guest rooms, pools, exercise facility, restaurant and bar, tennis courts, and room service. $$–$$$$

For More Information

Daytona Beach Area Convention and Visitors Bureau. 126 East Orange Ave., Daytona Beach 32114; (386) 255-0415 or (800) 544-0415; www.daytonabeach-tourism.com.

Port Orange and New Smyrna Beach

Along Hwy. 1 just south of Daytona Beach.

Canaveral National Seashore at Apollo Beach

Follow Rte. A1A across the south causeway and continue south about 6 miles; visitor center at 7611 South Atlantic Ave., New Smyrna Beach; (386) 428-3384; www.nbbd.com/godo/cns/Brochures/index.html. Park open 6 a.m. to 6 p.m. in winter, 6 a.m. to 8 p.m. in summer; visitor center open 9 a.m. to 5 p.m. Admission is $3 per person. May be closed during missile launchs, so call first.

This area is minimally developed with parking lots, nature trails, and restrooms. The south entrance is by foot only, and eventually you'll reach Klondike Beach. (More about Canaveral National Seashore appears under Titusville.)

Go-Kart City (all ages)

4114 South Nova Rd., Port Orange; (386) 761-2882. Open daily; hours vary according to demand. Admission for go-karts is $6.50 per ride (four laps), with multiride rates; "bullet" karts (faster) are $7.50 per ride. Golfing is $5 for adults, $4 for seniors and children 6 to 10, $2 for children 4 or 5.

Let 'em live their race-car fantasies on a ¼-mile track. Tots can buddy-ride **free** with parents. Non-racers can play games in the video arcade, or play eighteen holes on the minigolf course.

New Smyrna Beach Sugar Mill Ruins (ages 6 to 13)

1050 Old Mission Rd., New Smyrna Beach; (386) 427-2284; www.newsmyrnabeach.com/ resources/historic-ruins.html. Admission is **free.**

Sugar-coated history lessons continue. The county park makes low impact on the haunting, primitive beauty of undisturbed ruins and nature. This is a great place for a hike on the hammock trail, then a picnic away from it all.

Public Beach

Take the causeway at Rte. 44, turn left onto Peninsula Drive, and then right onto Flagler Avenue. Open sunrise to sunset daily. Admission is $5 per car.

The town of New Smyrna Beach has three marvelous beach accesses. The public beach is a small-town version of Daytona, where you can drive your car onto the 9-mile stretch of sand, while avoiding all the crowds and college boogie. Surfers and other boardsters like it here, especially at the north-end jetty, which also appeals to anglers.

Sugar Mill Botanical Gardens (ages 4 to 13)

Take Herbert Street west off Hwy. 1 and follow the signs; 950 Old Sugar Mill Rd., Port Orange; (386) 767-1735; www.dunlawtonsugarmillgardens.org. Open 8 a.m. to 6 p.m. daily. Admission is **free.** **To arrange a** **free** **guided tour, call (386) 767-0996.**

Remnants of Florida's sugar days persist despite the ravages of war and the elements. Twelve acres of peaceful gardens enshrine two distinctly different eras of Florida history. The site originally processed sugar, and several ruins remember the era. Forty years ago, it was turned into Bongoland, a now extinct theme park, although dinosaur statues remain. Throw in botanical gardens, and you have an offbeat attraction with enough variety for everyone in the family.

For More Information

Southeast Volusia Chamber of Commerce. 115 Canal St., New Smyrna Beach 32168; (386) 428-2449 or (877) 460-8410; www.sevchamber.com.

Titusville

About a half hour south of New Smyrna Beach on Hwy. 1.

The whole town, small as it is, revolves around the space theme, thanks to its role in hosting NASA. Still, Titusville remains natural and uncommercialized because it shares its

Ninja Turtles

May through September bring loggerhead, leatherback, and green turtles ashore. Mammoth, 300-pound mother turtles drag themselves above the shoreline in the stealth of night, leaving tractorlike tracks to mark their visit. Into their sandpit nests, they drop about a hundred eggs and are on their way, maternal duties complete. In summer you'll see their nests staked or wired off. Sixty days later, the eggs hatch, the baby turtles dig their way out of the sand, and then, like little ninjas, they scurry toward the moonlight reflected on the water.

shores with the pristine realms of two vast, nationally protected areas. Only for the few days surrounding a launch does the town fill with tourists as hotel rates rise. Otherwise, most of the trade is day-trippers, who come from the Orlando area just to tour the Space Center.

American Police Hall of Fame and Museum (all ages)

6350 Horizon Dr.; (321) 264-0911; www.aphf.org. Open 10 a.m. to 6 p.m. daily. Admission is $12 for adults, $8 for seniors and children ages 4 to 12, and free for kids ages 3 and under. Law enforcement officers are also admitted free.

Do your kids have a fascination with cops and robbers? If so, take them to see a real jail cell, electric chair, police cars, and weapons.

Canaveral National Seashore (ages 5 to 13)

Route 402; visitor center at 7611 South Atlantic Ave., New Smyrna Beach; (386) 428-3384; www.nbbd.com/godo/cns/Brochures/GenInfo/index.html. Open 6 a.m. to 6 p.m. in winter, 6 a.m. to 8 p.m. in summer. Admission is $3 per person.

Behold this wonderfully undiscovered beach world! Its 25-mile-long stretch has three sections. Easiest to reach and most family friendly is Playalinda Beach, still minimally developed with only pit toilets and beach walkovers. Thirteen parking lots line the 4-mile stretch. Secluded at its north end, it was once popular with nudists. Although the county has banned nudism, it still occurs on this most secluded of Florida beaches. Two other beaches, Apollo and Klondike, are most easily accessed from New Smyrna Beach (see New Smyrna listings).

Natural and gorgeous, Playalinda is the kind of beach you never want to leave. Sea turtles like it, too. Though they lay their eggs along the entire length of the East Coast and on the West Coast, too, this area begins a stretch of the state's heaviest concentration of turtle nests. With all this nature, it feels strange to look down the way and see a launchpad. The contrast is dramatic, but the duality seems to work. The beach does close around rocket launches, so call ahead.

Kennedy Space Center (ages 3 to 13)

Kennedy Space Center (follow signs off Hwy. 1 and head east on Rte. 405 to Rte. 3); (321) 449-4444; www.KennedySpaceCenter.com. Open 9 a.m. to 5:30 p.m. daily, except certain launch days and Christmas. Standard admission to the visitor complex is $38 plus tax for adults and $28 plus tax for children ages 3 to 11, and does not include the Astronaut Hall of Fame. The Space Center offers other combinations of tickets, plus deals on food and merchandise, and Astronaut Hall of Fame exhibits and simulators. Check the Web site for updates (and the next launch event).

This is why folks come to Titusville, and it's a great reason, especially for kids. It is, after all, the only space shuttle launch site in the world. For devoted space buffs, it's the ultimate, especially since the completion of its five-year, $130 million makeover. It takes several hours to fully tour the array of exhibits dealing with space exploration. Toddlers love the space-age playground. Older children are intrigued by flashy, multimedia presentations in the humorous Robot Scouts exhibit and by the futuristic look at humans on Mars in "Exploration in the New Millennium." Kids will love climbing aboard a replica of the space shuttle *Explorer* and meeting an astronaut in person.

With a Maximum Access pass, visitors get access into the two IMAX theaters with screens more than five stories high. *The Dream Is Alive* chronicles the history and drama of space travel. Guided bus tours take you past gates barring the general public, into NASA's inner workings and to three attractions. LC39 Observation Gantry is a multilevel deck looking out on Kennedy's two launchpads. At the Apollo/Saturn V Center, interactive displays and multimedia shows illustrate NASA's moon missions. See a real *Saturn V* orbiter and touch a moon rock. Gift shops and a wide variety of eateries throughout the Space Center provide souvenirs and sustenance.

For a special treat, sign up for the "Lunch with an Astronaut" program. You get to lunch with a real space hero, ask questions, and take pictures with those who have "the right stuff." As part of another program called ATX Astronaut Training Experience, visitors ages fourteen and older can take a whirlwind route through hands-on training, space flight preparation, and space shuttle simulators, and they even leave with cool ATX gear.

In the 1980s the six surviving *Mercury 7* astronauts conceived of a place where space travelers could be remembered—much like baseball players and other sports figures. Their dream was realized in 1990 as the U.S. Astronaut Hall of Fame, in Titusville, adjacent to the Space Center. It has become an official part of the Kennedy Space Center Visitor Complex, which spent $700,000 on improvements and celebrated a formal grand opening in 2003. The Hall of Fame tells the personal side of human space exploration history through artifacts once owned by astronauts, interactive exhibits, and astronaut training simulators. It also houses the world's largest collection of astronaut memorabilia,

Space Camp

The Space Center has a weeklong day camp for kids eight to fourteen, dubbed Camp Kennedy Space Center. It features an exciting array of fun activities and robust, hands-on learning, plus **free** twelve-month passes to the visitor complex for each camper and four **free** tickets for family members to the Astronaut Hall of Fame. Campers ride a 3D-360° simulator, G-Force Simulator, and ⅙ Gravity Trainer; climb a Zero-G Wall; operate a simulated Mars rover; meet an astronaut; and even design space exploration vehicles. Specially trained teachers lead the program, which is based at the Astronaut Hall of Fame, with occasional excursions to the nearby main campus at Kennedy Space Center visitor complex. Registration costs $295, plus tax, per camper, and includes all activities and transportation, hot lunches, afternoon snacks, and an official space center T-shirt. One spring session is available, and there are weekly sessions during summer, from June to August. Reservations are required; call (321) 449-4400 or write Camp Kennedy Space Center, Delaware North, Park Services, DNPS, Kennedy Space Center 32899.

exhibits, and tributes to the heroes of *Mercury, Gemini,* and *Apollo,* plus a fine collection of spacecraft, such as a *Mercury Sigma 7* capsule, *Gemini* training capsule, and an *Apollo 14* command module. Astronaut training simulators allow guests to feel the pressure of four times the force of gravity, ride a rover across Mars, and land a space shuttle.

Merritt Island National Wildlife Refuge (ages 5 to 13)
3.5 miles east of Titusville on Rte. 406; (321) 861-0667; www.fws.gov/merrittisland. The refuge is open daily during daylight hours; the visitor center is open 8 a.m. to 4:30 p.m. Mon through Fri and 9 a.m. to 5 p.m. Sat and Sun. Apr through Oct; the center closes on Sun. Admission is free.

Cross the Intracoastal Waterway—here the Indian River—to find a solitary world of wildlife that coexists with, and survives in spite of, the space-age neighbor that shares its realm. The refuge's 140,000 acres, together with bordering Canaveral National Seashore, provide habitat for 1,045 plant species, 310 bird species, and 21 threatened or endangered animal species, including the bald eagle, wood stork, manatee, and loggerhead turtle. Stop at the visitor center to get your bearings and background, then explore by car, foot, or bike along the trails.

North Brevard Historical Museum (ages 7 to 13)
301 South Washington Ave. (Hwy. 1 North); (321) 269-3658; www.nbbd.com/godo/history. Open 10 a.m. to 3 p.m. Tues through Sat. Admission is free or by donation.

Road **Markers**

Continuing down Rte. A1A, the resort towns reel off with their special brand of wide, firm beaches and attractions both classic and contemporary. This straight shot down the coast begins in the environs of Daytona Beach, just south of which it swings inland along Routes 40 and 17 to examine some hidden natural treasures around the town of DeLand. Then it's easy cruising down Hwy. 1 or parallel Rte. A1A along the so-called Space Coast and Treasure Coast, which are among the least discovered sections of Florida's eastern shores. A1A is the more scenic, but at times congested, route, especially around Melbourne Beach. Hwy. 1 is more utilitarian. Between Fort Pierce and Stuart, try Rte. 707 (Indian River Drive) for a scenic cruise. I-95 skirts the region inland from the shore, for a zippier trip.

Get a quick bite of history at this museum in the thick of downtown's historic renovation. It exhibits photographs, furniture, clothing, and other items that depict early local lifestyles. And since everything in the area must have a space spin, it displays the handprints of the original Mercury astronauts.

Titusville Playhouse (ages 4 to 13)

301 Julia St. off Hwy. 1 South; (321) 268-1125. Tickets cost $10 to $16, less for students and seniors.

Also downtown, you'll find the playhouse lodged in the Emma Parrish Theatre, a restored silent movie house from the turn of the twentieth century. It hosts the Rising Stars Children's Theatre.

Valiant Air Command Warbird Museum (ages 7 to 13)

6600 Tico Rd.; off Rte. 405; (321) 268-1941; www.vacwarbirds.org. Open 9 a.m. to 5 p.m. daily. Admission is $12 for adults, $10 for seniors and active military personnel, $5 for children ages 4 to 12; children under 4 free.

Although spaceships are more commonly associated with the area, you can get your fill of aviation history here. Displays preserve memories of aviation battle from World War I to the Vietnam War, including aircraft, uniforms, flying gear, and artwork.

Where to Eat

Kloiber's Cobbler Eatery. 337 South Washington Ave.; (321) 383-0689. In a historic department store setting, this family-run cafe sells the freshest in bakery goods, salads, soups, and deli sandwiches. Try the meat loaf sandwich on black bean–jalapeño cheese bread and some homemade ice cream or cobbler. Open for breakfast and lunch Mon through Sat and dinner Tues through Sat. $

For More Information

Titusville Area Chamber of Commerce.
200 South Washington Ave., Titusville 32780;
(321) 267-3036; www.titusville.org.

Detour: Christmas, Florida

Continue west on Rte. 50 to reach the town of Christmas, most famous for its postmark, which many seek for their holiday greetings.

Fort Christmas (ages 4 to 13)

1300 Fort Christmas Rd.; (407) 568-4149; www.nbbd.com/godo/FortChristmas. Park is open 8 a.m. to 8 p.m. in summer, 8 a.m. to 6 p.m. in winter. Museum is open 9 a.m. to 4 p.m. Tues through Sun. Admission is **free.**

The town's existence is based on the fort, which was constructed beginning on Christmas Day 1837, for the Second Seminole War, and later replicated. Visit the museum and enjoy a picnic in the play area.

Midway Airboat Tours (ages 8 to 13)

28501 East Colonial Dr. (Hwy 50); (407) 568-6790; www.airboatridesatmidway.com. Open 9 a.m. to 6 p.m. daily. Cost for forty-five-minute rides is $35 for adults and $25 for children 4 to 11; under 4 **free.**

Airboat rides are a loud but distinctively Floridian way to explore the state's inland waters. Excursions explore the rampant wildlife on the St. Johns River and connecting lakes.

Cocoa

About twenty minutes south of Titusville on Hwy. 1. Historic Cocoa Village lies along Brevard Avenue, just south of King Street (Route 520).

Astronaut Memorial Planetarium and Observatory at
Brevard Community College's Cocoa Campus (ages 5 to 13)

1519 Clearlake Rd.; (321) 433-7373; www.brevardcc.edu/planet. Schedule changes monthly. Planetarium admission is $7 for adults, $6 for seniors, $4 for children ages 4 to 12; under 4 **free.** Observatory and exhibits are **free.**

It offers planetarium programs, high-tech stargazing, and intergalactic movies three stories high.

Brevard Museum of History and Science (ages 5 to 11)

2201 Michigan Ave. (off Hwy. 1); (321) 632-1830; www.brevardmuseum.org. Open 10 a.m. to 4 p.m. Tues through Sat and noon to 4 p.m. Sun. June, July, Aug, open Thurs through Sat only, same hours. Admission is $6.00 for adults, $5.50 for seniors, $4.50 for children ages 5 to 16; 4 and under free.

This museum occupies twenty-two acres of interpreted environment. Trails lead through marsh, sand hills, and hammock. Indoors, kids can get their hands on science experiments in the Discovery Room; see displays from the Ice Age, pioneer days, and Space Age; and visit changing exhibits.

Horseback Trail Rides (ages 8 to 13)

1020 Camp Rd., Sharpes; 6 miles south of Rte. 405 off Hwy. 1; (321) 632-7085; www.florida horsebacktrailrides.com. Four scheduled rides depart between 9 a.m. and 5:30 p.m. daily. Rates are $35 per ninety-minute ride. No one under age 6 or over 225 pounds is permitted.

A horseback ride slows down the space-age pace to a clip-clop trip through primal woodlands. Call ahead for reservations and directions.

For More Information

Cocoa Beach Area Chamber of Commerce. 400 Fortenberry Rd., Merritt Island 32952; (321) 459-2200.

Cape Canaveral and Cocoa Beach

Head back north on Hwy. 1 and take Rte. 528, also known as Bennett Memorial Causeway, to cross Merritt Island to Cape Canaveral. Cocoa Beach lies south of Cape Canaveral on Rte. A1A.

Cocoa Beach Pier (ages 8 to 13)

401 Meade Ave., Cocoa Beach; (321) 783-7549; www.cocoabeachpier.com. Parking varies from $5 to $7 or a little more depending upon day, season, and special events. Admission to fishing end of pier is $1 for spectators; $5 for fishing adults, and $4 for seniors and children under age 12.

A local landmark, the pier measures 800 feet in length. Besides fishing, you'll find equipment rentals, restaurants, bars, shops, and live entertainment. It's also the site of festivals—such as the Labor Day Pro-Am Surfing Festival—launch watches, and informal gatherings.

Jetty Park (ages 4 to 13)

400 East Jetty Rd., north of Rte. 528, Cape Canaveral; (321) 783-7111; www.jettypark.org. The park is open until 9 p.m. for fishing. Day parking costs $7 per car, $15 per recreational vehicle.

One of the best locations for launch watching, this is also a great spot for beaching, camping, picnicking, pier fishing, and cruise-ship gazing. It has a general store, a playground, a bake shop, and concessions.

Ron Jon Surf Shop (ages 5 to 13)

Routes A1A and 520; 4151 North Atlantic Ave., Cocoa Beach; (321) 799-8820; www.ronjons .com. Open twenty-four hours daily.

Surf's up—about as up as it gets in Florida—at Cocoa Beach and vicinity. Much of the area's surfing reputation is based on the looming, visually loud presence of Ron Jon; it's the cathedral of water sports. The park around it displays ten sand sculptures of beach sports.

TRAXX at Jungle Village Family Fun Center (all ages)

South of Rte. 528 on Rte. A1A; 8801 Astronaut Blvd., Cape Canaveral; (321) 783-0595. Open 10 a.m. to midnight Sun through Thurs, 10 a.m. to 1 a.m. Fri and Sat. Fees are charged per attraction.

Life-size jungle animal sculptures herald your approach. The center assembles all the makings of a half-day's entertainment, with three varieties of racetrack, thirty-six-hole miniature golf course, laser tag, game arcade, and snack bar. Look for the elephant wearing sunglasses.

Where to Eat

Marlins Bar & Grill. Cocoa Beach Pier, 401 Meade Ave., Cocoa Beach; (321) 783-7549. Watch surfers while you chow down on wings, burgers, mahimahi, and seafood. Inside and outside seating; kids' menu. Open daily for lunch and dinner. $–$$

Where to Stay

Hampton Inn. 3425 North Atlantic Ave., Cocoa Beach; (321) 799-4099 or (877) 49-BEACH. With beach access and an above-the-rest view of the cruise-ship port and two waterfronts, this is one of Cocoa Beach's finest offerings. Pool and complimentary continental breakfast. $$–$$$

Melbourne and Melbourne Beach

Route A1A continues its crawl through resort town after resort town. Cocoa Beach blends into Melbourne Beach.

By the time you reach Rte. 518, the Eau Gallie Causeway, you may want to take a retreat to something more mentally satisfying in the charming, historic district of Eau Gallie.

Brevard Zoo (all ages)

8225 North Wickham Rd., Melbourne; off I-95's exit 73; (321) 254-9453; www.brevard zoo .org. Open 9:30 a.m. to 5 p.m. daily (gate closes at 4:15 p.m.). Admission is $12.50 for adults, $11.50 for seniors, $9.50 for children ages 2 to 12. Train fare is $3.00 for ages 2 and up.

Animals indigenous to Florida and Australia are at home here. See black jaguars, 600-pound tapirs, a giant anteater, kangaroos, dingoes, and two-toed sloths. At "Paws On" kids can try to outrun an alligator or outjump a frog. "Animal Encounters" petting zoo, a mini-train, and otter feedings give the place a personal, interactive touch. The Wetlands Outpost provides the opportunity to kayak.

For More Information

Melbourne/Palm Bay Area Chamber of Commerce. 1005 East Strawbridge Ave., Melbourne 32901; (321) 724-5400 or (800) 771-9922; www.melpb-chamber.org.

Sebastian

McLarty Treasure Museum (ages 7 to 13)

Sebastian Inlet State Park; 13180 Rte. A1A, Vero Beach; (772) 589-2147; www.floridastate parks.org/sebastianinlet/Info.cfm. Open 10 a.m. to 4:30 p.m. daily (last showing of the museum's film begins at 3:15 p.m.). Admission is $1 for persons ages 6 and older.

Part of the state park, the museum reveals the reason why this slice of coastline, from Sebastian Inlet south to Fort Pierce Inlet, is labeled the Treasure Coast. In 1715 a hurricane thrashed and dashed into the rocks a treasure-laden Spanish fleet returning from Mexico. Erected on the site of a Spanish salvage camp, the museum relates the story of the wreck and salvaging efforts and the Ais Indians who met the fleet's 1,500 survivors. It displays recovered treasure, from forks to pieces of eight. An observation deck lets you watch ongoing salvaging, most active in calm summer weather, or, if you're really lucky, migrating whales.

Sebastian Inlet State Park (ages 5 to 13)

970 South Rte. A1A, Melbourne; (321) 984-4852 or (561) 589-9659 for camping. Open twenty-four hours daily. Park entrance is $8 per vehicle of eight persons or fewer; $1 per extra passenger, cyclist, or pedestrian; $3 for a single-occupancy vehicle or motorcycle.

The coast's fame for surfing and turtle nesting continues. The surfing reputation crests at Sebastian Inlet, which slices through the middle of this park. The north side of the 587-acre park attracts beachers, surfers, and picnickers. Surfing contests are hosted year-round. A rock-barricaded "pool" in the inlet provides safe swimming for tots. The park accommodates anglers and boaters with its jetties, bridge catwalks, a bait shop, and a marina with a boat ramp, boat tour of the Indian River, and canoe and kayak rentals. South of the inlet, a small campground draws mostly fishing types, while a day-use area beach (no admission fee) is great for snorkeling and diving. Snorkeling gear is for rent in the park. In summer, rangers lead nighttime turtle walks to observe loggerheads and other sea turtles nesting on the beach.

For More Information

Sebastian River Area Chamber of Commerce. 700 Main St., Sebastian 32958; (772) 589-5969; www.sebastianchamber.com.

Vero Beach

About ten minutes south of Sebastian Inlet via Rte. A1A.

The true value of the Treasure Coast becomes apparent as you follow one of the most scenic portions of Rte. A1A south of Sebastian Inlet through Vero Beach to Fort Pierce Inlet.

North of Vero Beach along Indian River Shores, the beach parks are perfect for families: small, well maintained, and varied. Treasure Shores Park and Golden Sands County Park have playgrounds, lifeguards, picnic shelters, and barbecue grills. The wave action ranges from gentle to awesome. Admission and parking are **free.**

Vero Beach is a pretty, artsy town on its beach side, with lots of fun shops to explore. The beaches in the village are more crowded and narrow than those to the north. Jaycee Park, off Ocean Drive (Route A1A) at Mango Road, makes a nice picnic spot, with tables, grills, lots of trees, lifeguards on the beach, and a playground.

The town of Vero Beach spills onto the mainland, where museums and other cultural attractions await.

Central Florida Surf School (ages 7 to 13)

1085 Morningside Dr.; (321) 727-8464; www.surfschoolcamp.com. Most lessons are held at Fort Pierce Inlet State Park. Private lessons start at $100 per hour, two-hour minimum. Group lessons are $130 for a five-hour day (9:30 a.m. to 2:30 p.m.).

For one-on-one surfing lessons in the Vero Beach–Sebastian Inlet area, contact Lou Maresca at the Surf School. He also sells and rents equipment and rooms. Ask about summer and monthly camps.

Indian River Citrus Museum (ages 7 to 13)

2140 Fourteenth Ave., off Rte. 60 (Beachland Boulevard); (772) 770-2263; www.vero heritage.org/CitrusMuseum.html. Open 10 a.m. to 4 p.m. Tues through Fri. Admission is by donation.

In Indian River County, the other buzzword is citrus. Indian River produces some of the world's largest and juiciest oranges and grapefruit. How it won its reputation is the subject of photographs, antiques, farm tools, and memorabilia tracking the area's history from the early 1800s. You get a video viewing of modern-day techniques.

Indian River County Historical Society Exhibit Center
(ages 4 to 13)

2336 Fourteenth Ave.; (772) 778-3435; www.irchistorical.org/. Open 10 a.m. to 4 p.m. Mon through Fri. Admission is **free** or by donation.

If you're one who gets all steamed up over train memorabilia, you'll be happy here. It's set up in a historic railroad ticket office. You'll see a miniature railroad and other exhibits dealing with local history.

Where to Eat

Ocean Grill. 1050 Sexton Plaza; ocean-grill.com; (772) 231-5409. Overhanging the beach, a combination of nautical and medieval decor. Excellent lunches and seafood and steak dinners. Open for lunch Mon through Fri, dinner daily. Ask for a kids' menu. $$$–$$$$

Where to Stay

Disney's Vero Beach Resort. 9250 Island Grove Terrace; (800) 359-8000; www.dvcresorts.com. Part of the Disney Vacation Club network; 115-room inn with minigolf course, slide pool, restaurants, tennis, basketball, play area, river cruises. $$$–$$$$

Driftwood Resort. 3150 Ocean Dr.; (772) 231-0550. Funky place that began in the early 1900s as a way to put washed-up beach debris to use (thus, its name). Standard rooms, efficiencies, two-bedroom apartments—each with its own personality. Swimming pools and restaurant. $$–$$$$

For More Information

Vero Beach–Indian River County Chamber of Commerce. 1216 Twenty-first St., Vero Beach 32960; (772) 567-3491; www.IndianRiverChamber.com.

Fort Pierce

As you follow Rte. A1A, Fort Pierce begins on the south end of North Hutchinson Island, continues across the bridge (known as the North Bridge) onto the mainland (where A1A briefly merges with Hwy. 1), and spreads to still another island, the north end of Hutchinson Island, back on Rte. A1A. The bridge that crosses to Hutchinson is known as the South Bridge.

The Fort Pierce portion of Hutchinson Island (which also holds the beach adjuncts of Jensen Beach and Stuart) is the most developed, freckled with small resorts, surf shops, restaurants, and other tourism-related places. It has its share of beaches, with extensive boardwalks and picnic and fishing facilities.

Beach Horseback Riding (ages 10 and up)

Frederick Douglass Memorial Park, 3500 South A1A; (772) 468-0101. Rides available by reservation. Cost is $35 per person. Reservations required.

Hoof it down a stretch of pristine beach.

Fort Pierce Inlet State Park (ages 4 to 13)

Southernmost end of North Hutchinson Island; 905 Shore Winds Dr.; (772) 468-3985; www.floridastateparks.org/fortpierceinlet. Open 8 a.m. to sunset daily. Park entrance is $6 per vehicle of eight persons or fewer; $1 per extra passenger, cyclist, or pedestrian; $3 per single occupancy vehicle.

This is the place to go for beach recreation off the main road. You and the kids can sun yourselves on a choice of two beaches, fish, surf, have a picnic, hike into a coastal hammock, or play on the playground. Inlet Beach fronts the pass between North Hutchinson and Hutchinson Islands. Swift waters mean unsafe swimming conditions. On the ocean side, Jetty Park (aka North Beach) is protected from waves by its fishing jetty, making it safer for children. Lifeguards are on duty for added protection.

Harbor Branch Oceanographic Institution (ages 10 and up)

5600 Hwy 1 North; about fifteen minutes north of the North Bridge Causeway on the mainland; (772) 465-2400 ext 293; www.fau.edu/hboi. Open 10 a.m. to 5 p.m. Mon through Fri. 10 a.m. to 2 p.m. Sat. Admission is free.

Part of Florida Atlantic University, Harbor Branch is one of the leading centers for exploration of the world's oceans. Learn about the vital role they play in almost every aspect of our lives, even if we call Nebraska or North Dakota home. Displays, interactive exhibits, and videos inform and entertain. At the new Ocean Discovery Center you can become a "Marine Biologist in Training."

Jack Island Preserve (ages 10 to 13)

Off Rte. A1A (watch carefully for the entrance signs). Open 8 a.m. to sunset daily. Admission is free.

Part of Fort Pierce Inlet State Park (next entry), it juts into the Indian River. You can hike the peninsula's diked perimeter or trek into its center via a mile-long mangrove wetlands trail.

National Navy UDT-SEAL Museum (ages 7 to 13)

3300 North A1A; (772) 595-5845; www.navysealmuseum.com. Open 10 a.m. to 4 p.m. Tues through Sat (also Mon, Jan through Apr) and noon to 4 p.m. Sun. Admission is $6 for adults, $3 for children ages 6 to 12.

Within Pepper Park (see below) you can visit a museum that deals with a most unusual aspect of local history—the training of Navy frogmen in 1943 for the D-Day invasion. It tells the story of Underwater Demolition Teams and the Navy's SEAL (Sea Air and Land) program. Outside, a collection of specialized naval watercraft, a helicopter, and other large specimens begin this foray into special naval tactics.

Florida **Trivia**

Cocoons of the Deep Harbor Branch Oceanographic Institution is known for its underwater research using manned submersibles, like the one employed to explore the *Titanic* wreck. Its displays show the Link Trainer, a submersible simulator that is predecessor to today's amusement park motion simulator rides.

Pepper Park (all ages)

3300 North Rte. A1A, North Hutchinson Island. Open dawn to dusk daily.

A top choice for family recreation, it takes up both sides of the road, spreading from ocean to bayfront. The ocean part is older, with a nice beach and timeworn facilities, including tennis and basketball courts and picnic pavilions. Lifeguards supervise on the beach. The other side of the road crosses into a world tailor-made for fishing, hiking, canoeing, boating, and picnicking. Two boat docks, one of them for canoes, and six fishing piers reach into Wildcat Cove.

St. Lucie County Historical Museum (ages 4 to 13)

414 Seaway Dr.; off Rte. A1A alongside the South Bridge; (772) 462-1795; www.st-lucie. lib.fl.us/museum. Open 10 a.m. to 4 p.m. Tues through Sat. Admission is $4.00 for adults, $3.50 seniors, $1.50 for children ages 6 to 17; under 6 free.

At the north end of Hutchinson Island, take another peek at citrus and its local importance. Nicely framed vignettes show other aspects of local history, too, including one devoted to the sixteenth-century shipwreck of a Spanish treasure fleet and another of a Seminole Indian camp. Kids will love the 1919 fire engine and charming little pioneer home. The museum is located next to a waterfront park where you can picnic and fish.

Where to Eat

Mangrove Mattie's. 1640 Seaway Dr. (Hutchinson Island); (772) 466-1044. Seafood and pasta, and a picture-window view of Fort Pierce Inlet, beachers, and boat traffic. Lunch and dinner daily. $$–$$$

For More Information

St. Lucie County Tourist Bureau. 2300 Virginia Ave., Fort Pierce 34982; (772) 462-1535 or (800) 345-TGIF; www.visitstluciefla .com.

Jensen Beach

Take Rte. A1A ten minutes south of Fort Pierce on Hutchinson Island. To get to the mainland, cross the Intracoastal Waterway at Rte. 732.

Things get much quieter as you head south down Hutchinson Island. You'll see signs for beach accesses every few miles. Many have limited or no facilities and are favored by surfers and solitude-seekers.

Club Med Sandpiper

Northwest of Jensen Beach at 3500 S.E. Morningside Blvd., Port St. Lucie; (772) 398-5100 or (800) 258-2633; www.clubmed.com.

It is one of the few Florida resorts with a kids' program that includes infants, ages four to twenty-three months. Kids as young as four years old can get their fins wet on the Scuba Experience. The resort also caters to older children and adults, with circus courses in juggling, trapeze, and clowning. Each Thursday night the kids put on a circus under the real Big Top. Like all Club Meds, the emphasis is on activity, and there is plenty to do at this riverside property with its golf, river beach, swimming pools, trampoline, fitness center, sailing and waterskiing lessons, tennis courts, in-line skating and half-pipe ramp, pitch-and-putt course, basketball, volleyball, and beach shuttle. It has a French flair, and kids get exposed to people from many cultures. Ask about special family plans. $$$$ (Rates are per adult and include all meals and activities.)

Rosemeyer's Boat Rental (all ages)

Across the Jensen Beach Causeway at Jensen Beach Boulevard and Northeast Indian River Drive; 3321 Northeast Indian River Dr.; (772) 334-1000. Open 8 a.m. to 5 p.m. daily.

On-the-water opportunities are abundant on this part of the coast. Diving, surfing, windsurfing, and fishing—both deep-sea and back-bay—provide endless adventure of the H_2O variety. Create your own adventures with a boat rental from Rosemeyer's.

Sea Turtle Beach (all ages)

Jensen Beach Causeway at Rte. A1A. Open 8 a.m. to 8 p.m. daily.

This is the best beach for families who appreciate lots of activities. The vast stretch, 1,500 feet long, has lifeguards, extensive food concessions, volleyball, and picnic tables. The park manages to remain in a nicely maintained natural state despite its popularity.

Where to Eat

Conchy Joe's. 3945 Northeast Indian River Dr.; just across and north of the Jensen Beach Causeway; (772) 334-1130. Seafood and ribs. Bahamian style with view of the Indian River. Kids' menu. Lunch and dinner daily. $$–$$$

For More Information

Jensen Beach Chamber of Commerce. 1910 Northeast Jensen Beach Blvd., Jensen Beach 34957; (772) 334-3444; www.jensen chamber.com.

Stuart

Just south of Jensen Beach along Rte. A1A. Downtown centers around Osceola Avenue, north of and parallel to Rte. A1A.

Downtown Stuart has a rejuvenated appeal to shoppers and historians, but getting there from Hutchinson Island can be confusing. There's even an intersection called Confusion Corner. Most visitors, however, head to the beach, which occupies the southernmost portion of Hutchinson Island.

Bathtub Reef Beach (all ages)

Southeast McArthur Boulevard.

A favorite of families with small kids, it lives up to its name: A rare marine-worm reef creates a calm pond of Atlantic waters. However, facilities are a bit shabbier than at other local beaches. Lifeguards are around at peak activity periods. Posted notices warn of possible swimming dangers and surf conditions.

Elliott Museum (ages 7 to 13)

825 Northeast Ocean Blvd.; (772) 225-1961; www.elliottmuseumfl.org; Open 10 a.m. to 4 p.m. Mon through Sat and 1 to 4 p.m. Sun. Admission is $7 for adults, $2 for children ages 6 to 13.

On park grounds at Stuart Beach (see below), this museum presents a curious assortment of inventions by Sterling Elliott, including the stamp machine, automatic knot-tier, and four-wheel bicycle. There's also an impressive, eclectic collection of classic automobiles and Indian artifacts, and a vintage general store.

Florida Oceanographic Coastal Center (ages 4 to 13)
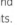

890 Northeast Ocean Blvd. (Route A1A); (772) 225-0505; www.floridaoceanographic.org. Open 10 a.m. to 5 p.m. Mon through Sat and noon to 4 p.m. Sun. Admission is $8 for adults, $4 for children ages 3 to 12.

Touch tanks, aquariums, a mounted fish collection, interactive puzzles and activities, and guided nature walks acquaint youngsters with local sea and land habitat and inhabitants.

Gilbert's Bar House of Refuge (ages 7 to 13)

301 Southeast McArthur Blvd.; off Rte. A1A; (772) 225-1875; www.elliottmuseumfl.org. Open 10 a.m. to 4 p.m. Mon through Sat and 1 to 4 p.m. Sun. Admission is $5 for adults, $2 for children ages 6 to 13.

Another unusual museum, this one dwells in a structure that once harbored nineteenth-century shipwreck survivors along these often cruel shores. The only remaining such structure where once stood ten, it today harbors turn-of-the-twentieth-century period furnishings from the time the Bessie family manned the lifesaving facility.

East Central Climes

Temperatures average between 62 to 88 degrees along this spell of coastline and are generally more temperate than inland since air and water temperatures are moderated by the Gulf Stream and the morning sea breeze. The average yearly humidity is 76 percent. Summer, of course, is hottest, most humid, and rainiest, but showers are usually brief. Winters may require long sleeves and pants legs, especially in the evening, but usually allow a just share of swimsuit time. Statistics show that the region enjoys an average of 230 days of sunshine per year.

Island Princess (ages 5 to 13)

Finest Kind Marina, 3585 SE St. Lucie Blvd., Stuart; (772) 225-2100; www.islandprincess cruises.com. Cost of two-hour tour is $21.95 for adults, $16.00 for children under age 12.

This yacht departs from the marina for several excursions. Recommended for children is Wednesday's two-hour nature cruise. You need not be a resort guest to enjoy it.

Stuart Beach (all ages)

Route A1A. Open sunrise to sunset. Admission is free.

Families love Stuart Beach, and why not? It has everything you could ever hope to find on a Florida beach: lifeguards, an outdoor cafe, a playground, a nature interpretation station, picnic shelters with grills, a volleyball net, basketball courts, and a concession where you can rent boogie boards, volleyballs, and basketballs.

Where to Stay

Hutchinson Island Marriott. 555 Northeast Ocean Blvd.; (772) 225-3700 or (800) 775-5936. Among Florida's top family destination resorts, 200 acres large, the Marriott is well respected for its golfing and kids' programs. There's a marina, four restaurants, bars, swimming pools, thirteen tennis courts, and any number of rental options, many of which front the beach. $$$–$$$$

Where to Eat

Prawnbroker Grill. Harbour Bay Plaza, 3754 Southeast Ocean Blvd.; (772) 288-1222.

Specializing in fresh seafood and steaks, with creative nightly specials and kids' menu. Dinner daily. $$$

For More Information

Stuart/Martin County Chamber of Commerce. 1650 South Kanner Hwy, Stuart 34994; (772) 287-1088 or (800) 524-9704; www.goodnature.org.

Hobe Sound

Head south on Rte. A1A, also known as Dixie Highway, about fifteen minutes from Hutchinson Island.

The teeny town of Hobe Sound makes a pleasant stop for antiques and crafts shoppers. Outside of town, the community is known for its natural treasures. Rte. 707 takes you through Jupiter Island with its mansions and its preserved beaches.

Blowing Rocks Preserve (ages 7 and up)

On Jupiter Island, 574 South Beach Rd., Hobe Sound; (561) 744-6668. Open 9 a.m. to 4:30 p.m. daily. Beach access fee $2 per person; free for children 12 and under. Guided nature walks on Sun at 11 a.m.

Blowing Rocks is named for the 50-foot plumes forced up after storms or during high tides. The preserve has beach dunes, mangrove wetlands, and tropical and upland trees. There is a butterfly garden with native plants.

Hobe Sound National Wildlife Refuge (ages 7 to 13)

Visitor center at 13640 Southeast Federal Hwy; (772) 546-6141; www.fws.gov/hobesound. The center is open 9 a.m. to 3 p.m. Mon through Fri. Admission is free. The island portion of the refuge is open sunrise to sunset daily. Admission to the refuge's beach portion, which lies on the north end of Jupiter Island (take Rte. 707/Bridge Road, east from Rte. A1A), is $5 per car.

It hosts environmental education programs, summer kids' camps, nature hikes, exhibits, and sea-turtle walks. Its beach is a prime nesting site for sea turtles. The tiny but packed full interpretative center on the mainland contains a big, old, soft vinyl manatee toy and glass boxes filled with a baby alligator, a baby crocodile, and snakes. Easy nature trails take you around the placid waterfront.

Jonathan Dickinson State Park (ages 5 to 13)

16450 Southeast Federal Hwy (Hwy. 1); (772) 546-2771; www.floridastateparks.org/jonathan dickinson. Open 8 a.m. to sunset daily. Park entrance is $6 per vehicle of eight persons or fewer, $1 per extra passenger, cyclist, or pedestrian.

Many people overlook Jonathan Dickinson because it lacks beaches. Its treasures are estuarine instead. Take the family there to camp, rent a cabin, hike, canoe, or enjoy pontoon tours into its 11,600 acres of forest—host to wildlife such as deer and Florida scrub jays.

Loxahatchee River Adventures (ages 6 to 13)

Jonathan Dickinson State Park; 16450 Southeast Federal Hwy; (561) 746-1466; www.florida parktours.com. Tours depart at 9 and 11 a.m. and 1 and 3 p.m. daily. Cost is $18.78 for adults, $11.50 for children ages 6 to 12, plus the car entrance fee to the park. Canoe rentals available beginning at $16 for two hours and $5 for each additional hour.

Guided pontoon rides from the park on the wild and scenic Loxahatchee River are provided four times daily.

More Things to See and Do
in East Central Florida

- **Andretti Thrill Park,** Melbourne; (321) 956-6706

- **Atlantic Race Park,** Daytona Beach Shores; (386) 226-8777

- **Brevard Museum of Art and Science,** Melbourne; (321) 242-0737

- **Manatee Observation and Education Center,** Fort Pierce; (772) 466-1600, ext. 3071

- **Maritime and Yachting Museum,** Jensen Beach; (772) 692-1234

- **Mel Fisher's Treasure Museum,** Sebastian; (772) 589-9875; www.melfisher .com/TreasureSales/Locations.asp

- **New Smyrna Speedway,** New Smyrna; (386) 427-4129

- **New York Mets Spring Training,** Port St. Lucie; (772) 871-2115

- **Ormond Memorial Art Museum and Gardens,** Ormond Beach; (386) 676-3347

- **Pirate's Cove Adventure Golf,** Ormond Beach; (386) 676-9326

- **Safari River Tours,** Debary; (386) 668-1002

- **Speed Park Motorsports,** Daytona Beach; (386) 253-FAST

- **Stuart Heritage Museum,** Stuart; (772) 220-4600

For More Information

Hobe Sound Chamber of Commerce. 8994 Southeast Bridge Rd. (P.O. Box 1507), Hobe Sound 33475; (772) 546-4724; www .hobesound.org.

Annual Events

Blue Spring Manatee Festival. Orange City; www.themanateefestival.com; (386) 775-3663. In January the park cohosts the Blue Spring Manatee Festival with entertainment, endangered species exhibits, and tours.

Seafest. Port Canaveral; (321) 459-2200. Seafood, arts, crafts, and entertainment three days in late March.

Daytona 500 NASCAR Stock Car Races. Daytona Beach; (386) 253-7223. The biggest motor sports event in Florida, held in April.

Ron Jon's/Robert August Easter Surfing Festival. Cocoa Beach; (321) 452-4145. Spring contests, entertainment, fun.

Central
Florida

Tourism in central Florida is dominated by the world of Disney and the kids' fantasyland of amusement parks that have sprung up on its shirttails. The Orlando-Kissimmee hub can provide enough for a month's worth of family vacation, if you and your wallet can take it.

You don't have to travel far from Walt Disney World and the Orlando area to find the real Florida, minus the animatronics. In the region's farthest reaches, you can discover snatches of the old Cracker days, when cowboys and orange growers scratched a living out of the swamps and prairies. Here, along the shores of year-round warm springs, Florida tourism was born.

This tour of central Florida takes you to both extremes—the time-frozen temperament and the futuristic façade.

Gainesville and Environs

East of I-75 at Hwy. 441.

Gainesville, once ranked the nation's best place to live by *Money* magazine, is first and foremost a college town, home of the University of Florida Gators—and birthplace of Gatorade! This keeps it youthful, spirited, and cultured. Natural attractions in its northern and southern environs keep it bonded to the environment.

Devil's Millhopper State Geological Park (ages 5 to 13)

4732 Millhopper Rd. (Route 232); (352) 955-2008; administrative office: 12720 Northwest 109th Lane; (386) 462-7905. Open 9 a.m. to 5 p.m. Wed through Sun; closed Mon and Tues. Make reservations for a free ranger-guided tour on Sat at 10 a.m. by calling (386) 462-7905. Admission to the site is $2 per vehicle or $1 per pedestrian or bicyclist.

Here is a special place where waterfalls and lush fern growth make you feel as though you've stumbled into the Garden of Eden. The unusual landscaping is due to a five-acre, 120-foot-deep sinkhole—232 steps to the bottom!

CENTRAL FLORIDA

Florida Museum of Natural History (ages 4 to 13)

University of Florida, UF Cultural Plaza, Hull Road and Southwest Thirty-fourth Street, Gainesville; (352) 846-2000; www.flmnh.ufl.edu. Open 10 a.m. to 5 p.m. Mon through Sat and noon to 5 p.m. Sun and holidays. Closed Thanksgiving and Christmas Day. Admission is free, but there may be fees for special exhibits.

This newly rebuilt museum teaches young learners about northern Florida limestone-based geology and the region's incredible dunes. Special exhibits rotate through the year. It's a not-to-be-missed attraction in Gainesville, with permanent exhibits showing ancient civilizations and fossils, a walk-through cave, and an Indian village.

Among the new additions is a butterfly rain forest where hundreds of the brightly colored winged beauties hover above waterfalls or flit from plant to plant. Weather permitting, kids may watch live butterflies released to the outside world Saturday and Sunday, at 2, 3, and 4 p.m. Admission to the Butterfly Rainforest is $9.50 adult, $7.00 seniors and students 13 to 17 and in college, $5.00 ages 6 to 12, 5 and under free.

Gainesville to Hawthorne Rail Trail (ages 8 to 13)

Parking at 3400 Southeast Fifteenth St. Parking and access to the trailhead is open 8 a.m. to sunset daily.

The 17-mile trail begins at Boulware Springs City Park and takes you through the Paynes Prairie wilderness to the town of Hawthorne. There are restrooms at mile 1 and mile 6.6.

Marjorie Kinnan Rawlings State Historic Park (ages 10 to 13)

Route 325, 21 miles southeast of Gainesville at Cross Creek; (352) 466-3672. The grounds are open 9 a.m. to 5 p.m. daily. You can enter the home by tour only, conducted every

TopPicks for Family Fun in Central Florida

1. Cavorting with Mickey Mouse at the Magic Kingdom, Walt Disney World

2. Riding the movies at Universal Studios Orlando

3. Entering the funny-paper world of Islands of Adventure, Orlando

4. Seeing 3-D at Disney Hollywood Studios, Walt Disney World

5. Looking into the future at EPCOT, Walt Disney World

6. Exploring underwater secrets at SeaWorld Adventure Park, Orlando

7. Kissing a dolphin at Discovery Cove, Orlando

8. Being a "science guy" (or gal) at Orlando Science Center, Orlando

9. Peeking into Florida's past at the Florida Museum of Natural History, Gainesville

Road Markers

This excursion roughly follows Hwy. 441 from the Gainesville area south to Orlando, then along I-4 through Kissimmee, and south on Hwy. 27 into the state's quirky midsection.

I-4 between Orlando and Tampa, often under construction (especially at the west end), can be a nightmare to drive, particularly in winter season. The construction is widening the road, so hopefully more lanes will disperse the traffic before the traffic catches up with the upgrade. In the meantime, it's best to avoid that route and take Hwy. 27 south, even if it does wind through towns and stoplights.

hour on the hour (except noon) from 10 a.m. to 4 p.m. Thurs through Sun (except Aug and Sept). Admission to the park is $2 per person; tours of the home are $3 for adults, $2 for children 6 to 12, and free for children under 6.

Prepare the kids with readings from *The Yearling,* then proceed to the home where the author once lived the spartan life. She's the region's local hero, and guides at the site dress in period costume to relate her life of farming oranges, hunting gators, and cooking cooter (turtle). Arrive early in the day because tours are limited in number, which means a long wait as the day rolls on.

Micanopy

As you make your way south on Hwy. 411, stop in Micanopy, where tourism first hit Florida. Today the town, which strings along Cholokka Boulevard parallel to the highway, has turned into a restored enclave for artisans and antiques vendors. Some of the shops sell vintage toys.

Morningside Nature Center (ages 5 to 13)

3540 East University Ave., Gainesville; (352) 334-2170; www.natureoperations.org. Open 9 a.m. to 5 p.m. daily. Admission to park and farm is free. Reenactments held Sat, except in summer.

Costumed actors re-create the lifestyles of a nineteenth-century farmer in its ten-acre Living History Farm, with an 1840 cabin and other vintage structures. Also in the 278-acre park, 5 miles of trails travel through cypress and pine forests, where more than 130 species of birds live. Spy some from the wildlife observation blind.

Paynes Prairie Preserve State Park (ages 5 to 13)

South of town on Hwy. 441; 100 Savannah Blvd., Micanopy; (352) 466-3397. The visitor center is open 9 a.m. to 4 p.m. daily. The park is open daily from 8 a.m. to sunset. Park entrance is $6 per vehicle of eight persons or fewer, $1 per extra passenger, cyclist, or pedestrian.

The park introduces visitors to northern Florida's social and natural history with inside exhibits and outdoor nature trails, living history, biking, canoeing, and camping. Sandhill cranes and alligators are common to its 22,000 acres of predominantly marshy terrain, plus the kids can try spotting American bison and Spanish horses. A visitor center with museum traces the region's Amerindian roots.

San Felasco Hammock State Preserve (ages 5 to 13)
Route 232, 4 miles northwest of town; 12720 Northwest 109th Lane, Alachua; (386) 462-7905. Open 8 a.m. to sunset daily. Park entrance is $2 per vehicle of eight persons or fewer, $1 per extra passenger, cyclist, or pedestrian.

This park presents still another unusual face of natural Florida, where springs play hide-and-seek amid the honeycombed limestone foundation and more than 150 species of trees occupy the forest along a nature trail. Wild turkeys, white-tailed deer, and bobcats also dwell here.

Santa Fe Community College Teaching Zoo (ages 4 to 13)
3000 Northwest Eighty-third St., Gainesville (near I-75); (352) 395-5611. Open 9 a.m. to 2 p.m. Sat and Sun, Mon through Fri by appointment. Admission is $4 adult, $3 senior and children 4 to 12, under 4 free.

No biggies like elephants, lions, and tigers to see, but about 200 birds, mammals, reptiles, and amphibians fill the cages and open pens on this ten-acre heavily wooded site. Led by zoology students, kids will have a learning experience as they view endangered and other wild animals from around the world.

Where to Eat

Emiliano's Cafe and Bakery. 7 Southeast First Ave., Gainesville; (352) 375-7381. Red-brick walls, a bakery, and sidewalk seating. Specialties have a Cuban-Caribbean flair. Lunch and dinner Mon through Sat, Brunch on Sun. $–$$

Harry's. 110 Southeast First St., Gainesville; (352) 372-1555. Cajun-style po'boys, soups, and other dishes in a New Orleans setting with sidewalk seating. Lunch and dinner daily. $–$$

Where to Stay

Lodging is typically inexpensive in Gainesville.

Bambi Motel Budget Host. 2119 Southwest Thirteenth St., Gainesville; (352) 376-2622 or (800) 34-BAMBI. Playground, pool, and thirty-four rooms. $

For More Information

Alachua County Visitors and Convention Bureau. 30 East University Ave., Gainesville 32601; (352) 374-5231 or (866) 778-5002; www.visitGainesville.net.

Ocala

About 35 miles south of Gainesville on Hwy. 441 or I-75.

One of the nicest ways to spend time in Ocala is looking at the scenery, whether from a car, a bike, or horseback.

Don Garlits Museum of Drag Racing (ages 5 to 13)

13700 Southwest Sixteenth Ave.; (352) 245-8661. Open 9 a.m. to 5 p.m. daily. Closed Christmas. Admission is $15 for adults, $13 for senior and students, $6 for children 5 to 12; under 5 free.

Race fans of a different stripe will want to look at the retired dragsters and the antique automobile displays here.

Horse Farms (all ages)

Horses are a recurring theme around town. The area's 400-plus horse farms raise 10 percent of North America's thoroughbred racehorses and provide some of the hill-heaving countryside's prettiest sights. Hwys. 441 and 301, and Routes 220, 225, 225A, and 475A are among the most scenic. Some of the farms allow visitors to tour. To tour the countryside by horse and buggy, call Ocala Carriage & Tours; (352) 867-8717; www.ocalacarriage .com. The company offers an hour carriage ride in the country for four, priced at $95. Reservations only.

Juniper Springs (all ages)

Route 40 east of Ocala; 3199 Northeast County Road 315, Silver Springs; (352) 625-3147 or (352) 236-0288. The park and its visitor information center are open daily 8 a.m. to 8 p.m. Park entrance fee is $4 per person over age 5.

The Ocala area has it up on all other parts of central Florida as far as natural attractions go. The continental United States' southernmost national forest, Ocala National Forest, is a 400,000-acre refuge for wildlife and sports folk alike. A gurgling land of warm (72-degree) springs and sand pines, it offers camping, swimming, hiking trails, wildlife sighting, canoeing, and diving in several recreational areas. Most popular and scenic is Juniper Springs, where an ancient waterwheel-powered mill edges see-through waters. A 7-mile canoe run takes you past alligators, limpkins, turtles, and other wildlife.

Silver Springs (all ages)

1 mile east of Ocala on Rte. 40; 5656 East Silver Springs Blvd., Silver Springs; (352) 236-2121; www.silversprings.com. Open 10 a.m. to 5 p.m. daily. General admission is $34.99 for adults, $30.99 for seniors, $24.99 for children ages 3 to 10; under 3 free. Includes boat rides and entrance into the museums and other attractions. Parking is $7.

One of the original glass-bottom boat rides took early visitors through the jungles and over the clear spring waters of Silver Springs. Besides the fish, turtles, snails and other marine life you glimpse through the glass, the Fort King River Cruise takes you to an Old Florida Cracker homestead. An Army stockade and Seminole village are also part of the interactive trip. The Lost River Cruise focuses on wildlife with an on-board naturalist. Florida's first tourist attraction continually grows and has kept up with the times by adding such rides as a Ferris Wheel, carousel, and gondola combo that rises 80 feet above the park, a net bridge, a bird show, a petting zoo, a Jeep safari, World of Bears, and Panther Prowl. The squeamish will want to sidestep the "Creature Feature" show, starring scorpions, bats, and giant Madagascar hissing cockroaches. Don't miss the white alligator

Movie Star

Silver Springs has starred in more movies and television shows than Harrison Ford. Six Tarzan movies, *Creature from the Black Lagoon*, *The Yearling*, *Never Say Never Again*, and *Smokey and the Bandit* are among major films shot on location at the park. It also starred in the *Sea Hunt* television series, episodes of *I Spy*, *One Life to Live*, National Geographic specials, and other movies, TV shows, and commercials dating back to the silent movie *The Seven Swans* in 1916.

exhibit. Big Gator Lagoon is home to more than twenty gators and crocodiles. Once the site of *Tarzan* filming, the park hosts a healthy population of free-roaming monkeys in addition to its contained animals. The tiny tots will like the playland. You can dine at one of seven food outlets; no food or drink is allowed to be brought into the park (except bottled water). Call for a schedule of special entertainment events.

Wild Waters Water Park (ages 4 to 13)
At Silver Springs; (352) 236-2121; www.wildwaterspark.com. Open in warm months, generally weekends in Apr, May, and Labor Day, daily June through Aug, 10 a.m. to 5 p.m Sun to Thurs, 10 a.m. to 7 p.m. Fri and Sat. Admission is $25.99 plus tax for adults, $22.99 for children shorter than 48 inches. **Free** to those 2 and younger. Parking costs $7.

Have a wet blast on the water slides and flumes—Thunderbolt, Hurricane, Silver Bullet, Osceola's Revenge, or Twin Twister—or in the wave pool with tubes. Tots can slide down a frog's tongue or play in the Cool Kids Cove. The Caribbean Sprayground squirts 'em down with misters and fountains.

Young's Paso Fino Ranch (ages 6 to 13)
8075 Northwest Rte. 326; (352) 867-5305. Trail rides start at 9 and 11 a.m. and 1 p.m. Mon through Sat, begin with instruction, and last about an hour. Cost is $38 per rider, and riders must be age 6 or up. Tours of the horse barns are $11 per person, 10 a.m. and 2 p.m. Mon through Sat. Call for appointment.

To actually ride a horse in these parts, stop here. You can take a tour of the barn, follow a wooded trail astride a gentle Paso Fino horse, or sit in on a horse show with dancing and live music, when scheduled. Children ages four or above are welcome, but they must be six or older to ride. Go in the spring when the foals are born, or in the summer for special kids' programs, that may include a hayride.

Where to Eat

Harry's. 24 Southeast First Ave.; (352) 840-0900. Jambalaya, red beans and rice, seafood gumbo, po'boys, and other Cajun specialties. Lunch and dinner daily. $–$$

Where to Stay

Days Inn–Silver Springs. 5751 East Silver Springs Blvd., Silver Springs; (352) 236-2575 or (800) DAYSINN. One hundred three rooms, pool, and restaurant. $

For More Information

Ocala–Marion County Chamber of Commerce. 110 East Silver Springs Blvd., Ocala 34470; (352) 629-8051; fax (352) 629-7651; www.ocalacc.com.

Mount Dora

Take Hwy. 441 south of Ocala 45 miles.

A picture-pretty town that refuses to join the twenty-first century, Mount Dora provides a restful contrast to the flurry of activity that awaits to the south. Downtown is a baker's window full of Victorian wedding-cake homes and browsable antiques shops. The chamber of commerce hands out historic tour maps.

Premier Boat Tours (ages 5 to 13)

Lakeside Inn, 100 N. Alexander, Mt. Dora (352) 343-0200. Departs at 11 a.m. and 2 p.m. daily Fare is $20 for adults, $10 for children ages 4 to 8, under 4 free.

To see Mount Dora's wild side, take Capt. Doolittle's twenty-one person pontoon boat canal tour between two lakes—Eustis and Dora—decorated with cypress trees and birds.

Where to Eat

The Gables Restaurant. 322 Alexander St.; (352) 383-8993. Salads, burgers, sandwiches, and entrees. Seating indoors and outdoors in the garden. Lunch and dinner daily. $–$$

Where to Stay

Lakeside Inn. 100 North Alexander St.; (352) 383-4101. Pretty historic property on the lake with pool, restaurant, lounge, tennis courts, nearby shopping, and a boardwalk to a natural island on the lake. $–$$$

For More Information

Mount Dora Area Chamber of Commerce. 341 Alexander St. (P.O. Box 196), Mount Dora 32757; (352) 383-2165; fax (352) 383-1668; www.mountdora.com.

Orlando

Located at the crossroads of I-4 and the Florida Turnpike. From Mount Dora, continue along Hwy. 441 for about a half hour to reach I-4.

Vacationland of the world, Orlando and its attractions come in two parts. Downtown you'll find culture, museums, and the showtime atmosphere of Church Street Station and environs.

Orlando's most publicized attractions and resorts lie south of downtown on the west side of town, along I-4 and International Drive. Although Disney World is not actually

Central Florida **Climes**

The average temperature ranges from 50 to 90 degrees. Humidity ranges from 55 to 88 percent. Winter months average daytime highs of 70 with low humidity. Thunderstorms cool hot, humid summer days. Be sure to take shelter at the first sound of an approaching thunderstorm, as central Florida is the nation's lightning capital.

contained within Orlando, it affects it deeply, and most people associate it with Orlando. The city itself was a quiet little town that went bonkers in 1971, when Disney moved in. The whole south end of town rides like an amusement park where sky beams, neon lights, larger-than-life sneakers and teddy bears, and sinking and upside-down buildings fight for your attention. It's a stream of fun, but be prepared to pay and stand in line for it.

Amway Arena (ages 6 to 13)

8600 West Amelia St.; 1 block off I-4; (407) 89-MAGIC or (800) 338-0005; www.orlandomagic .com. Off-season (single game) ticket prices from $10 to $95.

Basketball fans travel far (without penalty) to watch the Orlando Magic at Amway, formerly the T. D. Waterhouse Centre. The NBA team plays October through April.

Aquatica–Sea World's Water Park (all ages)

55800 Water Play Way, (467) 351-3600; 888-800-5447; www.aquaticabyseaworld.com. Open 8 a.m. to 10 p.m. daily. Tickets (gate) $47.87 adult, $41.48 ages 3 to 9.

Opposite Sea World along International Drive. The first new water park to open in Orlando in twelve years features thirty-six water slides, six rivers and lagoons, and more than 80,000 square feet of sandy beach. A one-of-a-kind experience is a 42-foot drop in an enclosed water slide through a lagoon of black and white Commerson's dolphins. Must be at least 48 inches tall for that ride. Small fry will have fun in Kata's Kookaburra Cove. Brilliant macaws and colorful fish are other live animals in the park.

Discovery Cove (ages 6 to 13)

6000 Discovery Cove Way; (877) 4-DISCOVERY; www.discoverycove.com. Open daily 9 a.m. to 5:30 p.m. All-inclusive admission with dolphin encounter is $259 to $279 per person, depending on the season, plus tax. Without dolphin encounter, admission runs $159 to $179 per person, depending on the season, plus tax.

Across the street from SeaWorld, its parent park, Discovery Cove expands the dolphin interaction program begun there into an all-inclusive (well, almost, anyway) resort experience. For the full price you get a dolphin encounter, which includes about forty-five minutes of instruction and forty minutes in the water with a dolphin, a trainer, and about eight other people. The package includes a cafeteria-style lunch, one **free** photograph taken as you enter the park, use of snorkel equipment (you keep the snorkel), and access to the park's freshwater river pool, saltwater ray and coral reef pools, aviary island, beach, lockers, showers, towels, and a seven-day pass to SeaWorld. The kids will love feeding the birds and petting the rays. Snacks, beverages, and dolphin interaction photos cost extra (at typical theme park prices). Admission is limited to 1,000 people per day, and reservations are required. Children must be age six or older to swim with the dolphins.

Gatorland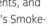

14501 South Orange Blossom Trail; (407) 855-5496 or (800) 393-JAWS; www.gatorland.com. Open 9 a.m. to 5 p.m. daily. Admission is $22.99 for adults, $14.99 for children ages 3 to 12, plus tax.

Not far from the hubbub, yet a world away, Gatorland holds on to Orlando's Cracker roots with gator-wrestling shows and native snake demonstrations. You'll see alligators from a foot long to 3 feet wide. There are also a wet and dry playground, after-dark events, and a crocodile land. If you dare, snack on some gator ribs or gator nuggets at Pearl's Smokehouse. It serves more normal fare as well and provides a smokehouse jungle gym for the kids.

Kelly Park (all ages)

North of Orlando in Apopka; 400 Kelly Park Rd., Apopka; (407) 889-4179. Admission is $3 per car or $5 per car for 3 or more people Open 8 a.m. to 8 p.m. in summer and 8 a.m. to 6 p.m. in winter.

Cool off in an inner tube or just a swimsuit. Picnic tables, grills, nature trails, volleyball courts, and horseshoes make for an old-fashioned family fun day. You can even camp overnight.

Lake Eola Park (all ages)

Rosalind Avenue and Robinson Street; (407) 246-2827. Paddleboat rentals are $10 for thirty minutes.

Much overlooked, but a great place for a picnic, this downtown refuge offers sculpture, lighted fountains, concerts, a pagoda, mossy oaks, a scenic walk, and graceful swan paddleboats.

Mennello Museum of American Folk Art (ages 5 to 13)

900 East Princeton St.; (407) 246-4278; www.mennellomuseum.com. Open 10:30 a.m. to 4:30 p.m. Tues through Sat, noon to 4:30 p.m. Sun. Admission is $4 for adults, $3 for seniors; $1 for students with ID, under 12 free.

For a day of culture, head to the Loch Haven neighborhood with its science museum, galleries, and other attractions. This small museum offers a dose in child-bright colors and an outdoor sculpture garden on the lake, featuring the work of Earl Cunningham and changing exhibits.

Top **Family** Resorts

1. **Holiday Inn Family Suites,** Lake Buena Vista

2. **Portofino Bay Hotel,** Universal Orlando

3. **Holiday Inn Sunspree,** Lake Buena Vista

4. **Hyatt Regency Grand Cypress,** Lake Buena Vista

5. **Grand Floridian,** Walt Disney World

6. **Polynesian Resort,** Walt Disney World

Orange County Regional History Center (ages 6 to 12)

65 East Central Blvd.; (407) 836-8500 or (800) 965-2030; www.thehistorycenter.org. Open 10 a.m. to 5 p.m. daily. Admission is $12 for adults, $9 for seniors and students with ID, $7 for children ages 5 to 12.

Moved downtown to the historic old city hall building, it has expanded to include more hands-on scenes of old Orlando, from 12,000 years past and ancient natives to Seminoles, pioneers, and Cinderella's Castle. Begin your sashay through time in the Orientation Theater, set on an Old Florida back porch.

Orlando **Museum of Art** (ages 5 to 13)

2416 North Mills Ave.; near Orlando Science Center; (407) 896-4231; www.omart.org. Open 10 a.m. to 4 p.m. Tues through Fri, noon to 4 p.m. Sat and Sun. Admission is $8 for adults, $7 for seniors and students, $5 for children ages 6 to 18. Locals admitted free from 1 to 5 p.m. on Thurs.

The kids can learn about art the fun way in the interactive Children's Gallery. The museum's permanent collection includes works by Georgia O'Keeffe, Andy Warhol, Roy Lichtenstein, and Childe Hassam, along with ancient art.

Orlando **Science Center** (ages 4 to 13)

777 East Princeton St.; (407) 514-2000 or (888) 672-4386; www.osc.org. Open 10 a.m. to 5 p.m. every day but Wed. Admission is $17 for adults, $16 for seniors and students with ID, $12 for children 3 to 11; 2 and under free. On Fri and Sat admission is lower after 6 p.m.

With all the flash and spark of Orlando, it winds you around four floors of touch, poke, and play exhibits. Lift a Volkswagen Beetle, walk into a giant mouth, spin a cloud, stick your head into a tornado, and stand inside a kaleidoscope. There's a special Kid's Town, where no one over 48 inches tall is allowed to enter. NatureWorks takes a walk on the wild side. Other exhibits include 1-2-3 Math, Physics Park, BodyZone, and Light Power. CineDome theater projects in-the-round films on a screen eight stories high, and live shows take place in the Adventure Theater. Some of the exhibits and the observatory present special programs, and traveling exhibits visit. Exhibits and programs were designed to meet school curriculum requirements. There's a lot to see here—it outlasts the attention spans of children under age ten.

Pirate's Dinner Adventure (ages 5 to 13)

6400 Carrier Dr.; off International Drive; (407) 248-0590 or (800) 866-AHOY; www.pirates dinneradventure.com. The box office and preshow room opens at 6:30 p.m. daily. Admission for dinner and show is $58.95 plus tax for adults and $38.95 plus tax for children ages 3 to 11.

The newest in the genre of dining experience pits swashbuckling buccaneers against one another in competition and mutiny—with feigned acts of hand-to-hand violence. The audience participates in the fun; children from the audience are used in many scenes. The stage is a floating pirate's brig. Entertainment is musical and dramatic with feats of circuslike skill. Dinner is a multicourse affair, with special kids' meals available and freely poured beverages (beer, wine, and cola—you can request something without caffeine for the kids). Before and after the show, you are treated to entertainment and partying with the pirates.

SeaWorld Adventure Park (all ages)

7007 SeaWorld Dr. (exit 29B westbound or 30A eastbound off I-4); (407) 351-3600 or (800) 4ADVENTURE; www.seaworld.com. Open 9 a.m. daily, with varying closing hours. Admission is $74.95 for adults, $64.95 for children ages 3 to 9 (tax not included). Parking is an additional $10 for cars, $12 for recreational vehicles. A "Pick Two" ticket for $79.95 plus tax, allows you to choose from several parks.

Killer whales, dolphins, sharks, and sea lions were the original stars at SeaWorld. The ever-evolving attraction has since added a sure-to-wow-'em Wild Arctic theme park with a simulated flight over the northlands and face-to-face encounters with polar bears (separated by Plexiglas). Breathing marine and wildlife now share the spotlight with a giant Manta Ray, located where the old aquarium once stood. Riders, strapped face down to its belly, swoop and soar over people, land, and water at speeds up to 56 mph. Those who prefer to keep their feet on the ground can visit the new aquarium where 300 living rays swim in a 186,000-gallon tank. Key West has moved to central Florida—sandy boardwalks, tropical blossoms, Bahaman cuisine, street entertainers, mangroves, and all. Journey to Atlantis is a thrilling flume ride and mythical sensory encounter all in one.

Top Family Beaches **and Parks**

1. **Juniper Springs,** Ocala National Forest

2. **Wekiwa Springs State Park,** Apopka

3. **Lake Kissimmee State Park,** Lake Wales

Smart **Travel**

- Admission prices are sky-high in the Orlando area, but you rarely have to pay full fare. Look for coupons in locally distributed brochures and materials, from hotel guest services, in restaurants, at other attractions, on the Internet, practically everywhere you look. Florida residents are often eligible for discounts. The Orlando Magicard offers discounts at seventy-six local establishments and is available through the Orlando/Orange County Convention and Visitors Bureau; (800) 551-0181. The Orlando FlexTicket packages admission to Universal Studios, SeaWorld, and Wet 'n' Wild theme parks and is available through individual park Web sites or by calling any of the participating parks.

- If you're including Disney or Universal Studios Escape in your Florida vacation, make it the grand finale. If you do Disney first, other attractions and activities pale. "Save the best for last."

- Don't be in a great hurry to get your toddler to Disney World. Although the Magic Kingdom does have its Mickey's Starland for teeny ones, it's generally most attractive to children ages seven and older. Young children have a hard time distinguishing fantasy from reality and can be scared even by the most seemingly benign attractions, such as Snow White. They also have a difficult time waiting in lines for an hour or more at a time. Universal's Islands of Adventure is the best major theme park for starters.

- When theme park–bound, bring backpacks and wear comfortable shoes and hats for the long haul. Suggested items: water spray bottle for hot days, sweaters for cool evenings, portable umbrellas or rain ponchos, apples and healthful snacks, frozen containers of drinking water and juice, sunscreen, bags of money. The wet rides at Universal's Islands of Adventure may require a change of clothes and locker rental.

- To save money, stamina, and sanity, consider taking an afternoon break from your theme park day. We usually leave about 2 p.m., go have lunch somewhere reasonably priced, go to the hotel to nap or chill out, then return when the weather has cooled and crowds have somewhat thinned.

- Many of the large theme park attractions don't serve kid-size portions in their restaurants and food stands, oddly enough (well, not so odd in a place where squeezing the last cent from your wallet seems to be the goal). Bring extra plastic cups so that you can split soft drink portions among little ones.

Split meals and snacks. One cheeseburger at Disney's Animal Kingdom easily fed two second-graders.

- When visiting large attractions, have a plan in case a child gets separated and lost. Instruct small children to stay put at the spot where he or she last saw the adults in the party. With older children, you can agree upon a spot to meet in case someone gets lost, or keep in touch with cell phones. Tuck notes into the pockets of small children with name of parents and home, cell phone, or hotel phone number.

- Disney T-shirts and other merchandise are sold at bargain prices at discount stores outside Disney World.

- To prevent scorching feet between rides at water parks, wear beach slippers.

The looping Kraken roller coaster, which is floorless and one of the tallest, fastest, and largest in Orlando, will thrill your teens. And older kids will love some of the parks' special programs, like Shark Deep Dive, where they descend into the shark tank with scuba or snorkel gear to see the massive creatures up close, or "sea trainer for a day," a day with the staff to see how marine animals are cared for and trained. The Waterfront, a five-acre entertainment, shopping, and restaurant complex designed to resemble a Mediterranean seaport, features street performers, musicians, and fun shows, like Kat 'n Kaboodle, with sixteen exotic species of trained cats doing amazing feats. You can also watch chefs flip pizza, cook on a Mongolian wok, and sample the cuisine of faraway places.

SkyVenture (all ages)

6805 Visitors Circle (across from Wet 'n' Wild off International Drive); (407) 903-1150; 800-759-3861; www.skyventureorlando.com. Open daily, 11:30 a.m. to 9 p.m. Sun through Thurs, 11:30 a.m. to 10 p.m. Fri and Sat. Indoor skydiving for $44.95 and up.

Kids don helmet, goggles, and flight gear for an ultimate role-playing experience as a skydiver. Besides equipment, Intro to Flying lasts about an hour; includes a hands-on training session, two flight rotations floating on wind up to 125 mph (each rotation equals one skydive), and a commemorative Flight Certificate. Release waver signed by parents or legal guardians required for children under age 18. Reservations suggested.

Universal Studios and Islands of Adventure Orlando
(ages 3 to 13)

1000 Universal Studios Plaza; (407) 363-8000 or (888) U-ESCAPE; www.universalorlando .com. Parks open at 9 a.m.; closing times vary. One-day admission to each park is $79.88 for adults, $67.10 for children ages 3 to 9 (tax included). Multiple-day, multipark passes save money, as do purchase of Internet-only specials from the parks' Web site. Multiday, multipark flex tickets are available for visits to Universal Studios, Islands of Adventure,

SeaWorld, Wet 'n' Wild, and Busch Gardens Tampa Bay. Florida residents can score special deals at certain times of the year. Admission to CityWalk is free. Parking fees are $12 for cars, $14 for large vehicles. Generally, no parking fees after 6 p.m.

With brashly entertaining parks, Universal Studios Orlando nears the top of the list of must-do attractions in Orlando. The original park, Universal Studios, features rides based on beloved blockbusters, such as *E.T., Jaws,* and *Men in Black,* with such recent additions as Disaster (replaced Earthquake) and a brand-new 17-story-high roller coaster with music of your choice, called Hollywood Rip Ride Rocket. However, the newest generation of technologically sophisticated attractions is even more fantastic, such as the psychological thrill ride Revenge of the Mummy or Shrek, namesake of the Oscar-winning film. It features a stunning four-dimensional film, which is amazing enough without the extra special effects that help guests realistically see, hear, and feel the action from their seats. Through the magic of "Ogrevision," the characters Princess Fiona, Donkey, and all the others come to life. Jimmy Neutron's Nicktoon Blast, a similarly high-tech attraction that takes you on a rocket trip to fight the evil Oublar from the planet Yokian, is a favorite, too. Preschoolers love the Funtastic World of Hanna-Barbera, Barney's Backyard, Fievel's Playland, and Curious George Goes to Town. Woody Woodpecker's Nuthouse Coaster is tame enough for the first-time thrill rider. Newest entry to the Kidzone is a ride through Krustyland with the Simpsons, America's favorite animated family. Shows and tours take you to back lots or Nickelodeon Studios, where visitors can tour a set. A new addition is the Blue Man Group, the poker-faced, blue-painted mimes who put on an eclectic all-ages show. It can be messy, and front rows get free ponchos.

Islands of Adventure appeals more evenly to all ages. Tots take a trip through the pages of *Cat in the Hat* at Seuss Landing. At Toon Lagoon, they are awed by the color and humor of their favorite funny-pages characters. Older adventurers love the monstrous roller coaster called the Incredible Hulk, which blasts them out of a dark tunnel from 0 to 40 mph in two seconds, only to drop them into thin air and then shoot them through water a couple of stories below. The park also boasts the world's first dual racing roller coasters, called Dueling Dragons, at the Lost Continent. The park holds lots of interactive areas as well, including the Jurassic Park Discovery Center, and offers a fun assortment of shows.

The Universal Express system makes it possible for one-day ticket-holders in either park to reserve a time on most attractions, saving time in line; they can hold only one reservation at a time. Resort guests enjoy "no-wait" privileges all day.

CityWalk is a lively complex of restaurants, movie theaters, and clubs. Two resorts complete the Universal scene, all accessible by water taxi, bus, or on foot.

Wekiwa Springs State Park (all ages)

Wekiwa Springs Road between Apopka and I-4; 1800 Wekiwa Circle, Apopka; (407) 884-2009. Open 8 a.m. to sunset daily. Park entrance is $6 per vehicle of eight persons or fewer, $2 per extra passenger, cyclist, or pedestrian.

Another cool place for a summer swim, it provides a playground, canoeing, hiking, picnicking, and camping within its 6,900 acres.

Wet 'n' Wild (ages 4 to 13)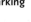

6200 International Dr.; (407) 351-WILD; 800-992-9453 www.wetnwild.com. Open daily; hours vary. Admission is $44.95 for persons ages 10 and older, $38.95 for children ages 3 to 9, seniors (60+); online discounted tickets for Florida residents. Tube rental $4. Parking costs $10 per car, $11 per recreational vehicle.

One of the most popular and spectacular of the region's many water parks, it boasts multi-passenger rides, a miniature park for kiddies, high-speed slides, a surf pool, and cable-pulled knee-boarding. Hydra Fighter lets riders create their own momentum by shooting water guns, but the line to get on moves painfully slow. Pools are heated in cold weather.

Wonderworks (ages 5 to 12)

Pointe Orlando, 9067 International Dr.; (407) 351-8800; www.wonderworksonline.com. Open daily 9 a.m. to midnight. Admission is $19.95 for adults ($22.95 with laser tag), $14.95 for seniors (65+) and children ages 4 to 12 ($17.95 with laser tag). Laser tag alone costs $4.95 per person.

The fun begins outside this tossed-upside-down building that creaks as if to topple when you walk by. With its disaster orientation, it may have stolen some of Orlando Science Center's thunder—but at a much higher price and less of a learning focus. Interactive games let you experience an earthquake, hang gliding, and aging. Dance on a keyboard and morph your voice to alien qualities. This place is lots of fun. An Outta Control Magic Comedy Dinner Show is available at 6 and 8 p.m. for $24.95 adult, $16.95 for kids ages 4 to 12 and seniors. Combo prices are $38.95 and $28.95, respectively.

Where to Eat

Cafe Tu Tu Tango. 8625 International Dr.; (407) 248-2222; www.cafetututango.com. Something for Mom, Dad, and the kids. An all-appetizer menu with an artist's theme. Lunch and dinner daily. $$–$$$

Flipper's Pizzeria. 7480 Universal Blvd.; (407) 351-5643. With four other locations. Yummy, handmade pizza, excellent salads with homemade dressings for Mom, even good desserts, and the prices are reasonable.

Flipper's even delivers to your hotel room if you're too tired to go out after a big day at the theme parks. $

One of the Largest McDonald's in All the World. 6875 Sand Lake Rd. (exit 74A off I-4); (407) 351-2185. Only in Orlando! McDonald's restaurant, pizzeria, and Mickey D's ice-cream parlor, plus a magnificent playland and two stories of video games. $

Tchoup Chop (pronounced chop-chop).
Royal Pacific Resort, 6300 Hollywood Way,
(407) 503-2467. The Polynesian-Asian menu,
conceived by celebrity chef Emeril Lagasse,
is a treat for adults, featuring such items as
blue crab claws, Kahlua pork, and a pineapple
upside-down cake that tastes like homemade.
It's not really suitable for young children, but
well-behaved teens and accompanying adults
can treat themselves to its luxurious calm and
gourmet fare after a hectic day at the theme
parks. $$$

Wild Jack's Orlando Grill & Co. 7364
International Dr.; (407) 352-4407. Kids love
the Wild West decor and cowboy boot–
shaped glasses. Prime steaks, fiery South-
western specialties, ribs, and wonderful
homemade soups and desserts. Open daily
for dinner. Reservations recommended.
$$–$$$

Where to Stay

Hyatt Regency Grand Cypress. 1 Grand
Cypress Blvd. (off Rte. 535 at I-4 exit 27);
(407) 239-1234 or (800) 233-1234; www
.hyatt.com. Near Disney, 1,500 acres and
750 guest accommodations in a luxury
atrium hotel, restaurants, golf, cave and
waterfall wrap pool with water slides, tennis,
horseback riding, pitch and putt-putt golf,

playground, and Camp Hyatt and Family
Camp programs. $$$$

Royal Pacific Resort. 6300 Hollywood
Way; (407) 503-3000 or (888) 273-1311; www
.universalorlando.com. Opened in June 2002
on a fifty-three-acre site directly across the
street from Universal's Islands of Adventure
park, it is a luxurious tropical retreat with
one of the city's largest swimming pools,
a 12,000-square-foot monster designed to
resemble a South Seas lagoon, complete with
extensive landscaping, water cannons, fake
beach, and water polo equipment. Its proxim-
ity to Universal is its best feature, but another
great perk for guests is that your room key
provides no-wait access to Universal parks
and rides, and other benefits such as **free**
use of the water taxi line. The hotel's restau-
rant, Tchoup Chop, is an elegant eatery that
makes a nice reward for adults who have
endured a whole day in a noisy theme park.
Hard Rock Hotel opened in January 2001 with
the same park privileges. $$$–$$$$

For More Information

**Orlando/Orange County Convention
and Visitors Bureau, Official Visitor
Center.** 8723 International Dr., Suite 101,
Orlando 32819; (407) 363-5872 or (800) 551-
0181; www.orlandoinfo.com.

Walt Disney World

Exit 67 off I-4 takes you to the bull's-eye of the Orlando area family target.

Here awaits a vacationland unto itself, 7,100 developed acres complete with umpteen
resorts, several major theme and water parks, stores, restaurants, nightlife complexes,
sports arenas—you name it. If you plan to spend several days at Walt Disney World,
look into its various pass options. For example, one-day, one-park tickets to the Magic
Kingdom, EPCOT, Animal Kingdom, or DisneyHollywood Studios cost $79 for guests
ages 10 and older, $68 for children ages 3 to 9; under 3 **free.** Seven day passes cost
$234 ($33.43 per day) per person. Florida residents can take advantage of discounted
rates. Other park admissions are listed separately. All ticket prices are subject to tax and

change. Parking at the attractions is $12/car, $13 or $16 for larger vehicles. For general information on any Walt Disney World attraction, call (407) W-DISNEY or visit www.disney world.com. Times vary according to season. Call or search "park hours" on the Web site for up-to-date information.

Disney Hollywood Studios (ages 6 to 13)

The park generally opens daily at 9 a.m.; closing hours vary throughout the year.

Thrill seekers line up first for the Twilight Zone Tower of Terror, whose thirteen-story elevator plunge makes their hair stand straight up. The little ones will love meeting Aladdin's genie, Belle of *Beauty and the Beast* fame, and other characters off the Disney screen. Even the older ones will get a kick out of the Muppet-Vision 3-D attraction. The Voyage of the Little Mermaid is sure to enchant, while Star Tours is a rollicking adventure through outer space with an absentminded droid in the cockpit. Lights, Motors, Action Extreme Stunt Show is a new attraction straight from Paris Disneyland. A live spectacle with specially designed cars, motorcycles, and Jet Skis sparked with pyrotechnics shows how action stunts are created for the movies. The nighttime Fantasmic! show stars Mickey Mouse. Don't miss one of the park's best coasters, Aerosmith's Rock 'n' Roller Coaster, which spins its riders through loops in the dark to the tunes of Aerosmith. Kids (and parents) with talent have a chance to display it in Disney's version of the *American Idol* show on TV. Win a "Dream Ticket" on the sixth and final show of the day, and it's an automatic audition with the real *American Idol* producers.

Disneyquest Indoor Interactive Theme Park (ages 5 to 13)

Downtown Disney West Side; (407) 824-2222; www.disneyquest.com. Open Mon through Thurs 11:30 a.m. to 10 p.m., Fri and Sat 11:30 a.m. to 11 p.m. Admission is $40 plus tax for guests age 10 and older, $34 plus tax for children ages 3 to 9.

Five stories of indoor interactive entertainment challenge visitors of all ages. The latest additions include a 3-D experience titled Pirates of the Caribbean: Battle for Buccaneer Gold and SongMaker, where up to four people can cut their own musical CD by mixing singers, lyrics, and a variety of musical styles. Kids will love taking home their personalized and self-designed CD in jewel case.

Disney's Animal Kingdom (ages 5 to 13)

Open 7 a.m. to 8 p.m.

Disney finally decided to follow the ecotourism trend, but of course in a big, big way. This largest of Disney theme parks concentrates on animals—real, imaginary, and extinct. Quite frankly, it doesn't measure up to Magic Kingdom or EPCOT, which charge the same entrance fee. The headliner attractions are DINOSAUR, Kali River Rapids, Kilimanjaro Safaris, and Expedition Everest. The first, the centerpiece of Dinoland, U.S.A., is a rollicking ride into the past with animatronic dinosaurs, a mild roller coaster, and typical Disney effects. The young ones especially will like playing in the nearby Boneyard

Disney Sports Trivia

- Wide World of Sports fields are always playable, thanks to drainage systems that remove 5 to 7 inches of rainfall per hour.
- Two of the largest air-conditioning units in all of Disney World cool the complex's field house.

play area, where they can slide, climb, and dig for bones. Africa's safari ride takes you to a wildlife preserve where real live animals—gazelles, elephants, Nile crocodiles, kudus, and giraffes—await around every corner and thin drama adds the Disney dimension. The new Expedition Everest thrills kids with hairpin turns on a high-speed train ride around Forbidden Mountain, which is guarded by a snarling Yeti. The best attraction is tucked into the roots of the impressive (though not alive) Tree of Life. It's Tough to Be a Bug is cute and fun 3-D entertainment (and the lines are much shorter!). Camp Minnie-Mickey is tot friendly, with character greeting areas and theme shows from *Lion King* and *Pocahontas*. Naturally, you'll find plenty of shops and food stands throughout the park.

Disney's Wide World of Sports (ages 5 to 13)

Admission for the Sports Experience, a multisport playground where kids can test their agility. A general admission ticket costs about $12 adult, $10 ages 3 to 9. Prices vary for premium event tickets, such as Atlanta Braves games.

Two hundred acres devoted to sports, it hosts the Atlanta Braves in spring training season (March through early April), Harlem Globetrotters training, and world-class tennis, soccer, karate, and other tournaments. The Sports Experience, formerly an attraction at Super Bowl host cities, has its permanent home here, allowing wannabe football players a chance to test their skills. Tiny future quarterbacks can play in the Kid's Zone with authentic NFL equipment.

EPCOT (ages 8 to 13)

Future World is open 9 a.m. to 7 p.m.; World Showcase, 11 a.m. to 9 p.m.

At EPCOT (Experimental Prototype Community of Tomorrow) younger children enjoy front-of-the-park Future World attractions. Honey, I Shrunk the Audience is especially popular. New for little ones is the Seas with Nemo and Friends, where a cruise in a clamobile ends with a Turtle Talk with Crush. Older kids will go for the new Mission: SPACE, which launches guests on a simulated space adventure. During this one-of-a-kind astronaut-like adventure in Future World, guests experience everything from a pulse-racing liftoff to "weightlessness" among the infinite reaches of outer space. Soarin' is another flight where you're suspended 45 feet in the air on a multi-passenger hang glider. Unlike Space, flyers over 40 inches tall glide over the more awe-inspiring sights of California. World

Showcase is more suited to parents and older kids. There you can tour eleven countries in one day, taste their culinary specialties, and buy their wares.

The Magic Kingdom (ages 6 to 13)

Normally open daily at 9:30 a.m. Closing times vary. Call ahead for exact times and a schedule of which attractions may be closed for repairs.

The park has to be on the wish list of every kid who has ever seen a Disney film or tape. It's the first place most families take their youngsters, but beware: Don't take them here at too early an age. The realistic effects of such classic attractions as Pirates of the Caribbean, the Haunted Mansion, and even Snow White's Scary Adventures can frighten preschoolers. If you do have tots, Mickey's Toon Town Fair is the best place for them, while you send the older kids off to survive Space and Splash Mountains. They'll also enjoy three new attractions featuring popular Disney characters. Goofy's crop duster takes off from a barn in Barnstormer at Goofy's Wiseacre Farm, while riders on Buzz Lightyear's Space Ranger Spin must save the toy universe from sinister Emperor Zurg. Sights, sounds, and sometimes yucky smells plague the new security recruit in Stitch's Great Escape while looking for the six-limbed alien. There is also the Spectro Magic Parade at night, dazzling with fiber optics and half a million lights. The Magic Carpets of Aladdin, in the Adventureland area of the park, has sixteen, four-passenger carpets circling around a giant Genie's bottle with funny-looking camels spitting refreshing squirts of water at airborne riders for extra fun. Check out the open-air marketplace called the Agrabah Bazaar where you can buy frosty fruit treats that are nutritious and delicious.

Walt Disney World Water Parks (ages 6 to 13)

Each of these water parks has its own theme. For an extra $20 at Typhoon Lagoon you can do a half hour of snorkeling-assisted scuba. Must be age 7 or older.

- Typhoon Lagoon. Admission is $45 for adults, $39 for children ages 3 to 9, plus tax; under 3 **free.** Speed down Mount Mayday in an enclosed slide.

- Blizzard Beach. Admission is $45 for adults, $39 for children ages 3 to 9, plus tax; under 3 **free.** Drop straight down at 55 mph.

Vacationland **Fun Facts**

- It takes more than a million yards of fabric to costume the cast at Walt Disney World.

- Shamu's swimming pool at SeaWorld holds 1.7 million gallons of water.

- Universal Studios' King Kong, the largest animated figure ever built, is covered with 7,000 pounds of fur.

Where to Eat

Disney World dining spans the realm of hot pretzel stands and gimmickry to fine dining and cutting-edge cuisine. Each park and each resort has its own selections, demonstrating a wide range of ethnic styles. Most are fit for families.

California Grill. Disney's Contemporary Resort, 4600 North World Dr., Lake Buena Vista; (407) 824-1576. Bright, sky-high setting, new California-style cuisine. Lunch and dinner daily. $$$

Character meals. For priority seating call (407) WDW-DINE. For a special treat, take the kids to a Disney character breakfast, lunch, or dinner to eat with Captain Hook, Cinderella, and other celluloid stars. These meals come at a premium, so to save money, look for the characters at the theme parks instead. Character meals are hosted by Magic Kingdom, EPCOT, Disney's Animal Kingdom, Downtown Disney Marketplace, Disney's Beach Club Resort, Contemporary Resort, Grand Floridian Resort, Polynesian Resort, Old Key West Resort, and Wilderness Lodge Resort. $$–$$$

Cinderella's Royal Table. Cinderella's Castle in Magic Kingdom. Buffet-style dining with Cinderella and friends. Breakfast. $$ (plus park admission)

Coral Reef Restaurant. EPCOT; (407) WDW-DINE. Kids will love dining "under the sea," with an eye-to-eye aquarium view. Seafood, naturally, is the specialty. Lunch and dinner daily. $$$

Disney Hollywood Studios. Sandwiches, burgers, seafood, and pasta. $–$$

ESPN Club. Disney's Boardwalk; (407) WDW-DINE. Welcome, sports fans, to the ultimate sports cafe, with seventy-five monitors, chili, burgers, barbecue pork sandwiches, salads, entrees, and desserts. Breakfast, lunch, and dinner daily. $$$

Rainforest Cafe. Downtown Disney, Walt Disney World, also at Disney's Animal Kingdom; (407) 827-8500; www.rainforest cafe .com. Tropical theme—complete with active volcano—and cuisine with live and animated wildlife. Lunch and dinner daily. $$–$$$

Where to Stay

Resort accommodations at Disney World cover all the bases, from the woodsy campground of Fort Wilderness to ones themed for sports, music, and luxury. One advantage to staying at a Disney resort, besides close proximity and **free** transportation to the parks, is early admission privileges on certain days and park ticket sales at hotel guest desks. Another is character meals and appearances. Children under age eighteen stay **free** in rooms with parents. For reservations for most Disney resorts, call (407) W-DISNEY or visit www.disneyworld.com.

Animal Kingdom Lodge. Feel like you're staying on an African wildlife reserve, with a view of grasslands, birds, and other animals outside your window. African architecture, hand-carved furnishings, restaurants, and pools. $$$$

Disney's All-Star Sports Resort. 1701 West Buena Vista Dr., Lake Buena Vista; (407) 939-5000. One of Disney's most affordable hotels, where oversized football, baseball, basketball, surfing, and tennis paraphernalia bedeck the property. There are 1,920 rooms. $–$$

Disney's Caribbean Beach Resort. 900 Cayman Way, Lake Buena Vista; (407) 934-3400. On a lake with seven beaches and a marina. There are 1,700 rooms, most with water views. Restaurant, bars, playground, whirlpool, and game room. $$$–$$$$

Grand Floridian. The ultimate in Disney grandeur, it evokes Florida's old wooden hotels of the railroad era. Kid activities and evening club, My First Facial in the spa for ages 10 to 14, beach, water activities, game room, character breakfast, teatime, and dinner, plus other dining options. $$$$

The Polynesian Resort. 1600 Seven Seas Dr., Lake Buena Vista; (407) 824-2000. Great for small kids because of its Minnie Mouse character breakfast and Neverland evening child-care facility. To enter, kids crawl through Wendy's (of Peter Pan fame) window. $$$$

Kissimmee and Lake Buena Vista

East of I-4 along Hwy. 192 (Irlo-Bronson Memorial Highway). Lighted mile markers help locate attractions along this busy strip.

A quiet cow town that burgeoned into Tourist Town, U.S.A., with the arrival of a certain mouse, Kissimmee has attractions that reflect its split personality. Hwy. 192, aka Irlo-Bronson Memorial Highway or Vine Street, is the town's main thoroughfare.

Boggy Creek Airboat Rides (all ages)

2001 E. Southport Rd., Kissimmee; (407) 344-9550, www.bcairboats.com. Open daily, 9 a.m. to 5 p.m., weather permitting. Continuous half-hour tours, $24.95 adult, $18.95 ages 3 to 10, under 2 free.

Skim over water and between tall grasses in a speedy, and noisy, ride to spot gators, turtles, birds, and other wildlife.

Congo River Golf (ages 4 to 13)

4777 West Hwy 192 (between mile markers 12 and 13, next to Sam's Club), Kissimmee; (407) 396-6900. Open 10 a.m. to midnight daily. Admission is $10.95 for adults for one course, $14.95 for both; children under10 $2 less. Paddleboat rides are $10 for a three-passenger boat.

Two eighteen-hole courses have different levels of play, but both are set amid giant waterfalls and mysterious caves. There's an arcade, an exhibit of twenty-five hungry gators to feed, and a paddleboat ride.

Green Meadows Farm (ages 2 to 10)

1368 South Poinciana Blvd., Kissimmee (5 miles south of Hwy. 192); (407) 846-0770; www.greenmeadowsfarm.com. Open 9:30 a.m. to 5:30 p.m. daily. Two-hour tours run continually until 4 p.m. Admission is $21 for adults and children ages 3 and older, $19 for Florida residents, $17 for seniors.

Some 300 farm animals call Green Meadows home. The kids (and you!) can pet 'em, milk 'em, ride 'em, and feed 'em. In this ultimate petting farm, kids mingle with the geese, sheep, donkeys, pigs, and goats. Price includes pony, miniature train, and tractor-pulled hayrides.

Holiday Inn SunSpree Resort

13351 Rte. 535 (exit 27 off I-4), Lake Buena Vista; (407) 239-4500 or (800) 366-6299; www .kidsuites.com.

In 1995 the resort came up with an entirely new concept for family accommodations. Its KidSuites are based on the belief that parents and children need their separate space— and beds—while on vacation. Bunk beds and media centers are part of cubby rooms separated by walls—decorated as forts, circuses, racetracks, and such—from the rest of the room. When considered with the hotel's excellent and wonderfully flexible kids' programs, they mount up to a near-perfect family vacation situation. Kids eat **free** with parents or in their separate kids-only restaurant. Swimming pools, a state-of-the-art video arcade with computer island, plus all sorts of special kid-oriented bonuses are also located on the property. Other accommodations are roomy suites with some kitchen facilities. $–$$$

Horse World (all ages)

3705 South Poinciana Blvd., Kissimmee; (407) 847-4343. Open 9 a.m. to 3:15 p.m. daily. Ride for $43.95 basic; $52.95 intermediate; $74.95 advanced plus tax (10 percent senior discount). Children age 3 or under can ride with an adult for $16.95 on the basic ride.

Reservations required. Here you can take bridle in hand. Trails thread through 750 acres of woodlands and are suitable for riders of all levels. Toddlers can enjoy pony rides and farm animals.

Kissimmee Trivia

- How do you correctly pronounce Kissimmee? Home-folks like to say Kiss-SIM-ee by day, and KISS-i-me by night.

- *Gasoline Alley* comic strip creator Frank King lived in Kissimmee for twenty-five years and drew inspiration for his cartoon scenes from local streets and buildings.

- Rodeo was brought to town by Milt Hinkle, bodyguard to Teddy Roosevelt and acquaintance of Wyatt Earp, Annie Oakley, Pancho Villa, and Geronimo.

Day Trip in Kissimmee

For three fun attractions one right after the other, take 192 East, and turn right on Poinciana Boulevard. After the kids visit the farm animals at Green Meadows and ride a pony at Horse World, they can end the day with a half-hour airboat ride. Poinciana Boulevard becomes E. Southport Road after Pleasant Hill Road and dead-ends at Southport Park by Lake Tohopeka-liga (approx 7½ miles).

Lakefront Park (ages 2 to 12)

250 Lakeshore Blvd., Kissimmee; (407) 847-2388; www.kissimmeeparksandrec.com.

This is a great place for a picnic lunch and family exercise on the lake; a marina rents fishing boats. Buy an ice-cream cone from the caboose stand, burn it off on the playground, and walk up Monument Avenue to give the kids a painless geography lesson at *Monument of States,* a 1940s sculpture composed of geological contributions from every state (except Hawaii and Alaska, which didn't join the Union until later).

Medieval Times Dinner and Tournament (ages 5 to 13)

4510 West Irlo-Bronson Memorial Hwy, Kissimmee; (407) 396-2900 or (888) WE-JOUST; www.medievaltimes.com. Showtimes vary. Admission to medieval village and dinner show is $63.08 for adults, $40.61 for children ages 3 to 12; tax included, gratuity extra. Birthday celebrants are admitted free with two paying adults. Seniors get a 10 percent discount.

Learn what it was like to live in the Middle Ages from authentically costumed village artisans—blacksmith, potter, and spinner—and visit the dungeon's museum of torture. Afterward, feast your eyes on a jousting match and your appetites on roasted chicken (which you're allowed to eat with your hands).

Old Town (ages 3 to 13)

5770 West Irlo-Bronson Memorial Hwy, Kissimmee; (407) 396-4888 or (800) 843-4202; www .old-town.com. Open 10 a.m. to 11 p.m. daily. Admission to the haunted house is $7 for adults, $5 for children, plus tax. Separate admission for other rides.

Mom can shop, Dad can eat, and the kids can ride go-karts, a Ferris wheel, a roller coaster, or an antique merry-go-round. Everyone hold hands while visiting the haunted house. A two-hour babysitting service is available in the children's play zone, Yellow Submarine. Where else can you still get Pepsi for a quarter?

Osceola County Stadium and Sports Complex (ages 5 to 13)

1000 Bill Beck Blvd., Kissimmee (off East Hwy. 192); (321) 697-3200. Tickets range $15 to $24.

The Houston Astros go into spring training here during March.

On a **Budget**

- **Florida Museum of Natural History,** Gainesville, **free** admission
- **Morningside Nature Center,** Gainesville, **free** admission
- **Kelly Park,** Apopka, admission $1 for adults, **free** for children
- **Downtown Disney's LEGO Imagination Center,** Walt Disney World Resort, **free** admission
- **Disney's BoardWalk,** Walt Disney World Resort, **free** admission

Pioneer Village (ages 4 to 13)

750 North Bass Rd., Kissimmee; (407) 396-8644. Open 10 a.m. to 4 p.m. Thurs through Sat, 1 to 4 p.m. Sun. Requested donation is $5 per adult, $2 per child.

Escape the futuristic madness of the local amusement parks with a step back in time. The museum maintains a bygone Kissimmee personality with eight historic buildings, including two late-1800s Cracker houses, old country store, and boardwalk into an eight-acre nature preserve. Picnic under one-hundred-year-old oak trees.

Reptile World Serpentarium (ages 3 to 13) K

5705 East Irlo-Bronson Memorial Hwy, St. Cloud; (407) 892-6905. Open 9 a.m. to 5 p.m. Tues through Sun, closed Mon; closed in Sept. Admission is $6.75 for adults, $5.75 for children ages 6 to 17, $4.75 for ages 3 to 5.

Watch demonstrations with cobras and other poisonous snakes.

Where to Eat

Cracker Barrel Old Country Store. 5400 West Irlo-Bronson Hwy, Kissimmee; (407) 396-6521 Old-fashioned country cooking for breakfast, lunch, and dinner. Kids menus. $–$$

Where to Stay

Holiday Inn Family Suites Resort. 14500 Continental Gateway, Lake Buena Vista, exit 67 east from I-4; (407) 387-KIDS or (877) 387-KIDS; www.hifamilysuites .com. This property has taken the KidSuites concept to new heights with two-bedroom suites, bunk beds, and their own electronic entertainment in the kids' room, a cute train station theme, interactive pool gizmos, and complimentary breakfast buffet. Besides Kid-Suites you can rent Cinemasuites (also "big" with families), Fitness Suites, and Business Suites. $$–$$$

For More Information

Kissimmee–St. Cloud Convention and Visitors Bureau. P.O. Box 422007, Kissimmee 34742-2007; (407) 847-5000 or (800) 327-9159; www.floridakiss.com.

Winter Haven

From Kissimmee, take I-4 west and turn south on Hwy. 27. Turn west on either Rte. 544, 542, or 540 and travel about 5 miles to Winter Haven.

Splash Island Water Park (all ages)

6000 Cypress Gardens Blvd., Winter Haven; (863) 324-2111. Open daily. Admission is $23.95 adult, $17.95 seniors and children ages 3 to 9. Combo admission to Water Park and Cypress Gardens Adventure Park is $29.95 for adults, $22.95 for seniors and children ages 3 to 9; 2 and under **free.** Parking is $10 for cars, $12 for RVs.

Reopened April 2009 after renovation, Cypress Gardens has permanently closed its rides and wildlife and returned to its roots. Lovely Southern Belles in period dress add even more color to flowering plants, bushes, and trees as they decorate the famed gardens.

Where to Stay

Best Western Admiral's Inn and Conference Center. 5665 Cypress Gardens Blvd., Winter Haven; (863) 324-5950; is just a stone's throw from the Splash Island Water Park and Cypress Gardens Adventure Park. There are 133 rooms and suites, a five-star restaurant, and a pool. No kid's programs but small pets are allowed, so kids may see at least one animal to make up for the Garden's loss. $$–$$$$

For More Information

Greater Winter Haven Area Chamber of Commerce. 401 Ave. B Northwest, Winter Haven 33882; (863) 293-2138 or (800) 871-7027; www.winterhavenfl.com.

Lake Wales

Along Hwy. 27 headed south.

Orange blossoms scent the air along heaving hillsides—yes, that's right, hills in Florida! Neatly plaited orchards envelope the pretty little town of Lake Wales, which lassos the body of water that gives it its name. For a scenic view of the water and its lakeside mansions and park, follow Lakeshore Boulevard.

Chalet Suzanne Country Inn and Restaurant (ages 7 to 13)

Off Hwy. 27; 3800 Chalet-Suzanne Dr.; (863) 676-6011 or (800) 433-6011; www.chaletsuzanne.com.

No trip to Lake Wales is complete without a stop here. Have a peek at the quaint old-world restaurant, inn, gift shops, and ceramic studio. Tours can be arranged through the soup cannery, where the restaurant's trademark dishes are packaged. Its signature romaine soup was sent into space with *Apollo 16*.

Historic Bok Sanctuary (ages 5 to 13)

3 miles north of Lake Wales near the intersection of Hwy. 27 and Rte. 60; 1151 Tower Blvd.; (863) 676-1408; www.boksanctuary.org. Open 8 a.m. to 6 p.m. daily (gates close at 5 p.m.). Admission is $10 for adults, $3 for children ages 5 to 12; under 5 free.

A trip to Bok Tower reaches an altitude of 298 feet. (In Florida, that's considered a mountain!) Exotic blossoms perfume leaf-muted pathways. Squirrels chatter atop enormous oaks. Carillons chime classical music. Lush greenery stirs the soul. Here, in 1929, Dutch immigrant Edward Bok built a 205-foot carillon tower to show his appreciation for the beauty he felt America had brought into his life. He planted the grounds around the "singing tower" in thousands of magnolias, camellias, azaleas, ferns, oaks, palms, pines, and plants from as far away as Asia. Best time to go is spring, when the flowers are blooming. More than 120 different wild bird species call the 157 acres home, including wood ducks. The fifty-seven-bell carillon tower, listed on the National Register of Historic Places, rings out classical harmonies every half hour starting at 10 a.m. Also on the National Register, under the original name of El Retiro, Spanish for "retreat," is a restored Mediteranean-style house. Built in 1929, the twenty-room mansion known as Pinewood adds an extra attraction to your visit. A mix of Moorish, Gothic, and Romanesque decor is displayed in carved wooden doors, wrought iron hangings, columns, and exposed beams. Ceramic tile from Tunisia is imbedded in the walls and floors. Tickets at $6 adults, $5 children can be purchased at the Visitor Center.

Lake Kissimmee State Park (all ages)

East of town off Rte. 60; 14248 Camp Mack Rd.; (863) 696-1112. Open 7 a.m. to sunset daily. Park entrance is $5 per vehicle of eight persons or fewer, $2 per extra passenger, cyclist, or pedestrian.

Reenactors play the part of cow hunters in a circa-1870 cow camp from 9:30 a.m. to 4:30 p.m. weekends and holidays. Bald eagles, squirrels, ospreys, sandhill cranes, alligators, and deer inhabit the 5,000-acre lake and the land that surrounds it. Spend the day hiking, fishing, canoeing—even stay the night in the sixty-site campground.

Lake Wales Depot Museum (ages 8 to 13)

325 South Scenic Hwy; (863) 678-4209. Open 9 a.m. to 5 p.m. Mon through Fri and 10 a.m. to 4 p.m. Sat. Admission is free or by donation.

The history of the area, including the building of the railroad that settled inland Florida, can be reviewed here. The museum is housed in three buildings, one of them the city's first structure, next to a historic railroad car.

Spook Hill (all ages)
Between North Avenue and Burns Avenue.

The kids will think it's fun to drive to North Avenue and Fifth Street, where mysterious forces seem to power your car uphill. Hokey, but entertaining.

Where to Stay

Westgate River Ranch. Off Rte. 60, 25 miles east of Lake Wales; 3200 River Ranch Rd., River Ranch; (863) 692-1321. Tennis, horseshoes, badminton, golf, fitness equipment, pools, tennis, horseback riding, rodeos, barbecues, hayrides, and a petting corral. Stay in your own recreational vehicle, or in an efficiency, hotel room, suite, or cottage. There's also a nine-hole golf course. $–$$

For More Information

Lake Wales Chamber of Commerce. 340 West Central Ave., Lake Wales 33853; (863) 676-3445; www.lakewaleschamber.com.

Sebring

About a forty-minute drive from Lake Wales on Hwy. 27.

Highlands Hammock State Park (all ages)
West of Sebring off Hwy. 27; 5931 Hammock Rd.; (863) 386-6094. Open 8 a.m. to sunset daily. Park entrance is $6 per vehicle of eight persons or fewer, $2 per extra passenger, cyclist, or pedestrian.

Far lovelier and a lot less noisy than the more-famous raceway, Highlands Hammock State Park gets its name from its ridge elevation. Hikers and cyclists get close to nature in cypress swamps and hardwood hammocks where alligators, otters, bald eagles, deer, and endangered scrub jays hide. You can rent a bike there or hop aboard a tram for a tour. It has picnic grounds, playgrounds, and camping.

Twelve-Hour Endurance Race (ages 10 to 13)
Sebring International Raceway, 113 Midway Dr.; (863) 655-1442.

Sebring's claim to fame is its annual race for world sports cars each March.

Where to Stay

Kenilworth Lodge. 836 Southeast Lakeview Dr.; (863) 385-0111 or (800) 423-5939. Historic landmark. Pool and complimentary breakfast. Kids stay **free** with parents. $–$$

For More Information

Greater Sebring Chamber of Commerce. 309 South Circle, Sebring 33870; (863) 385-8448; www.sebringflchamber.com.

More Things to See and Do
in Central Florida

- **Alexander Spring Creek,** Ocala National Forest; (352) 669-3522

- **Arabian Nights,** Kissimmee; (407) 239-9223 or (800) 553-6116

- **Audubon Center for Birds of Prey,** Maitland; (407) 644-0190

- **Bradlee-McIntyre House,** Orlando; (407) 332-0225

- **Discovery Science Center,** Ocala, (352) 401-3900

- **Disney's BoardWalk,** Walt Disney World Resort; (407) W-DISNEY

- **Downtown Disney,** Walt Disney World Resort; (407) W-DISNEY

- **Expo—The Children's Museum of Gainesville,** Gainesville; (352) 378-5492

- **Fantasia Gardens Miniature Golf,** Walt Disney World Resort; (407) 824-4321

- **Fun Spot Action Park,** Orlando; (407) 363-3867

- **Gainesville Raceway,** Gainesville; (352) 377-0046

- **Kissimmee Go-Karts,** Kissimmee; (407) 396-4800

- **Matheson Museum,** Gainesville; (352) 378-2280

- **Micanopy Historical Society Museum,** Micanopy; (352) 466-3200

- **Pirate's Cove Adventure Golf,** Orlando; (407) 352-7378

- **Retirement Home for Horses,** Gainesville; (386) 462-1001

- **Shell World,** Kissimmee; (407) 396-9000

- **Silver River Museum and Environmental Education Center,** Ocala; (352) 236-5401

- **Sleuth's Mystery Dinner Shows,** Orlando; (407) 363-1985

- ***Titanic:* The Exhibition,** Orlando; (407) 248-1166

- **Trainland,** Orlando; (407) 363-9002

Annual Events

Florida Strawberry Festival. Plant City; (813) 752-9194. Strawberry shortcake and country music highlight this eleven-day February-to-March event.

Kissimmee Bluegrass Festival. Kissimmee; (813) 783-7205. Three days of fiddling, bluegrass, and gospel music and barbecue in early March.

Florida High School Rodeo. Kissimmee; (407) 933-0020. Bull riding, calf roping, bareback riding, and more, two days late in May.

Kids Festival. Silver Springs; (352) 236-2121. Two days in mid-July of games and child-oriented fun.

Halloween Horror Nights at Universal Studios. Orlando; (407) 363-8000. Seventeen nonconsecutive days of special spook shows, haunted houses, mystery mazes, and roaming monsters and mutants in October.

Mickey's Very Merry Christmas Party. Walt Disney World Magic Kingdom; (407) 824-4321. Holiday goodies, fireworks, and a special night parade with snow; early in December.

West Central
Florida

The stretch of Gulf shoreline from the so-called Big Bend south to Sarasota and its environs undergoes many mood swings. At its northern reaches, mangrove coast replaces barrier island beaches, meaning less development and a more natural setting. Midway down begins the parade of islands that trickles down the coast to the southern tip of Florida. With the pretty islands in their sandy skirts come resorts, attractions, and sun-seeking tourists. Big-city Tampa and sister city St. Petersburg form the center of activity along this stretch. To the south, things get more exclusive around Bradenton and Sarasota, then more natural again on their outskirts.

Crystal River

On Hwy. 19, about 35 miles west of I-75.

To nature lovers and divers in the know, Crystal River is synonymous with the manatee—that endangered, blimpish, heavyweight darling of Florida marine mammals. The 1,300-pound creatures come each winter to feed on freshwater vegetation in the warm spring waters of aquarium-clear Crystal River, which hosts the largest herd in the state. Snorkelers and divers regularly spot the docile animals.

Crystal River Archaeological State Park (ages 4 to 13)

North end of town off Hwy. 19; 3400 North Museum Point; (352) 795-3817. Museum open 9 a.m. to 5 p.m.; grounds open 8 a.m. to sunset. Entrance fee is $2 per vehicle of eight passengers, $1 per pedestrian or cyclist.

Above water, you can usually spot the Crystal River's gentle giants from lofty lookouts, such as the one at this fourteen-acre park. Besides manatees, you can see six towering mounds—the highest, 30 feet tall—and artifacts left by ancient civilizations in the museum and throughout the grounds.

WEST CENTRAL FLORIDA

Crystal River

Archaeological State Park

Inverness

Homosassa

Brooksville

Weeki Wachee

Tarpon Springs

Dunedin

Clearwater Beach

Clearwater

Sand Key

Largo

Tampa

Indian Shores

Madeira Beach

St. Petersburg

St. Pete Beach

Anna Maria

Holmes Beach

Bradenton Beach

Bradenton

Zolfo Springs

Ona

Longboat Key

Sarasota

Osprey

Arcadia

Casey Key

Nokomis

Venice

Manasota Key

Englewood Beach

Fort Island Gulf Beach (all ages)
West of Hwy. 19 on Rte. 44; 1600 West Fort Island Trail; (352) 527-7677.

One of the few Gulf beaches you'll find this far north, it lies off the beaten path. Go for a picnic and a swim. Lifeguards are on duty in the summer.

Where to Eat
Oysters. 606 Hwy 19 Northeast; (352) 795-2633. Home-cooked specialties, sandwiches, and kids' menu. Breakfast, lunch, and dinner daily. $–$$

Where to Stay
Port Hotel and Marina. 1610 Southeast Paradise Circle off Hwy. 19; (352) 795-3111; www.porthotelandmarina.com. On the Crystal River, with bedrooms. $

For More Information
Citrus County Tourist Development Council. 801 Southeast Hwy 19; (352) 527-5223 or (800) 587-6667; www.visitcitrus.com.

TopPicks for Family Fun in West Central Florida

1. Spying animals and whooshing on roller coasters at Busch Gardens, Tampa

2. Feeling hurricane-force winds and other scientific phenomena at the Museum of Science & Industry, Tampa

3. Enjoying shark and manatee experiences at Mote Marine Aquarium, Sarasota

4. Learning at Great Explorations, The Hands-On Museum, St. Petersburg

5. Seeing what's under the sea at Florida Aquarium, Tampa

6. Exploring circus bygones at the Ringling Estate, Sarasota

7. "Driving" a fire truck at the Firefighters Museum, Tampa

8. Canoeing the Peace River, Arcadia

9. Watching manatees at their "salad bar" at Homosassa Springs Wildlife State Park, Homosassa

10. Snorkeling among Spanish-American War fort ruins at Egmont Key State Park, St. Pete Beach

Road Markers

This tour of west central Florida begins in its northern parts and follows Hwy. 19 to the beaches of Pinellas County. Traffic on 19 clogs around Port Richey, so avoid it during rush hours. (If you're headed to Tampa, cut over to I-75 north of Port Richey.)

Alternate Hwy. 19 branches off 19 at Tarpon Springs and continues south close to the coast. At Clearwater, where Rte. 60 intersects, turn west to reach the beaches. Rte. 699, a scenic coastal drive, threads the islands together. Most of the way it's four lanes, and traffic flows fairly well. Pinellas Bayway/Route 682 (toll road) connects Rte. 699 to I-275. Take this north to get to downtown St. Petersburg and Tampa.

South of there, this book's tour follows the parallel path of I-75 and Hwy. 41 to Bradenton, Sarasota, and their islands—with a few side trips here and there. If you're headed directly to Bradenton-Sarasota from Tampa's west shores, take I-275 south through St. Petersburg—it's the quickest and most scenic.

Weekend Getaway: Withlacoochee State Forest and Brooksville

Take Rte. 44 southeast to Hwy. 41. The town of Brooksville is located at the intersection of Hwys. 41 and 98.

Fort Cooper State Park (all ages)
Off Hwy. 41 south of Inverness; 3100 South Old Floral City Rd., Inverness; (352) 726-0315. Open 8 a.m. to sunset. Entrance is $3 per carload of eight people or fewer, $2 per cyclist or pedestrian.

The park is named for a Seminole War site since destroyed and hosts an annual reenactment of the war. A nature trail—where you might chance to spot deer, fox, rabbits, owls, and herons—and a nice sandy beach rim Lake Holathlikaha. Facilities are extensive: five primitive campgrounds, picnicking, swimming, canoe rentals, fishing, horseshoes, volleyball courts, and a playground.

Nobleton Canoe Rental (ages 6 to 13)

Off I-75 exit 62, right outside the state forest northern entrance; 29196 Lake Lindsey Rd.,
Nobleton; (352) 796-7176, (352) 796-4343, or (800) 783-5284; www.nobletoncanoes.com.
Open 9 a.m. to 7 p.m. Fri through Mon; closed Tues through Thurs. Shuttle and two- to
five-hour trips cost $35 to $50 for two to three people.

Canoe or kayak the blackwater Withlacoochee River on trips ranging from five to thirteen
persons. The scenery is gorgeous. Explore the offshoot waterways and bays to discover
the richest wildlife. Parks along the way provide pit stops. Nobleton also rents pontoon
boats and fishing boats, and gives airboat rides. Pub and cafe are on-site,

Rogers' Christmas House & Village (all ages)

103 Saxon Ave., Brooksville; (352) 796-2415 or (877) 312-5046. Open 10 a.m. to 5 p.m. daily.
Admission is free.

Get in the holiday spirit any day of the week or year (except Christmas Day, of course).
Just look for the signs. Five clustered cottages are stuffed like Christmas stockings with
yuletide goodies. The Storybook Land cottage makes a big impression with toys inspired
by fairy tales and kid classic tales.

Withlacoochee State Forest (all ages)

The Withlacoochee State Forest Headquarters is located on Hwy. 41, north of Brooksville;
15019 Broad St., Brooksville; (352) 754-6777 or (352) 754-6896 (for camping and recreational
information). The visitor center is at 15003 Broad St.; (352) 754-6896; www.fl-dos.com.

Florida's second-largest state forest, Withlacoochee's 120,000 acres are divided into
six tracts, with three main campgrounds and various recreation areas. You'll find picnic
areas, a boat ramp, nature trails, canoeing, snorkeling, and camping. The 46-mile paved
Withlacoochee State Trail (352-394-2280) follows an old train route through the park and
accommodates bikers and hikers.

Where to Eat and Stay

See the Crystal River and Homosassa listings
for dining and lodging options.

Homosassa

South of Crystal River about ten minutes on Hwy. 19.

Homosassa Springs Wildlife State Park (all ages)

Off Hwy. 19, 4150 South Suncoast Blvd.; (352) 628-5343. Open 9 a.m. to 5:30 p.m. daily
(ticket sales close at 4 p.m.). Admission is $13 plus tax for visitors ages 13 and older, $5
for children ages 3 to 12.

Where freshwater and salt water intermingle, aquatic life is diverse. See the diversity
from an underwater observatory. Here, you're in the fishbowl, and the marine life swims

Manatee Facts

- Marine mammals are members of the elephant family.

- Adults average 10 feet in length and weigh 800 to 3,500 pounds.

- Vegetarians, they eat 80 to 500 pounds daily of sea grasses, hydrilla, water hyacinths, and water lettuce.

- They are gentle, nonaggressive, and slow moving.

- Enemies: man, propellers, and red tide

- Endangered status: fewer than 3,000 survive today in Florida waters.

free. From the floating observatory, you can listen to manatees talking underwater via telephones and watch them chomp away at their "salad bar." In the park's virgin Florida forest, you'll see local fauna both caged and roaming loose: turtles, bobcats, black bears, deer, ospreys, and other birds. A boat ride tours you around the watery premises, and a children's education center holds, among other curiosities, a live two-headed turtle. Daily educational programs demonstrate the habits of alligators, crocodiles, snakes, and manatees.

Yulee Sugar Mill Ruins Historic State Park (all ages)

South of the park on County Road 490, west of Homosassa Springs; (352) 795-3817. Open 9 a.m. to 5 p.m. daily. Admission is free.

Here, the state has preserved relics from Florida's sugar production era. The crumbling mill structures provide a lovely background for a picnic, sheltered by time-dignified live oaks. Explore at your leisure along a self-guiding path.

Where to Eat

Emily's Family Restaurant. Hwy. 19 North; Cardinal Street, Homosassa Springs; (352) 628-6559. From burgers to sirloin steaks, it's no-frills American cooking. Kids' menu. Breakfast, lunch, and dinner daily. $–$$

Where to Stay

Homosassa Riverside Resort. Hall's River Road off Hwy. 19; 5297 South Cherokee Way; (352) 628-2474. Motel with marina overlooking the Homosassa River. $$–$$$

For More Information

Citrus County Chamber of Commerce, Homosassa Branch. 3495 South Suncoast Blvd. (P.O. Box 709); Homosassa Springs 34447-0709; (352) 628-2666; www.citrus countychamber.com.

Top Family **Resorts**

1. **Innisbrook Resort,** Tarpon Springs

2. **The Colony,** Longboat Key

3. **Saddlebrook Resort,** Tampa

4. **Holiday Inn Tampa Busch Gardens,** Tampa

5. **Tradewinds Sirata Beach,** St. Pete Beach

6. **Holiday Inn Hotel & Suites,** Longboat Key

7. **Don CeSar Beach Resort & Spa,** St. Pete Beach

8. **Radisson Suites Resort of Sand Key,** Clearwater Beach

Weeki Wachee

About fifteen minutes south of Homosassa on Hwy. 19.

Weeki Wachee Springs State Park (ages 2 to 9)

Intersection of Hwy. 19 and Rte. 50; 6131 Commercial Way, Spring Hill; (352) 592-5656 or (877) GO-WEEKI; www.weekiwachee.com. Open 10 a.m. to 3 p.m. daily, during the spring and summer; Thurs through Sun, fall and winter. Admission is $13 for adults, $5 for children ages 6 to 10, plus tax; 5 and under are free. With Buccaneer Bay, $24.95 for adults, $16.95 for children. (Prices and hours are subject to change.)

Having recently joined the Florida State Park system, Weeki Wachee is in a transition period. However, the springs' famous mermaids who have been staging underwater shows since 1947, remain. You watch from the comfort of an underwater theater with windows onto the clear spring waters. Other shows include Misunderstood Creatures featuring assorted reptiles, plus there's a river cruise. Buccaneer Bay water park is open daily from June through August 23, offering springs, beach swimming, bumper boat rides, and flume slides in summer and some holidays. Canoe and kayak rentals are available. Call ahead, or click on the Web site, before your visit for more information. Parking is $3 per car, $10 for an RV or bus.

Where to Stay

Comfort Inn Weeki Wachee. 9373 Cortez Blvd.; (352) 596-9000 or (800) 228-5150. Pool and free continental breakfast. $–$$

For More Information

Hernando County Welcome Center. 30305 Cortez Blvd., Brooksville 34602; (352) 754-4405 or (800) 601-4580; www.co.hernando.fl.us/visit.

Office of Tourism Development. 26 South Brooksville Ave., Suite B, Brooksville 34601; (352) 540-4323.

Tarpon Springs

Take Alternate Hwy. 19 off Hwy. 19 north of town, about 35 miles south of Weeki Wachee.

Highly seasoned by its Greek influences, Tarpon Springs is a throwback to the Old World. The Greek community of spongers that settled here in the early 1900s still holds sway; its culture centers around the old sponge docks on Dodecanese Boulevard, off Alternate Hwy. 19 at the north end of town.

Dodecanese Boulevard represents the more touristy aspects of Tarpon Springs. It's a good place to sample Greek food and pastries, but for a less commercialized look at the town and its Greek heritage, head south on Alternate Hwy. 19. Downtown Tarpon Springs, at Rte. 582 (Tarpon Avenue), is a designated National Historic District where vintage structures house antiques shops, cafes, and galleries.

Fred Howard Park (all ages)

Go west on Klosterman Road (Route 880) to the south and follow the signs to the park.

For family recreating, you can't beat this park with its 150 acres of beautiful beach, oak-canopied picnic facilities, playgrounds, and windsurfing west of the docks.

Island Wind Tours (ages 5 to 13)

600 Dodecanese Blvd.; (727) 934-0606. Tours begin at $10 for adults, $5 for children 6 to 10, and free to those 5 and under.

Pinellas **Suncoast**

For information contact the St. Petersburg/Clearwater Area Convention and Visitors Bureau, 14450 Forty-sixth St. North, Clearwater 33762; (727) 464-7200 or (800) 352-3224; www.floridasbeach.com.

Pinellas County encompasses a long stretch of Gulf coastline, from Tarpon Springs to St. Pete Beach, encompassing also the metropolises of Clearwater and St. Petersburg. Known as the Pinellas Suncoast, its islands rank as some of Florida's sunniest and most popular destinations. The business of tourism for the entire coast falls under the auspices of the bureau listed above. Towns and communities have their own visitor bureaus and chambers of commerce as well, which are listed with each town.

On a Budget

- **Rogers' Christmas House & Village,** Brooksville, **free** admission
- **St. Nicholas Greek Orthodox Cathedral,** Tarpon Springs, **free** admission
- **Jolley Trolley,** Clearwater Beach, fare $2 per person
- **Heritage Village and Pinewood Cultural Park,** Largo, **free** admission
- **Suncoast Seabird Sanctuary,** Indian Shores, **free** admission (or by donation)
- **Tampa Electric's Manatee Viewing Center,** Apollo Beach, **free** admission
- **Manatee Village Historical Park,** Bradenton, **free** admission
- **DeSoto National Memorial Park,** Bradenton, **free** admission

From the docks, you can depart on excursions to pristine Anclote Key State Preserve for a half day of secluded beaching or an hour of watching birds, dolphins, and manatees. Other tour boats docked in the vicinity stage sponge-diving demonstrations.

Simply Kayaking (all ages)

(727) 481-0184; www.simplykayaking.com. Call to reserve a two-hour guided trip. Departure times are dependent on weather and tides. Rates run $49 per person.

Snacks, water, and a CD of digital photos to commemorate your cruise of serene bayous are included in the price. Single, double, and three-person kayaks are available.

St. Nicholas Greek Orthodox Cathedral (all ages)

348 North Pinellas Ave.; (727) 937-3540. Admission is free.

This replica of St. Sophia Cathedral in Constantinople, Turkey, is open to visitors from 10 a.m. to 4 p.m. Stained-glass windows and painted icons (which are said to weep on occasion) carry Greek inscriptions. Gilded frames, silver plating, and marble adorn the interior. Anchoring the town's historic district, the cathedral's onion dome and tower dominate the Tarpon Springs skyline. During services you must wear appropriate dress.

Suncoast Primate Sanctuary (all ages)

4600 Alt. US 19, Palm Harbor; (727) 943-5897; www.suncoastprimate.org. Open 10 a.m. to 4 p.m., Thurs through Sat; Admission is $10 for adults, $5 for ages 3 to 10.

Birds, reptiles, goats, and lemurs join numerous chimps, orangutan, and other monkeys, in this twelve and a half acre park that abuts the Pinellas Trail. What was once Noell's Ark Chimp Farm, a campy and infamous roadside attraction in 1971, evolved into an assisted living home of last resort for elderly or injured animals and abandoned exotic pets. Cheeta, one of the more famous chimps, was used in Tarzan movies in the early 1930s. Maintained largely by volunteers, the nonprofit sanctuary was reopened to the public in 2008. Once past Klosterman Road heading south, keep looking to the left or you'll miss it.

Tarpon Springs Aquarium (all ages)

At the west end of the sponge docks; 850 Dodecanese Blvd.; (727) 938-5378; www.tarpon springsaquarium.com. Open 10 a.m. to 5 p.m. Mon through Sat, noon to 5 p.m. Sun. Admission is $6.75 for adults, $6.00 for seniors, $4.75 for children ages 3 to 11.

Watch from any of three window views as a diver hand-feeds sharks in the 120,000-gallon tank at this family-run aquarium. Other tanks let you feed and pet stingrays, face up to a moray eel, and observe piranhas. No touching with these toothy, and hungry, fish!

Where to Eat

Costa's Restaurant. 521 Athens St.; (727) 938-6890. Authentic Greek seafood and other specialties. $–$$

Hellas Restaurant. 785 Dodecanese Blvd.; (727) 943-2400. Cry "opa!" as flaming cheese begins your Greek meal in view of the Anclote River. The adjoining bakery tempts with baklava and other sweets. Lunch and dinner daily. $–$$

Where to Stay

Innisbrook Resort and Golf Club. 36750 Hwy 19, North Palm Harbor; (727) 942-2000 or (800) 456-2000; www.innisbrookgolfresort .com. A golfing and tennis focus with schools to teach both. Fine kids' program centered around a playground, nature preserve, water park pool, and miniature golf course. Luxury condo and hotel accommodations. $$–$$$$

For More Information

Tarpon Springs Chamber of Commerce. 11 East Orange St., Tarpon Springs 34689; (727) 937-6109; www.tarponsprings.com.

Dunedin

A half hour south of Tarpon Springs on Hwy. 19.

The community of Dunedin is still patterned in the plaids of its Scottish heritage, but these days it is more visited for its terrific state parks and its downtown historic antiques shopping district.

Annual Highland Games (ages 4 to 13)

(727) 733-6240. Call for dates.

The games pay homage to Dunedin's heritage. Competitions include piping, drumming, hammer throw, and *clachneart* (stone of strength).

Caladesi Island State Park (all ages)

1 Causeway Blvd.; (727) 469-5942 for park information; (727) 734-1501 for ferry schedule. Entrance fee $6 per vehicle with up to eight passengers. Ferries depart from Honeymoon Island (see below) for Caladesi Island every hour on the hour beginning at 10 a.m. (On busy weekends, the ferry runs every half hour.) Passengers are assigned a four-hour return time but are allowed to cross back earlier. The last trip leaves from Honeymoon Island at 4 p.m. Round-trip ferry fare from Honeymoon Island is $10 for adults, $6 for children ages 4 to 12. Private boaters can dock for the day or overnight for a fee.

One of the most outstanding, pristine beaches in the United States and a regular on top-ten lists, Caladesi is worth the cost of ferry and admission. The sand is soft as a feather pillow. With its playground, nature trail, concessions, and picnic area, the park provides a day's worth of entertainment on its own.

Downtown Dunedin (ages 6 to 13)

Brochure available from the Dunedin Chamber of Commerce, 301 Main St., Dunedin 34698; (727) 733-3197. Open 8:30 a.m. to 4:30 p.m. Mon through Fri.

Take a 15-block historic walking tour. Many of Dunedin's historic buildings have been restyled as antiques shops, which attract collectors, especially for the springtime Antiques Fair. Most of the shops are open daily.

Dunedin Historical Museum (ages 8 to 13)

349 Main St.; (727) 736-1176. Open 10 a.m. to 4 p.m. Tues through Sat. Suggested donation is $2 for adults.

The downtown tour takes in Dunedin's old train depot, which houses a collection of railroad and pioneer day memorabilia, photographs, and artifacts.

Hammock Park (all ages)

1900 San Mateo Dr.; (727) 298-3271. Admission is **free.**

The eighty-five-acre preserve has nature trails, picnic shelters, and a playground.

Honeymoon Island State Park (all ages)

North of Dunedin; 1 Causeway Blvd.; (727) 469-5942. Open 8 a.m. to sunset daily. Park entrance is $8 per vehicle with up to eight passengers, $4 for a single passenger, and $2 for extra passengers, bicyclists, and pedestrians.

Spend the day fishing, following hiking trails to osprey habitat, or having a picnic. (There's also a snack shop and a new interactive nature center.) The beach isn't so great—it's rocky, even though the staff regularly cleans up—especially when compared with the one at Caladesi Island State Park, a ferry ride away from Honeymoon.

Knology Park (ages 5 to 13)

373 Douglas Ave.; (727) 733-9302. Tickets cost $13 to $25.

Baseball fans visiting in March and early April should plan on catching the Toronto Blue Jays in spring training here.

Top Family Beaches and Parks

1. **Caladesi Island State Park,** Dunedin

2. **Pier 60 Park,** Clearwater Beach

3. **Pass-A-Grille Beach,** Pass-A-Grille

4. **Siesta Key County Beach,** Siesta Key

5. **Egmont Key,** Fort DeSoto Park

Pinellas Trail (ages 5 to 13)
(727) 464-4751.

Passing right through the middle of town, the 37-mile paved pathway gives joggers, skaters, and cyclists a clear route between Tarpon Springs and St. Petersburg along an old railroad route.

Where to Eat

Kelly's . . . For Just About Anything. 319 Main St.; (727) 736-5284. Casual restaurant with excellent food, offering everything from burgers to fancy salads for Mom and terrific gooey desserts. It sits just off the Pinellas Trail, so you can eat, and then take the kids to air out along the quiet, safe trail on foot, bicycles, or skates. Breakfast, lunch, and dinner daily. $–$$

Where to Stay

Holiday Inn Express. 975 Broadway (alternate Hwy. 19); (727) 450-1200. Great for kids because it backs up to the Pinellas Trail and has a pool, **free** continental breakfast, and fun-decorated rooms. $–$$

For More Information

Greater Dunedin Chamber of Commerce. 301 Main St., Dunedin 34698; (727) 733-3197.

Clearwater and Clearwater Beach

South of Dunedin 4 miles on Alternate US 19. To get to Clearwater Beach, turn west on Rte. 60.

Clearwater is a sprawling, metropolitan extension to St. Petersburg. Clearwater Beach occupies a barrier island to the west and heads a succession of linked islands that runs about 30 miles down the face of Clearwater and St. Petersburg.

Captain Memo's Pirate Cruise (ages 4 to 13)

Clearwater Marina; 25 Causeway Blvd., Slip 3, Clearwater Beach; (727) 446-2587; www
.captmemo.com. Fares (including beverages) are $35 for adults, $38 in evening, $30 for
seniors and juniors ages 13 to 17, $25 for children ages 3 to 12, 2 and under **free** (tax is
additional).

Clearwater Marina harbors any number of options for exploring nearby islands and
waters. A good one for young seafaring adventurers, Captain Memo's sets sail aboard
a vessel of swashbuckling allure four times daily for sightseeing and partying. Kids wear
pirate hats, engage in water-pistol battles, get their faces painted, and dance the mac-
arena. Cannons fire at passing watercraft. It's all kinds of fun.

Celebration Station (all ages)

24546 Hwy 19 North, Clearwater; (727) 791-1799; www.celebrationstation.com. Open 10
a.m. to 11 p.m. Mon through Thurs, 10 a.m. to midnight Fri and Sat, and 11 a.m. to 11 p.m.
Sun. Hours subject to change. Rates vary according to activities.

A playground for the whole family, it has a spread of miniature golf, batting cages, bumper boats, go-karts, games, shows, and a pizza parlor.

Clearwater Marine Aquarium (ages 4 to 13)

Turn right off Memorial Causeway onto Island Way at Island Estates and follow the signs
to 249 Windward Passage, Clearwater; (727) 447-0980 or (888) 239-9414; www.cmaquarium
.org. Open 9 a.m. to 5 p.m. Mon through Thurs, 9 a.m. to 7 p.m. Fri and Sat, and 10 a.m.to
5 p.m. Sun. Admission is $11.00 for adults, $9.00 seniors (60+), $7.50 for children ages 3 to
12. Sea Life Safari two-hour boat tours cost $21.35 for adults, $19.95 for seniors, $13.75 for
children ages 3 to 12.

Kids will enjoy the daily dolphin shows (at noon, 2, and 4 p.m.) and a touch tank, and
learning interactive techniques at this research and rehab facility. Aquariums contain
exotic fish, and recovering dolphins, otters, and huge sea turtles swim around in tanks.
Marine biologists guide its Sea Life Safari Cruises (727-462-2628 or 800-444-4814).

Jolley Trolley

Office at 483 Mandalay Ave., Clearwater Beach; (727) 445-1200. Pickups every thirty minutes daily. Fare is $2 for adult, $1 for ages 4 to 12, 3 and under **free.**

The trolley travels around Clearwater Beach and Clearwater.

Pier 60 Park (all ages)

Intersection of Causeway and Gulfview Boulevards; (727) 462-6466. Parking automated.
Open twenty-four hours. Admission to the fishing pier is $6.30 for adults, $5.25 for seniors
(65+), $5.00 for children under age 16; 50 cents if sightseeing.

Clearwater Beach has some of the best beaches of all the Suncoast. They're wide, white,
plushly sandy, and full of family things to do, especially Gulfview, where a nightly sunset
celebration convenes on Pier 60 with jugglers, clowns, magicians, face painters, and musicians. It's also a great place for fishing. The playground is way cool in many ways—it's

sheltered from the sun by a tin roof, and it has the newest in play equipment and interactive fountains. Volleyball is the sport of Clearwater Beach, site of major beach volleyball tournaments. Much of the volleyball action takes place at Pier 60, a full-service beach with lifeguards and concessions for food, beach supplies, and water-sports rentals.

Sand Key Park (all ages)

Parking is by meter at 25 cents for twenty minutes.

The town of Clearwater Beach continues onto Sand Key, across the south-end bridge. Often listed among Florida's top beaches, Sand Key Park is a family favorite with lots of green areas for picnicking and playing. The wide, sugar-sand beach is patrolled by lifeguards and offers water-sports rentals.

Where to Eat

Frenchy's Rockaway Grill. 7 Rockaway St. off Gulfview Boulevard, Clearwater Beach; (727) 446-4844. Colorful furnishings, sunset views, casual fare, and beach location. Lunch and dinner daily. $–$$

Gondolier Pizza Italian Restaurant. 674 South Gulfview Blvd., Clearwater Beach; (727) 441-3353. Relaxed, 160-seat restaurant specializes in lovely lasagnas, ravishing ravioli, and all sorts of pizza, too. Breakfast, lunch, dinner; open until midnight, seven days a week. $–$$

Where to Stay

Days Inn. 504 S. Gulfview Blvd., Clearwater Beach; (727) 441-1722; www.daysinn.com. On the bayside, near the beach. $$–$$$$

Marriott Suites of Sand Key. 1201 Gulf Blvd., Clearwater Beach; (727) 596-1100 or (800) 228-9290. Across the street from Sand Key Park with kid-proofed family suites and a clubhouse for kids' activities. A macaw named Lisa is available for tuck-ins. Microwave ovens and small refrigerators in the suites, waterfall swimming pools, and beach shuttle. $$$

For More Information

St. Petersburg/Clearwater Area Convention and Visitors Bureau. 14450 Forty-sixth St., Suite #108, Clearwater 33762; (727) 464-7200 or (877) 352-3224; www.floridas beach.com.

Sand Key

Just south of Clearwater Beach on Rte. 699.

A number of small resort and residential communities string along Sand Key south of the town of Clearwater Beach. Indian Rocks Beach is a picturesque town with small public beach accesses and reasonably priced restaurants suited to the family.

If you take a left on Sixteenth Avenue and a right on Bay Palm Boulevard, you'll wander into the historic heart of Indian Rocks Beach.

West Central Climes

In the northern reaches of this region, the average year-round temperature is 70 degrees. Winter temperatures average 60.1 degrees, and summer temperatures 82.4 degrees. Crystal River, for instance, averages 294 days of sunshine.

Sunshine is such a constant around St. Petersburg, in the middle part of this region, that it made the *Guinness Book of World Records* with a 768-day run of consecutive sunny days, from February 8, 1967, to March 17, 1969. It averages 361 sunshiny days a year and a temperature of 73 degrees. Summer highs reach 90.3 degrees; winter lows, 49.5.

Summers mean thunderstorms and the rare hurricane. Winters are cool and dry.

Hubbard's Sea Adventures (ages 4 to 13)

150 John's Pass Boardwalk, Madeira Beach; (727) 398-6577 or (800) 755-0677; www.hubbards marina.com. Cost for excursions is $16.82 to $26.90 for adults, $8.41 to $13.45 for children ages 3 to 11. Tax is additional. Request pay in cash or traveler's checks.

Take sunset, dolphin watch, Shell Key barbecue, and Egmont Key excursions aboard a deck boat for fun and informative narratives. Snorkel gear rentals are available. Boats have restrooms and covered seating.

John's Pass Village and Boardwalk (all ages)

150 John's Pass Boardwalk, Madeira Beach; (727) 394-0756; www.johnspass.com.

Madeira Beach, also known as Mad Beach, is where the action happens. Most of it centers around John's Pass. Here, an angling charter industry has grown into a shopping and restaurant district with a ramshackle fish-house motif. It boasts its catches of grouper, a large Florida fish with tasty white meat. Snag one on a deep-sea fishing charter. Eat it and other local seafood in the village's many restaurants and at the annual John's Pass Seafood Festival in October.

Pinewood Cultural Park (ages 7 to 13)

12175 125th St. North, Largo; (727) 582-2100, (727) 582-2123; www.pinellascounty.org/ heritage. Florida Botanical Gardens open daily 7 a.m. to 7 p.m.; Heritage Village open 10 a.m. to 4 p.m. Tues through Sat, 1 to 4 p.m. Sun. Village and gardens free, but donations are welcomed.

Spend a day immersed in Old Florida history. Two bridges and separate entrances lead to where a village of living history in a twenty-one-acre park adjoins a multicolored themed gardens. At Heritage Village, a self-guided tour or docents in period dress lead you through such homes as an 1852 log cabin, and a thirteen-room Victorian house of seven gables. A one-room schoolhouse, general store, blacksmith shop, and more than a dozen other historic structures take you back in time. Assorted festivals and events occur throughout the year.

Suncoast Seabird Sanctuary (all ages)

18328 Gulf Blvd., Indian Shores; (727) 391-6211. Open 9 a.m. until dark daily. One-hour tours are conducted at 2 p.m. every Wed. Admission is free, but donations are appreciated.

While "doing the beaches," you must stop in to deliver best wishes to recovering patients of the feathered variety. It's right on the beach, and it's usually flocked with pelicans. In the cages you'll find hawks, sandhill cranes, owls, pelicans, and a variety of other injured birds on the mend.

Where to Eat

Crabby Bill's. 401 Gulf Blvd., Indian Rocks Beach; (727) 595-4825. A local favorite serving fish-house fare on long picnic tables for lunch and dinner daily. $–$$

Friendly Fisherman Seafood Restaurant. 150 John's Pass Boardwalk, Madeira Beach; (727) 391-6025. View of bay waters and just-caught fish. Breakfast, lunch, and dinner daily. $$

For More Information

Tampa Bay Beaches Chamber of Commerce. 6990 Gulf Blvd., St. Pete Beach 33706; (727) 360-6957 or (800) 944-1847; www.tampabaybeaches.com. Represents the little towns sprinkled along the barrier islands along the Gulf of Mexico, from Sand Key in the north to St. Pete Beach in the south.

St. Pete Beach

South of Sand Key and Treasure Island along Rte. 699.

Egmont Key State Park (all ages)

From Fort DeSoto Park (see below), you'll spy a small, slender island, site of a sister fort during the Spanish-American War. This fort is sliding into the sea, creating one of the coast's foremost snorkeling sites. There's no bridge to the island, but a ferry from Fort DeSoto Park and several charters out of St. Pete Beach make trips. The beach is luxuriously long and perfect for swimming and shelling. Still-intact fort ruins give the kids something to explore on land. There are also nature trails that lead to a still-functioning lighthouse that dates back to 1858.

Fort DeSoto Park (all ages)

Southeast of St. Pete Beach (follow the signs); 3500 Pinellas Bayway South, Tierra Verde; (727) 582-2267 for the campground; www.fortdesoto.com. Open sunrise to sunset. There's a 35-cent toll to get to the park as of this writing, but the toll is expected to rise.

Campers will love it here. It has a nattily maintained campground within a wildlife sanctuary that occupies five keys. The 1,136-acre county park's namesake fort, which never saw battle, was built for the Spanish-American War. Next to it, a fishing pier juts out 1,000 feet into the Gulf. Another in the bay measures 500 feet. The park has two beaches with nice picnic areas and playgrounds. You can watch traffic into deep Tampa Bay from the fort, pier, and beach. Swift currents make swimming dangerous in parts. North Beach is popular with shellers.

Gulf Beaches Historical Museum (ages 6 to 13)

115 Tenth Ave.; (727) 552-1610. Open 10 a.m. to 4 p.m. Fri and Sat, and 1 to 4 p.m. Sun, during summer. From Sept to May, it's open Thurs, Fri, and Sat 10 a.m. to 4 p.m., and 1 p.m. to 4 p.m. Sun. Admission is free.

When you're ready to take a break from the beach, browse the bygones through photos and memorabilia. Or play a little shuffleboard in the park nearby.

Merry Pier (all ages)

Pass-A-Grille Way; (727) 360-1348; www.shellkeyshuttle.com about the Shell Key shuttle. The shuttle departs from the pier three times daily. Fare is $22 for adults, $11 for children ages 12 and under, plus tax. Parking is $2.

On the bay side, you can catch a ten-minute shuttle to Shell Key, an unbridged key with no facilities, but lots of seashells and wildlife. You can also catch a fishing or sunset cruise charter, rent a fishing boat, or drop a hook from the pier, which is free and equipped with all the necessities.

Pass-A-Grille Beach (all ages)

Gulf Way between First and Twenty-first Avenues. Parking in the area is metered at 25 cents for fifteen minutes.

The village of Pass-A-Grille spreads a great beach. The facilities are minimal, but the sand and water are extremely user-friendly.

Where to Eat

Skidder's Restaurant. 5799 Gulf Blvd.; (727) 360-1029 or (727) 367-7825. Friendly restaurant popular among tourists and locals alike, specializing in pizzas as well as more complex dishes like steak Diane glamorous with satiny gravy; finish with rice pudding. Open for breakfast, lunch, and dinner. $–$$

Wharf Seafood Restaurant. 2001 Pass-A-Grille Way; (727) 367-9469. Locals' haunt serving fish, shrimp, crab cakes, and crab claws for lunch and dinner daily. $–$$

Woody's Waterfront Cafe & Beach Bar. Corey Avenue and Sunset Way; 7308 Sunset Way; (727) 360-9165. Off the beaten path, casual, and waterfront. Burgers and seafood baskets. Lunch and dinner daily. $$

Where to Stay

Rooms are plentiful up and down the strip.

Don CeSar Beach Resort & Spa. 3400 Gulf Blvd.; (727) 360-1881 or (800) 282-1116; www.doncesar.com. At the island's south

Battle Facts

During the Spanish-American War, Tampa Bay was deemed a strategic military post. Col. Teddy Roosevelt set up headquarters for his Rough Riders at the ornately luxurious Tampa Bay Hotel, and the town became the staging point for 30,000 American troops. Forts were built on Mullet Key (at today's Fort DeSoto Park) and Egmont Key, but nary a shot was fired in battle.

end, the most noticeable landmark is this vintage bubblegum-pink palace. It has a good kids' program, a great beach with water sports galore, two swimming pools, and an old-fashioned ice-cream parlor. A good time to visit is when the resort hosts its sandcastle building contest in late June or early July. $$$–$$$$

Sirata Beach Resort and Conference Center. 5300 Gulf Blvd.; (727) 363-5100 or (800) 344-5999; www.sirata.com. Part of a three-resort complex on St. Pete Beach under the TradeWinds umbrella that shares facilities, this one is the most family-suited with its own Island Cafe providing a kids' play space. Daily kids' program; 380 rooms and one-bedroom suites. $$–$$$$

St. Petersburg

From St. Pete Beach, head east on Pinellas Bayway/Route 682 (toll) to I-275, which travels through St. Petersburg. I-175 and I-375 peel off and skewer the downtown area. The trip from St. Petersburg to I-75 crosses the Skyway Bridge, a suspended work of art especially impressive when lit at night. The bridge that it replaces has been turned into the World's Longest Fishing Pier.

Downtown St. Petersburg hugs Tampa Bay on a peninsula that faces its sister city, Tampa. An old city once known for its elderly population, St. Petersburg has been rejuvenated in recent years. In its sprightly new form, it has much to offer family visitors along its waterfront.

Boyd Hill Nature Park (all ages)

1101 Country Club Way South; (727) 893-7326. Open 9 a.m. to 8 p.m. Tues through Thurs, 9 a.m. to 6 p.m. Fri, 7 a.m. to 6 p.m. Sat, and 11 a.m. to 6 p.m. Sun. Admission is $3 for adults, $1.50 for children ages 3 to 16; tram tour is $2 extra.

Add nature lessons to your family picnic at this park, tucked away in south St. Petersburg. Lizards and squirrels scamper while kids conquer the tree-house-like playground, explore the nature center, and bike or hike trails. Ask for the butterfly checklist and make a game of spotting different species. A daily tram tour departs at 1 p.m.

Great Explorations, The Hands-On Museum (all ages)

1925 Fourth St. North; (727) 821-8992; www.greatexplorations.org. Open 10 a.m. to 4:30 p.m. Mon through Sat and noon to 4:30 p.m. Sun. Admission is $8 for seniors (55+), $9 ages 1 and older; under 1 **free.**

Kids will like this fast-forward, entertaining, and highly stimulating museum. They can make their own cartoons via computer animation, test a real lie detector, or wear themselves out on a climbing wall. A less frenzied play area is set aside for children six and younger. "I Can Construct," a new two-story tree house featured on several TV shows, introduces interactive activities related to construction, architecture, and engineering.

The Pier (all ages)

800 Second Ave. Northeast; (727) 821-6443; www.stpete-pier.com. Open 10 a.m. to 8 p.m. Mon through Thurs, 10 a.m. to 9 p.m. Fri and Sat, and 11 a.m. to 7 p.m. Sun. Pier Aquarium open 10 a.m. to 8 p.m. Mon through Sat, noon to 6 p.m. Sun. Admission to the Pier is **free;** parking is $3.00. Admission to the Pier Aquarium is $5.00 for adults, $4.00 for seniors and students 7 and older; 6 and under **free.** On Sun, admission is $2.50 for all.

The Pier is a hub of local activity, with charters and rental boats departing from its docks and land tours taking off from its approach. Around the outside perimeter, fishermen cast, just as they did from its six predecessors since 1899. Today, kids enjoy fishing or feeding the pelicans, and they can wear themselves out on rented bikes. At the Pier Aquarium on the second floor kids can become an "Official Fish Feeder" during the 3 feedings and touch sea horses and hermit crabs. Exhibits include "Nemo," other exotic fish, and huge tanks full of marine life.

Salvador Dali Museum (ages 8 to 13)

Exit 22 off I-275 at 1000 Third St. South; (727) 823-3767; www.salvadordalimuseum.org. Open 10 a.m. to 5:30 p.m. Mon through Thurs and Sat (extended to 8 p.m. on Thurs), 10 a.m. to 4 p.m. Fri and noon to 5:30 p.m. Sun. Admission is $17 for adults; $14.50 for seniors (65+), $12.00 for children ages 10 to 17, $4.00 for ages 5 to 9, and **free** for children 4 and under. Thurs after 5 p.m. admission is $5.00.

Downtown's most impressive treasure, it is home to the world's largest collection of original works by its namesake surrealist artist, he of melting clocks fame. Some of his works extend from floor to ceiling, others are small preliminary pencil sketches. Special exhibits complement permanent ones.

St. Petersburg Historic Sunken Gardens

1825 Fourth St. North; (727) 551-3100; www.stpete.org/sunken. Open 10 a.m. to 4:30 p.m. Mon through Sat and noon to 4:30 p.m. Sun. Admission is $8 for adults, $6 for seniors (55+), $4 for children ages 2 to 11.

Down a sinkhole in the middle of the city, you'll find cool, quiet respite amid thriving plant life at Sunken Gardens, a tourist attraction since 1935. See butterflies, birds, and bird and reptile shows three times daily. Garden tours available.

Smart **Travel**

- Traveling families should always be on their guard against crime, but especially in and around large cities such as St. Petersburg and Tampa. Keep doors locked always when driving and when getting out at gas stations and rest stops to safeguard against carjacking and theft. Avoid travel at night, especially in dimly lit and unfamiliar areas.

- In summer, plan dry outdoor activities for mornings. By afternoon you'll be looking for water, air-conditioning, and an umbrella.

- Many resorts throughout Florida let kids under a certain age stay **free** with parents. Be sure to indicate the number of children in your family and their ages when you're making reservations.

- If traveling with toddlers, ask to have your room childproofed when making your reservation. If the hotel or resort does not have a childproofing kit or plan, request that matches be removed and ask for a room on the ground floor if there are open balconies. Bring your own childproof outlet plugs. And don't forget the night-lights.

St. Petersburg Museum of History (ages 4 to 13)
335 Second Ave. Northeast; (727) 894-1052; www.spmoh.org. Open 10 a.m. to 5 p.m. Tues through Sat, 1 to 5 p.m. Sun, Closed. Mon. Admission is $9 for adults, $7 for seniors, $5 for those 7 to 17, and **free** for those 6 and younger. All $5 on Sat.

With a vintage airplane hanging from the ceiling and period clothes you can "try on," this museum has plenty to offer family members. The airplane is a replica of the circa-1910 Benoist airboat—the first recorded airplane to fly a commercial route by crossing from Tampa to St. Petersburg. To try on the costumes, you stand behind glass pull-out displays and see yourself in the mirror. Other vignettes realistically depict life throughout the history of St. Petersburg.

Science Center (ages 5 to 13)
7701 Twenty-second Ave. North; (727) 384-0027; www.sciencecenterofpinellas.com. Open 1 to 4 p.m. Mon through Fri. Admission is $5 per person and includes self-guided tours, planetarium shows, and the Environmental Learning Zone.

This is a neighborhood, Mr. Wizard kind of place where kids learn about marine science, animals, astronomy, chemistry, and archaeology. A touch tank with marine life; a room with small animals, birds and reptiles, including alligators; and a sixteenth-century Native American village are some of the exhibits kids can explore.

Tropicana Field (ages 4 to 13)

1 Tropicana Dr.; (727) 825-3250 or (888) FAN-RAYS. The Tampa Bay Devil Rays regular single-game tickets range from $8 to $210; spring training tickets are $7 to $20. Parking is free. Kids will enjoy the cool kid page at the Devil Ray Web site, www.devilrays.com.

Major league baseball's Tampa Bay Devil Rays hosts fans here in air-conditioned comfort, April through September. A play area relieves monotony for the too-small-to-appreciate. The Devil Rays spring training games have been moved to the Port Charlotte area.

Where to Eat

Cha Cha Coconuts. The Pier, 800 Second Ave. Northeast; (727) 822-6655. Colorful, panoramic view from the Pier's fifth floor, sandwiches, and seafood for lunch and dinner daily. $–$$

The Pier Food Court. 800 Second Ave. Northeast; (727) 895-4460. Bakery goods, pizza, steaks, burgers, and ice cream, all reasonably priced and above standard fast-food fare. Often you're entertained by minstrels. Open daily. $

Skyway Jacks. 2795 Thirty-fourth St. South; (727) 866-3217. Popular, old-fashioned diner, homemade Southern-style eats. The kids will like the big chicken out front and the chocolate chip pancakes. Breakfast and lunch. $

Where to Stay

Renaissance Vinoy Resort. 501 Fifth Ave. Northeast; (727) 894-1000; www.renaissance hotels.com. Grand historic hotel with plush rooms, marina, tennis courts, swimming pools, golf, and fitness center. $$$–$$$$

For More Information

St. Petersburg/Clearwater Area Convention and Visitors Bureau. 14450 Forty-sixth St., Suite 108, Clearwater 33762; (727) 464-7200 or (877) 352-3224; www.floridas beach.com.

Tampa

Continuing through St. Petersburg, I-275 crosses Tampa Bay on the Howard Frankland Bridge, plunging into Tampa's core.

The west coast's biggest town, Tampa is a megacenter of transportation, commerce, and communication, as well as tourism. Visitors often combine a trip to the Pinellas Suncoast with a visit to Tampa, and vice versa, to get a taste of the best Florida has to offer: culture, year-round sports, amusement parks, and beaches. There's even some outdoor adventure to be had in Tampa.

This tour delves into the northern and western parts of the city and heads to the vibrant, revitalizing downtown area. From the west side of downtown, Hwy. 92 will take you across the Gandy Bridge to St. Petersburg and on to I-275 south.

Adventure Island (ages 3 to 13)

Next door to Busch Gardens; 4500 Bougainvillea Ave.; (813) 987-5600; www.adventureisland .com. Hours vary by season and day. It closes Nov through Feb and is open weekends only

in fall and spring. Admission is $39.95 for adults, $35.95 for children ages 3 to 9. (Tax is additional.) Combination tickets for one day each at Busch Gardens and Adventure Island are $159.95 and $54.95, plus tax. Parking is $10, Free with a season pass.

As far as water theme parks go, it's a splash above most. With rides like Flash Attack, Gulf Scream, Aruba Tuba, Rip Tide, Calypso Coaster, and Caribbean Corkscrew, to name a few, it's a fun day for all ages. The park fills up early with families who come to grab picnic tables and shade, but only coolers of less than 16-quart size are allowed. Snack bars and cafes are also on-site.

Busch Gardens (all ages)
3000 Busch Blvd.; (813) 987-5082; www.buschgardens.com. Hours vary by season and by day; call for a schedule. Admission is $69.95 for adults, $59.95 for children ages 3 to 9 (tax is additional). Parking is $11 for cars, $13 for recreational vehicles, trucks, and campers.

The attractions grow grander as you head east. Busch Gardens, one of Florida's top family attractions, is an all-day affair with monstrous adventure rides and African animals wandering 300 acres. The park is divided into nine different African-themed areas—such as Morocco, the Congo, Egypt, and Timbuktu—with shops and restaurants to go along with the animals, shows, and rides. You can view the entire grounds by skyride or train. Especially interesting are the Myombe Reserve gorilla and chimp area. Some of the rides get you moderately wet to drenched, so you may wish to bring extra clothes and rent a locker. A lovable tot's playland is dragon-themed. The newest addition is Jungala, which combines a native village, 3-story playland with the latest ride, a zip line, and jungle animals. Kids can even play tug-of-war with a Bengal tiger, just as shown on TV. Edge of Africa devotes fifteen acres of land to habitats for African animals, which visitors can view close up and from afar. Truck tours of the Serengeti start at an extra $33.99 per person (must be over five years of age; make reservations once in the park). The newest ride is the "floorless" SheiKra, a dive coaster where, at 200 feet up, a 90-degree straight drop gives an unobstructed view at 70 mph. Too thrilling? Try the Cheetah Chase, a family ride made for that first coaster experience.

Canoe Escape (ages 5 to 13)
9335 East Fowler Ave., Thonotosassa; (813) 986-2067 or 44-TAMPA; www.canoeescape .com. Open 9 a.m. to 5 p.m. weekdays and 8 a.m. to 5 p.m. weekends. Self-guided trips start at $23 per person (two-person minimum); $44 and up per solo kayak.

Recipe for a **Tampa Cuban Sandwich**

Mind you, this differs from a Miami Cuban sandwich.

Take one loaf Cuban bread, baked with a palm leaf laid on top. Fill with roast pork, baked ham, Genoa salami, cheese, pickles, and mustard. Nothing else. Toast in a special Cuban sandwich press.

Canoeing on the Hillsborough River is a great way to explore local ecology. Ibises, alligators, ospreys, and herons course among the gigantic oaks and cypress trees. Canoe Escape provides outfitting and shuttle service for two-hour to full-day excursions.

Columbia Restaurant (ages 6 to 13)
2117 East Seventh Ave.; (813) 248-4961.

The most noticeable and renowned of Ybor City's restaurants is this Latin-Baroque-style jewel. You must have a look at it; you can't miss its rococo tile exterior. Stop in for lunch or dinner any day and marvel at the architecture of its many rooms and the authenticity of its Spanish cuisine. Kids love the dramatic, live flamenco dancers, who perform six nights a week. $$$–$$$$

Florida Aquarium (ages 4 to 13)
701 Channelside Dr.; (813) 273-4000; www.flaquarium.org. Open 9:30 a.m. to 5 p.m. daily. Admission is $19.95 for adults, $16.95 for seniors (60+), $14.95 for children ages 3 to 11. Wild Dolphin Eco-tour is $21.95 for adults, $19.95 for seniors, $17.95 for ages 3 to 11. Parking is $6. Combination tickets are also available.

Under a shell-shaped glass dome, exhibit areas showcase the state's different aquarian environments. You can look below the surface of a mangrove estuary to see mullet and snook; above the water line, native owls and vegetation create the effect of the damp environment. Another display demonstrates beach life—waves and all. An interactive addition allows children to dig for beach treasures and build a reef. Awes & Jaws features more than twenty additional species of sharks and rays and hands-on ways to learn about the animals' power and anatomy. Frights of the Forest contains leeches, scorpions, vampire bats, and other under-loved critters. The complex's most colorful section gives you a magnificent window into reef life. Many of the exhibits are conveniently at kid's-eye level. The 149 passenger boat ride sails daily, weather permitting.

Gasparilla Invasion (all ages)
(813) 353-8108; www.gasparillapiratefest.com.

Downtown is the site of the best festival, which takes place in February—a re-creation of the legend of the local pirate hero, Gasparilla. Invasion Day thunders with the harbor landing of hundreds of swashbuckling pirates aboard the tri-masted *Jose Gasparilla*, followed by a boisterous parade along Bayshore Boulevard. Monthlong festivities include street dances, foot races, Ybor City's concurring Fiesta Day street festival and illuminated night parade (813-248-3712), and the Florida State Fair at Florida Expo Park (813-621-7821 or, in Florida, 800-345-FAIR).

Glazer Children's Museum (ages 1 to 10)
Ashley Drive, in downtown Tampa; (813) 277-3199; www.glazeermuseum.org. Under construction to replace Kid City, closed December 2008 and scheduled to open in summer 2010. Hours and admission unavailable at this time.

The three-story, 53,000-square-foot building expects to offer permanent and traveling interactive exhibits, programs, and special events. It will front the new Tampa Museum of Art, also under construction, in Curtis Hixon Waterfront Park.

Henry B. Plant Museum (ages 8 to 13)

401 West Kennedy Blvd.; (813) 254-1891; www.plantmuseum.com. Open 10 a.m. to 4 p.m. Tues through Sat, noon to 4 p.m. Sun. A donation of $5 per adult, $2 per child under age 12, is requested Jan through Nov.

Your little ones are bound to be intrigued at the sight of this skyline-dominating building: It looks like something out of *Aladdin*, with its silver minarets and ornate profile. Built in 1891 by its namesake as a railroad luxury hotel, the Moorish-Byzantine-style landmark is today maintained in its original splendor on the campus of the University of Tampa. Period pieces furnish the Grand Salon, Solarium, Guest Room, and others.

Hillsborough River State Park (ages 5 to 13)

Take Hwy. 301 north to Thonotosassa; 15402 Hwy 301 North, Thonotosassa; (813) 987-6771. Open 8 a.m. to sunset daily. Park entrance is $6 per vehicle of eight persons or fewer, $2 per extra passenger, cyclist, or pedestrian.

This park holds memories of Florida's long and painful Seminole Indian conflicts during the 1800s at the Fort Foster living history site (winter only). For families, it also holds the opportunity within its 3,000 acres for outdoor bonding along its canoe trails, nature paths, and at its campsites.

La Casita House Museum (ages 8 to 13)

1804 East Ninth Ave. Tours 11 a.m. and 3 p.m. Mon through Sat when docents are available. Combined admission for the Ybor City Museum State Park and La Casita is $4 per person.

In Preservation Park you can see how cigar factory workers once lived. La Casita, ca. 1895, is a furnished "shotgun" cottage—named for its straight-through design—one of a group of six in the park's reconstructed streetscape.

Legends Field (ages 5 to 13)

4330 North Dale Mabry Hwy; (813) 879-2244 or (800)-96YANKS. Tickets range from $3 to $5.

Tampa is big on sports—the major-league type—most of which are found in northwest Tampa. The new Yankees complex seats 10,000 for March exhibition games and off-season rookie and semiprofessional baseball. It replicates New York's Yankee Stadium.

Lowry Park Zoological Garden (ages 2 to 11)

1101 West Sligh Ave.; (813) 935-8552; www.lowryparkzoo.com. Open 9:30 a.m. to 5 p.m. daily. Admission is $19.95 for adults, $17.95 for seniors, $14.95 for children ages 3 to 11, 2 and under free. The River Odyssey ecotour is $14 for adults, $13 for seniors, $10 for ages 3 to 11. Combo tickets are available.

The top zoo in the U.S. for kids (*Parents* magazine, 2009, *Child* magazine, 2004) has the koala bear from Australia to the Kangaroo Walkabout section. Other child favorites in these fifty-six acres of exotic and native animals in their natural habitats are the "happy feet" penguins from southwest Africa. Kids can feed a giraffe, ride a camel, and pet a goat or a stingray. Exhibits include such endangered animals as manatees, Florida panthers, Sumatran tigers, and an Indian rhinoceros. But the zoo is not all wildlife. A 2008 addition is "Gator Falls," a water flume ride that ends with a 30-foot drop over a new alligator habitat.

Museum of Science & Industry (MOSI) (ages 4 to 13)

4801 East Fowler Ave.; (813) 987-6100, (800) 995-MOSI, or (877) 987-IMAX; www.mosi.org. Open 9 a.m. to 5 p.m. daily. Admission (including one IMAX movie) is $20.95 for adults, $18.95 for seniors, $16.95 for children ages 2 to 12.

MOSI, the largest science center in the southeastern United States, gives you a feel for tornadoes, the birthing process, and hurricanes. Kids In Charge, a challenging interactive children's science center for ages twelve and under that opened in 2006, was largely planned by kids ages ten to seventeen. Some 450 other exhibits deal with Florida's environment and natural history, health, flight, and space in a creative, interactive manner, using computer and other games. The IMAX domed screen shows and a planetarium will enchant the entire family with 180-degree views of volcanoes, the planets, and the Amazon rain forest. Explore a butterfly garden and stroll more than 3 miles of backwoods trails. This is one of Florida's most high-tech interactive museums.

Raymond James Stadium (ages 5 to 13)

3501 West Tampa Bay Blvd.; (813) 673-4300.

This is home to National Football League's Tampa Bay Buccaneers (813-879-2827; www.tampasportsauthority.com) in fall and winter.

St. Petersburg Times Forum (ages 5 to 13)

Near the Florida Aquarium; 401 Channelside Dr.; (813) 301-6500 or (813) 301-2500 for box office; www.tampabaylightning.com.

The 2004 Stanley Cup champion Tampa Bay Lightning hockey team plays its games at this immense $153 million arena.

Tampa Bay History Center (all ages)

801 Old Water St.; (813) 228-0097; www.tampabayhistorycenter.org. Open daily, 10 a.m. to 5 p.m. Admission is $12 for adults; $10 for seniors (65+), children ages 13 to 17, and students with ID; $7 ages 4 to 12; 3 and under free.

Here you'll find 500 years of recorded history and 12,000 years of human inhabitation moved into a brand-new four-story, 60,000-square-foot building overlooking the waterfront in January 2009. Neon images of regional history, a flamenco dancer, a Tarpon Springs sponge diver, and a streetcar welcome visitors. Galleries display memorabilia from the days of the Seminole Indians, Crackers and Cowboys, and Cigar City. On the second floor kids have hands-on fun in an interactive Discovery Center. A library, museum store, and the Columbia Restaurant cafe for inside or outside meals add to a structure built to be "green."

Tampa Electric's Manatee Viewing Center (all ages)

Big Bend and Dickman Roads, I-75 exit 47 south of Tampa in Apollo Beach; (813) 228-4289; www.manatee-teco.com. Open daily 10 a.m. to 5 p.m. Nov through Apr. Admission is free.

Watch manatees during their migration to warmer waters in winter. An observation platform, educational displays, and a video familiarize visitors with the behavior of Florida's "gentle giants."

Tampa Firefighter's Museum (ages 3 to 12)

720 Zack St., (813) 964-6862. Open Tues through Sat 10 a.m. to 2 p.m. Free.

This new attraction in an old firehouse contains a variety of exhibits include "Little Mac," a 1949 Pumper. Kids will have fun donning bunker gear to make like a fireman on a replica of a fire truck.

Tampa Theatre (ages 5 to 13)

711 Franklin St.; (813) 274-8981; www.tampatheatre.org. Requested donation for one-hour tour (held Wed and Sat at 11:30 a.m.) is $5 per person.

In the heart of downtown, it's the old, not the new, that dazzles. You shouldn't miss this ornately bedecked gem. It has been restored to its 1926 grandeur and stages films, concerts, and other special events. Guided tours and open houses allow you into its Gothic interior. Tours include a mini-concert and film. Rumor has it the theater comes with its own resident ghost, which has been featured on national TV.

TECO Line Streetcar (all ages)

(813) 254-HART; www.tecolinestreetcar.org. One-way fares are $2.50 for adults; $1.25 for seniors, children ages 5 to 17, and people on Medicare or with disabilities; children 4 and under traveling with an adult ride free.

Mr. Fink, the Afterlife Projectionist

Foster "Fink" Finley was Tampa Theatre's projectionist for twenty-five years, until his death in 1970. Not willing to give up his job in the afterlife, Fink has been accused of slamming doors and fooling around in the projection booth, causing his first replacement to quit. Other manifestations involve keys: Fink likes to jiggle them and turn them in keyholes for workers opening up the theater. The phenomena once drew the attention of a nationally known parapsychologist, who visited with a crew from NBC and registered otherworldly activity around the theater's stage.

Florida Trivia

Trivia for Bladers Bayshore Boulevard, touted as the world's longest continuous sidewalk, is perfect for in-line skating, offering scenic skate-by views of the waterfront and its lovely old homes. However, be careful crossing the street, as Tampa is among the nation's most dangerous cities for pedestrians.

Not many cities have zippy yellow, fully air-conditioned streetcars that clank their way around, but Tampa invested $53 million in a new 2.3-mile streetcar track linking downtown, the Channelside District, and Ybor City. Opened in October 2002, it boasts eight shiny streetcars, duplicates of the original Birney cars that traversed Tampa until their demise in 1946. This is a fascinating expedition for kids, many of whom have never been on a real streetcar, relatively cheap, and perfect for families who want to leave their cars behind and walk around town. Streetcars go right past the Florida Aquarium and through Ybor City.

Ybor City

Take exit 1 off I-4 West.

A Latin essence lingers from Ybor City's heyday as a Cuban cigar-making district. The era brought an intermingling of many other cultures, including German, Italian, and Jewish, which is reflected in the district's acclaimed restaurants. The competition is always on to see who makes the best Cuban sandwich. Black bean soup and Cuban coffee are other specialties. The entire 110-block Ybor City district is filled with historic cigar factories and workers' homes, many of them reborn as shops, galleries, and restaurants. Kids will like Game Works, a Steven Spielberg video game land at the Centro Ybor shopping and entertainment venue. For a walking tour visit the chamber of commerce, listed at the end of this section.

Ybor City Museum State Park (ages 8 to 13)

1818 East Ninth Ave.; (813) 247-6323. Open 9 a.m. to 5 p.m. daily. Admission is $4 per person and includes a tour of La Casita House Museum (see above).

Ybor (EE-bore) City was founded by Vincente Martínez Ybor. This Spanish entrepreneur began the city's cigar industry there in 1886. The political, social, and cultural factors that influenced the district's boomtown era are exposed in a period bakery building, complete with the ovens where the community's supply of Cuban bread was baked. A video, cigar-making exhibits, and gardens complete the tour.

Where to Eat

La Tropicana. 1822 East Seventh Ave.; (813) 247-4040. While in Ybor, do as the Cubans do: Take the family out for Cuban sandwiches, black beans and rice, and other local specialties at this Latin quarter fixture. Lunch and dinner daily. $

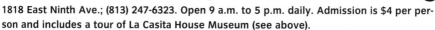

Mel's Hot Dogs. 4136 East Busch Blvd.; (813) 985-8000. Classic Chicago-style dog, bagel dog, bacon dog, corn dog, and many others. Lunch and dinner daily. $

Where to Stay

New Clarion Hotel of Tampa. 2701 East Fowler Ave.; (813) 971-4710 or (800) 4-CHOICE; fax (813) 977-0155. Close to the city's major kids' attractions and popular with families because of its suites, food court, and pirate ship water playground. $$–$$$

Saddlebrook Resort. 5700 Saddlebrook Way, Wesley Chapel; north of Tampa; (813) 973-1111 or (800) 729-8383; www.saddle brookresort.com. A destination in itself, especially for golfers and sports lovers. Thirty-six holes of golf, three swimming pools (including its central Super Pool), forty-five tennis courts, volleyball, basketball, lawn games, a fitness center, a spa and sauna, a kids' program, and a variety of dining options. $$–$$$$

For More Information

Tampa/Hillsborough Convention and Visitors Association. 400 North Tampa St., Suite 2800, Tampa 33602; (813) 223-1111 or (800) 826-8358; www.visittampabay.com.

Ybor City Chamber of Commerce. 1800 East Ninth Ave., Tampa 33605; (813) 248-3712; www.ybor.org.

Day Trip: Ona, Zolfo Springs, and Arcadia

From I-75, a triangular side trip east of Bradenton via Rte. 64 (known here as the Florida Cracker Trail) sneaks you into some unusual, back-road Florida attractions.

Arcadia (all ages)
About 20 miles south of Zolfo Springs on Rte. 17.

Best known for its biannual rodeos in March and July, Arcadia is worth a visit even when the rodeos are not in session because of its lovely old architecture and numerous antiques shops. Pick up a self-guided historic tour guide from the chamber of commerce.

Peace River State Canoe Trail (ages 6 to 13)

Contact Canoe Outpost, on Rte. 661 outside Arcadia, 2816 Northwest County Road 661, Arcadia; (863) 494-1215 for outfitting and livery service. Open at 8 a.m. daily. Cost per canoe for two people on day trips, with shuttle, is $40. Extra person costs $10, except kids age 12 and under, who go free.

Day and overnight trips on the scenic Peace River, shuttle service, and camp gear rentals are available.

Pioneer Park (all ages)

Continue along Rte. 64 to juncture of Rte. 17 in Zolfo Springs; (863) 735-0330. Park entrance is free.

Amazing
Florida Facts

If you take county roads 64, 66, and 68 across the state from Bradenton to Fort Pierce, you'll be following the old Florida Cracker Trail. As late as 1937 cowboys on horseback, drove their cattle past little towns like Myakka, Ona, Zolfo Springs, and Lorida. Existing roads were still mostly dirt, and few bridges spanned the rivers and creeks. When fording high water, it was said they could sink up to their necks.

Here is a pleasant spot where you can explore buildings from the past, picnic, camp, and canoe or fish in the Peace River.

Solomon's Castle (ages 4 to 13)

Turn right on Rte. 665 and continue to 4533 Solomon Rd., Ona; (863) 494-6077; fax (863) 993-0755; www.solomonscastle.com. The castle is open 11 a.m. to 4 p.m. Tues through Sun. It closes between July 1 and Oct 1. Admission is $10 for adults, $4 for children ages 12 and under. The Boat in the Moat restaurant is open the same hours.

Behold a most unexpected sight rising out of the cow pastures and orange groves—a full-size castle made completely out of recycled materials, mostly cast-off aluminum offset newspaper plates. The creator and king, Howard Solomon, is a whimsical fellow with a quick humor and a castle full of stained-glass windows, bizarre sculptures, and other oddities. Have lunch in the pirate ship he built next to his castle.

Watermelon Festival (all ages)

DeSoto Park, west of Arcadia on Rte. 70; (863) 494-4033.

What could be more fun than spitting watermelon seeds—with permission? Seed spitting and watermelon eating are just two of the activities at the Memorial Day weekend event.

Where to Eat and Stay

See Bradenton or Sarasota listings for dining and lodging options.

For More Information

DeSoto County Chamber of Commerce. 16 South Volusia Ave., Arcadia 34266; (863) 494-4033; www.desotochamber.net.

Bradenton

From Tampa, follow I-75 south about 5 miles from the I-275 intersection. From Arcadia, follow Rte. 70, then take I-75 north to the Bradenton exit, number 224.

In the 1800s, the Bradenton area was settled by sugar planters. Today it's known as the doorstep to sunny vacation isles. Rte. 64 drops you into downtown Bradenton, which is slowly restoring and reviving its past days of grandeur. Old Main Street, the city yacht basin, and Waterfront Park form the backbone of the downtown district.

DeSoto National Memorial Park (ages 4 to 13)

Seventy-fifth Street Northwest, north of Rte. 64, P.O. Box 15390, Bradenton 34280; (941) 792-0458; www.nps.gov/desoto/index.htm. Open 9 a.m. to 5 p.m. daily. Admission is free.

Hernando DeSoto is the local trademark historical figure. He supposedly first came ashore at the mouth of the Manatee River, where the United States has established its out-of-the-way DeSoto National Memorial Park. Displays, a re-created Indian village, an audio-narrated interpretive trail, and in-season living history guides recall the life and times of the sixteenth-century explorer and unfettered Florida.

Florida Heritage Festival (all ages)

(941) 747-1998.

In April the entire county celebrates its past during Florida Heritage Festival. A reenactment of DeSoto's 1539 landing highlights the events.

Gamble Plantation Historic State Park (ages 6 to 13)

Route 301 near the interstate; 3708 Patten Ave., Ellenton; (941) 723-4536; www.floridastate parks.org/gambleplantation. Visitor center open 8 a.m. to 4:30 p.m. (closed 11:45 a.m. to 12:45 p.m.) Thurs through Mon. Visitors can view the home by tour only at 9:30 and 10:30 a.m. and on every hour between 1 and 4 p.m. Admission to the visitor center is free; entry to the mansion is $6 for adults and $4 for children ages 6 to 12.

The sugar days left their residue most notably here. Built ca. 1840 in Greek Revival style out of local oyster shell, sand, and, some believe, molasses, its eighteen stately columns welcome visitors to an era "gone with the wind." Abandoned in 1856, the mansion was rescued from neglect in 1925 by the United Daughters of the Confederacy, who declared it a Civil War shrine for sheltering Confederate secretary of state Judah P. Benjamin when on the lam after the war. A museum in the visitor center tells the story of the property through the eras.

Manatee Village Historical Park (ages 4 to 13)

1404 Manatee Ave. East; (941) 741-4075. Open 9 a.m. to 4:30 p.m. Mon through Fri, and the second and fourth Sat of the month. Closed Sun. Admission is free.

Several buildings with local historical significance form the preserved community in its pleasant, oak-shaded park setting. The County Courthouse is the oldest building, completed in 1860. Others include a church, Cracker farmhouse, one-room schoolhouse, smokehouse, boat works, and general store. A museum of artifacts, photographs, and hands-on exhibits for children resides in the general store. The Stephens House is stocked with period kitchen items, furniture, and farm implements. Staff dress for the times to enhance the feel of authenticity.

McKechnie Field (ages 5 to 13)

Ninth Street and Seventeenth Avenue West; (941) 748-4610. Tickets are $17 to $19 for box seats, $16 to $18 for reserved, and $10 to $11 for grandstand.

This is the site of the Pittsburgh Pirates' spring exhibition games, played mostly in March.

Pirate City (ages 5 to 13)

1701 Twenty-seventh St. East; (941) 747-3031. Practice 8 a.m. and 12:30 p.m. daily.

You can catch the Pirates at practice here during exhibition season.

South Florida Museum (ages 4 to 13)

201 Tenth St. West; (941) 746-4131; www.southfloridamuseum.org. Open 10 a.m. to 5 p.m. Tues through Sat, noon to 5 p.m. Sun in May, June, and Aug through Dec. Open daily Jan through Apr and July. Closed Thanksgiving, Christmas Day, and New Year's Day. Admission is $15.95 for adults, $13.95 for seniors, $11.95 for children ages 4 to 12; children under age 4 are free when accompanied by a paying adult.

The museum focuses on southwest Florida's natural and cultural history with life-size dioramas and dramatic exhibits. See fossil, bird, and shell collections, along with full-scale replicas of a sixteenth-century manor house. Other exhibits address Native American, Spanish conquistador, and Civil War days, and include Discovery Place, a childrens' hands-on activity center. The brightest star of the museum is Snooty the manatee, the oldest manatee born in captivity Feeding times for Snooty and his friends are 11:15 a.m. and 1, 2:45, 3:45 p.m. Summer brings space camp and other children's activities to the museum.

Where to Eat

Mattison's Riverside at Twin Dolphin Marina. 1200 First Ave. West; (941) 748-8087. Floribbean cuisine indoors and outside. Riverfront view. Lunch and dinner Mon through Sat, dinner all day Sun. $$–$$$

Where to Stay

Most folks, when vacationing in the vicinity, head to Anna Maria Island (see page 157) or Longboat Key (page 158) for resort accommodations.

Courtyard by Marriott. 100 Riverfront Dr.; (941) 747-3727; www.marriott.com\SRQBD. Lovely Spanish-motif hotel on the river with restaurant, pool, and 153 rooms and suites. $$–$$$

For More Information

Bradenton Area Convention and Visitors Bureau. P.O. Box 1000, Bradenton 34206; (941) 729-9177 or (800) 4-MANATEE; www.flagulfbeaches.com.

Anna Maria Island

Continue on Rte. 64 over the Anna Maria Island Causeway, about thirty minutes from downtown Bradenton.

A beachy, relaxed island, it holds three separate communities. Anna Maria lies northernmost. Most of its attractions round its northern tip.

Gulf Drive (Route 789) is the best one to take south, through the more commercial and upscale community of Holmes Beach and its popular beaches, and Bradenton Beach, at the island's south end.

Anna Maria Island Historical Society Museum (ages 8 to 13)
402 Pine Ave.; (941) 778-0492. Open 10 a.m. to 1 p.m. Tues through Sat, June through Oct; 10 a.m. to 4 p.m. the rest of the year. Closed Mon and Sun. Admission is free or by donation.

The town's past is preserved at a 1920s icehouse. Inside, you'll browse among photographs, maps, records, books, a shell collection, a turtle display, and vintage videos. Have a chuckle at the old jail next door.

Bayfront Park (all ages)
Northeast end of Bay Boulevard.

The Anna Maria City Pier extends 700 feet into Anna Maria Sound at the northeast end of the island and has food and bait concessions. The park, one of the island's most secluded, fronts the bay with picnic facilities, a playground, and recreational opportunities. It affords a magnificent view of St. Petersburg's Sunshine Skyway Bridge.

Coquina Beach
Gulf Drive, Bradenton Beach.

Popular Coquina Beach wraps around the pass and provides beachgoers with lifeguards, picnic areas, concessions, boat ramps, good snorkeling, a playground, a mangrove nature trail, and lots of shady Australian pine trees.

Manatee County Park
Gulf Drive, Holmes Beach.

This is the island's hot spot in more ways than one. Families love it here because of all the facilities: playground, picnicking, lifeguard, snack bar, fishing pier, restrooms, and showers.

Where to Eat

Melinda's Café. 5315 Gulf Dr., Holmes Beach; (941) 778-0411. Lunch on homemade soups, sandwiches, and salads every day but Mon. Open 7 a.m. to 4 p.m. for breakfast and lunch. $–$$

Rotten Ralph's. Galati Yacht Basin, 902 Bay Blvd. South, Anna Maria; (941) 778-3953; www.rottenralphs.com. View of the marina and bay, Old Florida–style ambience indoors and out, fresh seafood. Lunch and dinner daily. $–$$$

The Sandbar. On the beach at 100 Spring Ave., Anna Maria; (941) 778-0444. Deck (best for families) or indoor seating with offerings casual to gourmet. Lunch and dinner daily. $$–$$$

Where to Stay

Rod & Reel Resort. 877 North Shore Dr., Anna Maria; (941) 778-2780; www

.rodandreelmotel.com. Small, quiet bayside retreat with modern efficiencies. $–$$

Seaside Inn and Beach Resort. 2200 Gulf Dr. North, Bradenton Beach; (941) 778-5254 or (800) 447-7124; www.seasideresort.com. Small charming property (ten rooms and suites) on the beach. $$–$$$

For More Information

Anna Maria Island Chamber of Commerce. 5313 Gulf Dr. North, Holmes Beach 34217; (941) 778-1541; fax (941) 778-9679; www.annamariaislandchamber.org.

Longboat Key

A short bridge on Rte. 789 spans the pass from Anna Maria Island to Longboat Key.

A much more exclusive island, Longboat Key's northern end is nonetheless family friendly with a public beach access, affordable accommodations, and the casual fish-house restaurants of the community known simply as the Village. To get to the Village, turn east off Gulf of Mexico Boulevard (Route 789) onto Broadway Street.

If you drive around the neighborhood of the Village, which was Longboat Key's original settlement, you'll probably spot a peacock or two, part of a colony of wild peacocks that have made themselves at home here. Look on roofs.

Back on Rte. 789, cyclists ride the 12-mile-long island along the paved bike path. The view is of majestic homes and meticulously manicured, blossomy yards.

Where to Eat

Mar-Vista Dockside Restaurant & Pub. 760 Broadway St.; (941) 383-2391. Genuine Old Florida atmosphere, fresh seafood by the boatload, and island attitudes. Lunch and dinner daily. Kids' menu. $$–$$$

Moore's Stone Crab Restaurant. 800 Broadway St.; (941) 383-1748. Lodge-style, Southern-fried dining on the water. Lunch and dinner daily. Kids' menu. $$

Where to Stay

The Colony Beach & Tennis Resort. 1620 Gulf of Mexico Dr.; (941) 383-6464 or (800) 282-1138; www.colonybeachresort .com. Premier destination resort with self-catering suites, complimentary kids' program, and fabulous beach and restaurants. It's the number-one rated tennis resort in the United States, with twenty-one hard and clay courts, two lit for night play. $$$$

Amazing
Florida Facts

St. Petersburg made aviation history on New Year's Day 1914 when Anthony "Tony" Jannus flew the first paying passenger across the bay to Tampa. It was the beginning of commercial airline flights in the United States. Twenty years later, St. Pete became the hometown of National Airlines, and its Ryan monoplanes carried mail and passengers across the state to Daytona Beach. By 1980 National had an international network covering 29,000 miles and 41 cities in five countries.

For More Information

Longboat Key Chamber of Commerce. Whitney Beach Plaza, 6854 Gulf of Mexico Dr., Longboat Key 34228; (941) 383-2466; fax

(941) 383-2466; www.longboatkeychamber .com

Sarasota

Continue down Rte. 789.

As you cross the next bridge to a new cluster of islands, the address changes to Sarasota. City Island, just north and east of the bridge from Longboat Key, protects Sarasota's environmental soul. The Sarasota Bay Walk, Mote Marine Laboratory and Aquarium, and Sarasota Bay Explorers concentrate on the area's flora and fauna.

On the west side of Rte. 789, or John Ringling Parkway, Lido Key holds some very nice beaches that attract sun lovers in throngs. Tucked into the island's bayside crook, St. Armands Key is the site of the famous shopper's arena known as St. Armands Circle. Here you get your first inkling of the great impact one man had on Sarasota. That man was John Ringling, circus mogul. Though Sarasota tries at times to forget the raucousness of its circus era—thirty-odd years during which the "Greatest Show on Earth" wintered in town—the memories lurk everywhere. In the park areas around St. Armands Circle, you'll find classic statues, reminders of Ringling's love of art, and plaques commemorating some of the circus's greatest performers. Also of interest to kids are the shopping center's various ice-cream and candy shops.

Bayfront Park (ages 6 to 13)
Bayfront Drive, downtown Sarasota.

Shop here for adventure charters in Sarasota's waters—everything from sightseeing to shark fishing. Merely stroll along the docks and take your pick. There is also an open-air restaurant in the park.

Cà D'Zan (ages 7 to 13)

Ringling Estate, 5401 Bay Shore Rd.; (941) 351-1660; www.ringling.org. Open daily 10 a.m. to 5:30 p.m. Admission fees allow admittance to all Ringling attractions: $20 for adults; $17 for seniors; $7 for children ages 6 to 17, for military, and Florida students and teachers (with identification); 5 and under free. Tour reservations are suggested; call (941) 358-3180.

You must peek into Ringling's incomparable "House of John" (Cà D'Zan in Italian) palace. Using the Doge's Palace in Venice as a model, Ringling spared no expense building a monument to success and excess in the 1920s. Baroque, Gothic, and Renaissance elements contribute to an overall look of breathtaking opulence and ornateness throughout the thirty-room, $1.5 million mansion that John built, which has undergone a seven-year, $16 million renovation. Also on the grounds, you can visit the rose garden, three gift shops, and Banyan Cafe.

Casey Key & Nokomis Beach

Take Blackburn Point Road west off South Hwy. 41.

For a scenic detour, follow the skinny, snaky road that threads through lovely Casey Key, a refuge for well-heeled escapists for several decades. At the island's south end, Nokomis Beach has more than pretty views to offer families, namely fun-filled beaches and great fishing. Bustling Nokomis Beach and its sand volleyball courts lie at the junction of Albee Road. Keep heading south to North Jetty Park, which is a little more out of the mainstream but still with lots to do. It has a picnic area, restrooms, lifeguards, and concessions, and, most important, throngs of fish in the narrow pass that separates it from Venice Beach to the south.

Ed Smith Stadium (ages 6 to 13)

East of Hwy. 41; 2700 Twelfth St.; (941) 954-SOXX.

Catch some Cincinnati Reds spring training action.

G. Wiz (ages 3 to 13)

Blivas Science and Technology Center, 1001 Boulevard of the Arts; (941) 906-1851; www .gwiz.org. Open 10 a.m. to 5 p.m. Mon through Sat, and noon to 6 p.m. Sun. Admission is $9 for adults, $8 for seniors, $6 for ages 3 to 18. Free admission for the first Wed of the month 5 to 8 p.m.

One would expect Sarasota's version of a hands-on museum to be brighter, artsier, edgier than the rest—and it is. Two floors of exhibits have the kids doing everything from sprint racing to creating cartoons. The cool outdoor playground makes a fun outing on its own. The museum continually grows with state-of-the-art exhibits.

Historic Spanish Point (ages 8 to 13)

500 North Tamiami Trail, Osprey; (941) 966-5214; www.historicspanishpoint.org. Open 9 a.m. to 5 p.m. Mon through Sat and noon to 5 p.m. Sun. Admission is $9 for adults, $8 for Florida residents and seniors, $3 for children ages 6 to 12. Tram tours are $3 extra, make reservations two days in advance.

This attraction occupies eras from 2150 b.c. through a.d. 1918. Within its thirty acres on Little Sarasota Bay, you can explore a prehistoric Indian shell mound, pioneer homestead, late Victorian home, old cemetery, reconstructed chapel and citrus packinghouse, and archaeological exhibit. By the end of the ninety-minute tour, you become well acquainted with the pioneering Webb family and Sarasota matriarch Bertha Palmer. Local actors give living-history performances Saturday and Sunday during the winter season (January to mid-April). Guided walking tours are available daily and tram tours by reservation Monday through Friday.

John and Mable Ringling Museum of Art (ages 8 to 13)

Ringling Estate, 5401 Bay Shore Rd.; (941) 351-1660; www.ringling.org. Open daily 10 a.m. to 5:30 p.m. Admission fees allow admittance to all Ringling attractions: $20 for adults; $17 for seniors; $7 for children ages 6 to 17, for military, and Florida students and teachers (with identification); 5 and under free. Admission to the art museum is free for everyone on Mon, by provision of Ringling's will. Audio tour $5. Family guides are available for download on the Web site. Recommended books that might be helpful in raising your kids' interest include *Once Upon a Picture* by Sally Swain, and *If I Ran the Circus*, by Dr. Seuss.

Just off Tamiami Trail lies Sarasota's preeminent attraction, the sixty-six-acre bayfront estate that John Ringling left to the state upon his death. The art museum is responsible for giving Sarasota its reputation for the artistic. Designated as the State Art Museum of Florida, it specializes in late Medieval, Renaissance Italian, and Spanish baroque works. The most impressive exhibit flaunts a collection of five original Rubens tapestries. Definitely too highbrow for youngsters (and for adults bored by religious paintings), it does have hands-on activities Saturday and Sunday from 1 to 3 p.m.

Mote Marine Laboratory and Aquarium (all ages)

1600 Ken Thompson Parkway; (941) 388-2451 or (800) 691-MOTE; www.mote.org. Open 10 a.m. to 5 p.m. daily. Admission is $17 for adults, $12 for children ages 4 to 12, under 4 free.

This highly respected facility specializes in the research and rehabilitation of marine mammals. Kids especially love its 135,000-gallon shark tank, stocked with sharks and fish typical of the area, such as grouper, snook, jewfish, pompano, and snapper. Aquariums, a ray touch tank, and a separate touch tank hold more than 200 varieties of common and unusual species. A mollusk tank holds a rare preserved giant squid. In a separate building, visitors can watch recovering whales, dolphins, manatees, or whatever happens to be a guest patient at the time and visit with the two resident manatees, Hugh and Buffett. Quench your thirst at the old-fashioned soda fountain in the retro 1950s-style Deep Sea Diner.

Oscar Scherer State Park (all ages)

1843 South Tamiami Trail, Osprey; (941) 483-5956. Open 8 a.m. to sunset daily. Park entrance is $5 per vehicle of eight persons or fewer, $2 per extra passenger, cyclist, or pedestrian.

Go here for wilderness camping, canoeing, and getting back to nature. River otters and alligators inhabit the waters; threatened scrub jays, bobcats, and bald eagles inhabit the land. Campers are secluded in a setting of palmettos, pines, lovely moss-draped oaks, and creek. The nearly 1,400-acre park also offers picnicking, hiking, freshwater swimming, and fishing opportunities. In October, Oscar Scherer Day is a Sunday filled with living history, craft demonstrations, guided walks, food, and live music.

Ringling Museum of the Circus (ages 4 to 13)

Ringling Estate, 5401 Bay Shore Rd.; (941) 351-1660; www.ringling.org. Open daily 10 a.m.to 5:30 p.m. Admission fees allow admittance to all Ringling attractions: $20 for adults; $17 for seniors; $7 for children ages 6 to 17, for military, and for Florida students and teachers (with identification); 5 and under free. Tour reservations are suggested; call (941) 358-3180.

The kids are likely to enjoy most the property's circus museum, especially the calliopes, costumes, oversized clowns' props, wagons, and circus grounds model. Kids love the miniature circus where tiny figures portray a typical day in circus life during the 1920s and 1930s.

Sarasota Bay Explorers (ages 4 to 12)

Mote Marine Aquarium, 1600 Ken Thompson Parkway; (941) 388-4200. Cruises depart daily from behind Mote at 11 a.m., 1:30 p.m., and 4 p.m. Boat tickets cost $26 for adults, $22 for children ages 4 to 12. Combination tickets for Mote and the cruise are $36 and $29. Reservations are recommended.

A pontoon tour of bay waters between City Island and Siesta Key, it features a trawl-net toss, binocular-ogling at rookery islands, and naturalist narration. The Nature Safari is a new tour that takes kids ages six to twelve on a "wade and walk" journey to seek a variety of marine life in shallow water. The Newest addition is a Pirate Cruise. Custom and kayak tours are also available.

Sarasota Bay Walk (ages 4 to 13)

1550 Ken Thompson Parkway (left off Rte. 789), City Island. Admission is free.

This quiet, self-guided tour of the bay, estuaries, lagoons, and upland gives lessons about coastal ecology along boardwalks and shell paths.

Sarasota Classic Car Museum (ages 7 to 13)

5500 North Tamiami Trail; (941) 355-6228; www.sarasotacarmuseum.com. Open 9 a.m. to 6 p.m. daily. Admission is $8.50 for adults, $7.50 for seniors, $6.50 for kids ages 6 to 12, and under 6 free.

Fun for kids and parents, it displays more than one hundred antique, celebrity, and classic cars, including John Lennon's Mercedes-Benz and Rolls Royces that belonged to circus king John Ringling, patriarch of Sarasota. By tour, you can see a collection of old player pianos, phonographs, music boxes, hurdy-gurdies, and record albums. The kids will especially get a kick out of the museum's first exhibit, a precursor to today's video arcades. Its old-timey games still take nickels and dimes.

Sarasota Jungle Gardens (all ages)

3701 Bay Shore Rd.; (941) 355-5305; www.sarasotajunglegardens.com. Open 10 a.m. to 5 p.m. daily. Admission is $14 for adults, $13 for seniors, and $10 for children ages 3 to 12.

It gives the kids a place to stretch their legs while enjoying exotic and predatory bird and reptile shows, a mounted butterfly collection, a jungle-themed playground, a small petting zoo, monkeys, flamingos, swans, wallabies, and other animals. Mom and Dad will enjoy the peace of lush vegetation in a sixteen-acre garden setting.

Sarasota Ski-A-Rees Show (ages 4 to 13)

City Island, behind Mote Marine; (941) 388-1666; www.skiarees.com. 2 p.m. Sun. Admission is **free.**

Amateur performances in the bay.

Siesta Key County Beach (all ages)

Midnight Pass Road at Beach Way Drive, Siesta Key.

South of downtown Sarasota, cross via Rte. 72 to Siesta Key, home of the whitest sand beaches south of the Florida Panhandle. Its silky white sands are plush and an active family's dream come true. The park holds picnic tables, volleyball nets, tennis courts, a fitness trail, ball fields, a soccer field, playgrounds, lifeguards, and rental and food concessions. The parking lot, large as it is, fills early in high season, so get there at the top of the morning.

Tony Saprito Fishing Pier (ages 4 to 13)

Ringling Causeway Park.

As you cross the Ringling Causeway to the mainland, stop here for some rod-and-reeling. A bait store across the road provides whatever you've neglected to bring with you.

Van Wezel Performing Arts Hall (ages 5 to 13)

777 North Tamiami Trail; (941) 953-3366; www.vanwezel.org.

Downtown Sarasota is known for its theaters and art galleries. Most is highbrow stuff, opera and experimental. For something more kid-friendly, head to the monthly Saturday kids' show, November through April. The hall itself, in the shape of a purple scallop shell, exudes a bit of circus razzmatazz and Big Top drama.

Where to Eat

Old Salty Dog. 1601 Ken Thompson Parkway; (941) 388-4311. Near Mote Marine, on the water. Seafood and sandwiches. Lunch and dinner daily. $–$$

Phillippi Creek Village Oyster Bar. 5353 South Tamiami Trail; (941) 925-4444. Famous for its combo seafood steamer pots, but the sandwiches and other seafood items are tops, too. Sit inside an old Southern-style fish house or creekside on the patio or floating dock. Lunch and dinner daily. $–$$$

Weekend Getaway:
Myakka River State Park

Inland about 9 miles on Rte. 72; 13207 Rte. 72, Sarasota; (941) 361-6511 for park information; (941) 365-0100 for tour information. Open 8 a.m. to sunset daily. Park entrance is $6 per vehicle with up to eight passengers, $4 for a single passenger, and $2 for extra passengers, bicyclists, and pedestrians. One-hour boat and tram tours cost $10 for adults, $6 for children ages 6 to 12.

Myakka River State Park affords opportunity for camping, canoeing, and communing with nature in 35,000 acres of forest and wetlands. A 25-foot-high boardwalk lets you explore wildlife at treetop level. It's fun to tour the park via tram or boat or to take a guided walk. Canoe and bike rentals are also available.

Where to Stay

Lido Beach Resort. 700 Ben Franklin Dr.; (941) 388-2161 or (800) 441-2113; www .lidobeachresort.com. Near the public beach entrance, with pool and outdoor restaurant. Kitchens or kitchenettes in rooms. $$–$$$$

For More Information

Sarasota Convention and Visitors Bureau. 655 North Tamiami Trail, Sarasota 34236; (941) 957-1877 or (800) 522-9799; www.sarasotafl.org.

Venice

About five minutes south of Nokomis on Hwy. 41.

Don't pass this small town by—it has more to offer than meets the eye. Its best features lie west of Hwy. 41, in the vicinity of West Venice Avenue. Follow it through a charming shopping district and neo-Mediterranean-style neighborhood to get to the beaches, known near and far for their abundance of shark's teeth.

Stop at one of the local stores for a book about collecting shark's teeth and a "Florida snow shovel"—a screen scoop used to sift the shark's teeth from the sand. The chamber of commerce hands out basic information and sometimes specimens.

Brohard Park and Venice Fishing Pier (all ages)

1600 South Harbor Dr.; (941) 316-1172. Admission to the pier is $1 for adults, 50 cents for children.

Head where collecting and beaching are best. At 750 feet, the pier is one of the state's longest.

Caspersen Beach (all ages)

South of Brohard Park on Harbor Drive; (941) 316-1172.

This is more secluded than Brohard Park, but with most of the same amenities: picnic areas, dunes walkovers, restrooms. You can walk to Manasota Beach from here, 1 mile away. (By car, it takes close to a half hour to reach.)

Sharks Tooth & Seafood Festival (all ages)
Sharky's on the Pier restaurant is headquarters for this annual bash held in April. Get your picture taken in the mouth of a shark, look at mounds of shark's teeth and other fossils, browse among crafts booths, and eat your fill of shark shish kebob and other local seafood specialties.

Venice Little Theatre for Young People (ages 5 to 13)

140 West Tampa Ave.; (941) 488-1115.

It provides off-season theatrical instruction (ages eight to sixteen) and Christmas and springtime performances for youngsters.

Where to Eat

Sharky's on the Pier. 1600 South Harbor Dr. (P.O. Box 267), Venice 34284; (941) 488-1456. On the pier with indoor and outdoor seating. Lunch and dinner daily. $$

Snook Haven Retreat. Exit 191 off I-75; 5000 East Venice Ave.; (941) 485-7221. Rural and casual on the Myakka River with canoe rentals and Sunday barbecues. Lunch and dinner daily. $–$$

Where to Stay

Hampton Inn and Suites Venice. 881 Venetia Bay Blvd.; (941) 488-5900; fax (941) 488 6746; www.hamptoninnvenice.com. Nice hotel located near local attractions. $–$$

For More Information

Venice Area Chamber of Commerce. 597 Tamiami Trail South, Venice 34285-1908; (941) 488-2236; www.venicechamber.com.

Manasota Key and Englewood Beach

South of downtown Venice, turn south on Rte. 776. Turn west on Manasota Beach Road.

The island's northern section, which lies in Sarasota County, holds a wildlife preserve, discreet mansions blocked from view by natural vegetation, ancient Amerindian mounds, and public beaches. The south end is more inviting to families, with affordable resorts and active beach parks.

More Things to See and Do
in West Central Florida

- **The Manatee Toy Co.,** Crystal River; (352) 795-6126

- **Old Mill House Gallery and Printing Museum,** Homosassa; (352) 628-1081

- **Wild Bill's Airboat Tours,** Inverness; (352) 726-6060

- **Nabor Doll Factory and Museum,** Homosassa; (352) 382-1001

- **Captain Bligh's Landing,** Clearwater Beach; (727) 443-6348

- **Florida International Museum,** St. Petersburg; (727) 822-3693 or (800) 777-9882

- **Tampa Museum of Art,** Tampa; (813) 274-8130

- **Marie Selby Botanical Gardens,** Sarasota; (941) 366-5731

Chadwick Park Beach (all ages)

Beach Road (Route 776), Englewood Beach. Open 6 a.m. to 11 p.m. daily. Parking is $1.

Located right where the south bridge meets the Gulf, it is convenient also because of its recreational and picnic facilities. There are volleyball and basketball courts, play areas, and food concessions, but no lifeguards. Shops, restaurants, and water-sports rentals are located nearby. It gets to be a high school hangout in the evening.

Manasota Beach (all ages)

8570 Manasota Beach Rd. Open 8 a.m. to 8 p.m. daily.

The northernmost beach has lots of amenities, including lifeguards, picnic pavilions with grills, volleyball, and a boat launch. By foot, this beach lies about a mile south of Venice's Caspersen Beach.

Middle or Blind Pass Beach (all ages)

3 miles to the south at 6725 Manasota Beach Rd. Open 8 a.m. to 8 p.m. daily.

This beach feels less cramped by sand erosion and is prettily landscaped.

Oyster Creek Regional Park (all ages)

6791 San Casa Dr., Englewood; (941) 475-3904.

The new park has a public swimming pool, nature trails to explore, a rink for skating, tennis courts, and baseball fields. Even dogs will find a section all their own.

Where to Eat

Lock & Key Restaurant and Pub. 2045 North Beach Rd., Englewood; (941) 474-1517. Casual indoor/outdoor dining with a waterfront view. Voted Englewood's best restaurant ten years in a row. Kids' menu. Open daily for lunch and dinner. $–$$

Where to Stay

Weston's Resort. 985 Gulf Blvd., Englewood Beach; (941) 474-3431. Eighty-three-unit beach-to-bay property with fishing dock, boat slips and rentals, two swimming pools, tennis courts, barbecue grills, and shuffleboard. Studio efficiencies to three-bedroom apartments. $–$$$

For More Information

Englewood Area Chamber of Commerce. 601 South Indiana Ave., Englewood 34223; (941) 474-5511 or (800) 603-7198; www.englewoodchamber.com.

Annual Events

Epiphany. Tarpon Springs; (727) 937-3540. On January 6 the Greek town's young men dive for the cross; a Greek celebration follows. **Free.**

PAL Sailor Circus. Sarasota; (941) 361-6350; www.sailorcircus.org. Students from grades three to twelve perform professional circus feats during a two-week season March to April and over the Christmas and New Year's holidays.

Children's Art Festival. Sarasota; (941) 355-5101. For one day mid-March, families can enjoy hands-on art activities and musical and dramatic performances.

Manatee Heritage Days. Bradenton; (941) 741-4070. The month of March is devoted to the celebration of local history and traditions throughout the county. **Free.**

Festival of States. St. Petersburg; (727) 898-3654. During March and April, events include parades, school bands, kids' art displays, clown school, and baseball clinics.

Suncoast Offshore Grand Prix. Sarasota; (941) 371-2827. A national attraction, with powerboat racers from around the world in June. **Free.**

John's Pass Seafood Festival. Madeira Beach; (727) 398-5994. For one weekend late in October, enjoy seafood and kids' attractions such as the Catch Tank, a costume contest, and haunted house. **Free.**

Sarasota Medieval Fair. Hunsader Farms, Bradenton; (888) 303-FAIR; www.sarasotamedievalfair.com. Watch thirteenth-century knights in full armor joust for ladies faire on two weekends in November. A marketplace offers trinkets and food.

Santa Parade and Snow Fest. St. Petersburg; (813) 274-8615. The first weekend of December brings snowball fights, ice-skating, a parade, kids' games, and a visit from St. Nick. **Free.**

Southwest Florida

A s Florida's last region to be settled and developed, southwest Florida manages to maintain more natural decorum than its other coastal counterparts. Greater thought and care went into community and resort planning, so the focus remained on wildlife and its habitat. Once a playground for wealthy adventurers in the early part of the last century, it still holds itself highly exclusive in parts. For families this may mean steeper prices, but also more opportunity for water adventures and nature discovery away from the crowds and the lights. Those with young kids especially favor the Gulf of Mexico's lazy waves over the frothy challenge of Atlantic Ocean breakers on the East Coast.

This route begins on the west shores of quiet Charlotte County, south of Sarasota County and off the well-trod path. It continues through old towns, unblighted countryside, highly touted resort communities such as Sanibel Island and Naples, and new urban development, ending at the west coast access to the Florida Everglades. The lower Gulf Coast tour takes occasional back-road stabs at southwest Florida's more hidden inner parts. TopPicks for Family Fun in Southwest Florida

Boca Grande and Vicinity

From Englewood, follow Rte. 776 to Rte. 775. Cape Haze, access point to Palm Island, lies along this route. Gasparilla Island, home to Boca Grande, lies to the west on Rte. 771. Causeway toll is $3.50.

The historic town of Boca Grande begs to be explored. A longtime escape destination for the nation's wealthy, it remains exclusive, while its reputation for tarpon fishing adds a maritime flavor. The Gasparilla Inn, grande dame of southwest Florida, still reserves rooms for the Vanderbilts each winter. An old circa-1910 depot and a 1928 movie theater now hold shopping centers. Restaurants range from fun and casual to spiffy.

SOUTHWEST FLORIDA

Boca Grande Bike Trail (ages 5 to 11)

The best way to explore Gasparilla Island is by bike. A 7-mile bike path follows the trail of the old railroad that once shipped phosphate from inland Florida to Boca Grande's deep port. Don't miss riding under the tree canopy on Banyan Street. Have a gape at the gracious Gasparilla Inn on Fifth and Palm Streets, where the Vanderbilts and their ilk have come to winter since the 1910s. Keep a watchful eye out for iguanas, a colony of which lives on the island. Motorized golf carts are also allowed on the path.

The Boca Grande Fishing Guides Association (ages 10 to 13)
www.fishingboca.com.

Boca Grande Pass is a mecca for tarpon fishing in spring and summer. To hook up with a charter, contact this group. Be prepared to dig deep into your pockets, especially if you're among those who try for the purse in the World's Richest Tarpon Tournament in July. Top prize: $150,000.

TopPicks for Family Fun in Southwest Florida

1. Seeing the (electric) light at the Edison-Ford Winter Estates, Fort Myers

2. Experiencing a thunderstorm and hurricane at Imaginarium: Hands-On Museum and Aquarium, Fort Myers

3. Watching the big cats snacking at the Zoo at Caribbean Gardens, Naples

4. Interacting with nature at the Conservancy of Southwest Florida's Natural Science Museum and Naples Nature Center, Naples

5. Kayaking through J. N. "Ding" Darling National Wildlife Refuge, Sanibel Island

6. Hiking through ancient forest at Corkscrew Swamp Sanctuary, Naples

7. Experiencing the world of shells at Bailey-Matthews Shell Museum, Sanibel Island

8. Petting a snake at Calusa Nature Center and Planetarium, Fort Myers

9. Getting out on the water with Grande Tours, Placida

10. Paddling into nowhere along the Wilderness Waterway canoe trail, Everglades National Park

Road **Markers**

I-75 zips you along the coast's eastern edge, connecting to Alligator Alley, the aptly named arterial that crosses the Everglades to reach Fort Lauderdale. Hwy. 41, also known as Tamiami Trail, meanders—often clogs—as it makes its way through towns and cities. It also penetrates Everglades territory south of I-75 and hits the east coast at Miami.

The region's northern destinations require back-road treks off the main arterials. Directions appear under each destination.

Boca Grande Lighthouse Museum and
Gasparilla Island State Park (all ages)

Gulf Boulevard; (941) 964-0060; www.barrierislandparkssociety.org. Entrance fee to park $3 for a vehicle with up to eight persons. Parking is $2 per car. Museum open 10 a.m. to 4 p.m. Wed through Sun June through Oct and daily Nov through May. Admission is **free** or by donation.

The park around this hundred-year-old lighthouse provides a good place for a picnic and swim. Stay out of the waters in Boca Grande Pass; they're deep and swift. Inside, look at photographs, artifacts, and exhibits depicting the island's multifaceted past.

Grande Tours (ages 5 to 13)

12575 Placida Rd. (P.O. Box 281), Placida 33946; (941) 697-8825; www.grandetours.com. Kayak rentals start at $25 for two hours. Kayaking ecotours cost $50 for a two-and-a-half-hour session. Don Pedro Island Shuttle is $27 per person, Captain's Choice is $35 per person. All tours by reservation.

Naturalist-interpreted deck boat and kayaking excursions tour the Myakka River and Charlotte Harbor Aquatic Preserve. The large flock of white pelicans that are among the seasonal visitors to Placida, are an eye-catching sight. The Sea Life Excursion (Captain's Choice) features seine net pulling to collect and study marine life. The Don Pedro Island Shuttle cruises to a barrier island for shelling, fossil hunting, and swimming at an 8-mile-long beach with facilities and grills; you bring your own food and drink. The staff specializes in fishing trips for the kids.

Island Bike 'n Beach (ages 5 to 11)

333 Park Ave., Boca Grande; (941) 964-0711. Open daily. Rates range from $7 an hour to $59 a week.

Rent bikes and golf carts here.

Loose Caboose

The Depot Mall, Park Avenue, Boca Grande; (941) 964-0440.

Stop in for a dip or two of homemade ice cream or a fruit smoothie.

A Woodyard **Adventure**

It was a hot July the day we pitched a borrowed tent on a strip of sand in Boca Grande. Bathed in sunlight, the Charlotte Harbor bay was a deep blue against a cloudless sky.

A string of glistening white powerboats streaming up the channel made the picture complete. Why, I wondered, were they in such a rush? The answer came when not one, but two water spouts appeared on the horizon. I watched, open-mouthed, as the tornado-like funnels swirled toward us and their daddy herded the kids into the van. Wind tore at the tent, and rain flooded its floor, as the two of us tried to hold it together. Then it was over as fast as it had begun. Needless to say, we scurried home and spent the rest of the weekend drying out the tent, and ourselves, in our own backyard.

Rum Bay Restaurant

Palm Island, Palm Harbor Island Resort Reception Area; 7092 Placida Rd., Cape Haze; (941) 697-0566. Water taxi available from noon to 6 p.m. Mon through Sat, 10 a.m. to 6 p.m. Sun, and costs $6 per passenger, 2 and under **free.** Reservations required.

You can begin an adventure in lunching at the ferry landing for Rum Bay Restaurant. The water taxi runs every thirty minutes, and the trip takes less than fifteen minutes. The restaurant is part of an exclusive getaway island resort with a family-friendly attitude. The tropical restaurant also serves dinner and is known for its baby back ribs. $$–$$$

Where to Eat

South Beach. 777 Gulf Blvd., Boca Grande; (941) 964-0765. Squatting right on the beach, this is a great place for casual lunches sandwiched into sunning time. Seafood and sandwiches. Also open for lunch and dinner daily. $$$

Where to Stay

The Innlet. 1251 Twelfth St. East (P.O. Box 248), Boca Grande 33921; (941) 964-2294. Pool, restaurant, and play area; boat-accessible location. $$–$$$

Palm Island Resort. 7092 Placida Rd., Cape Haze; (941) 697-4800 or (800) 824-5412; www.palmisland.com. Luxury beach villa accommodations, five pools, eleven tennis courts, restaurants and bar, island store, full-service marina, boat rentals, charter service, nature trail, bicycle and water-sports equipment rentals, and kids' program. $$$$

For More Information

Boca Grande Chamber of Commerce. P.O. Box 704, Boca Grande 33921; (941) 964-0568; www.bocagrandechamber.com. Information center at Courtyard Plaza at island's north end.

Port Charlotte and Vicinity

Along Hwy. 41 at exits 167 and 170 off I-75. From Boca Grande, follow Rte. 771 northeast; Hwy. 41 is about a thirty-minute drive away.

Port Charlotte is a new town that grew up around Hwy. 41 with little character. To bypass it, take Collingswood Boulevard off Rte. 776. Turn left on Edgewater Drive and continue to Hwy. 41 at the south end of town.

Charlotte Sports Park (all ages)

2300 El Jobean Rd.; (941) 743-2425.

This is spring training ground for the Tampa Bay Rays. This newly renovated stadium can seat about 7,500 fans. A kids' playground to keep little ones happy while parents watch the game and a tiki bar to celebrate a win are among the amenities.

Fish Cove Adventure Golf (ages 4 to 13)

4949 Tamiami Trail, Port Charlotte; (941) 627-5393. Open 10 a.m. to 10 p.m. Sun through Thurs, 10 a.m. to 11 p.m. Fri and Sat. Admission for eighteen holes of golf is $9.50 (plus tax) for ages 13 and older, $8.50 for seniors, $8.00 for ages 5 to 12, and $3.25 for 4 and under.

Two eighteen-hole putt-putt golf course. Add $3.00 each for all thirty-six holes.

Port Charlotte Beach (all ages)
South end of Port Charlotte at the east end of Harbor Boulevard; (941) 627-1628. Open 8 a.m. to 5 p.m. Parking is 50 cents an hour. Admission to swimming is $2.50 (plus tax) for persons 18 and older, $1.50 for ages 3 to 18.

Clustered around the man-made beach, a variety of facilities and activities will keep the family entertained for an entire day. Bring a picnic lunch or buy from the concessions. Play volleyball, basketball, tennis, or horseshoes. There's also a playground, boat ramps, a fishing pier, and a swimming pool.

For More Information

Charlotte County Chamber of Commerce. 2702 Tamiami Trail, Port Charlotte   33952; (941) 627-2222; fax (941) 627-9730; www.charlottecountychamber.org

Punta Gorda

South of Port Charlotte across the Peace River, about ten minutes along Hwy. 41. Downtown Punta Gorda lies close to exit 164 off I-75.

Across the wide mouth of the Peace River lies the old waterfront and historic downtown area of Punta Gorda. Gilchrist Park runs along the river on Retta Esplanade and has picnicking, a playground, a tennis court, and bike paths. The restored buildings of old cattle town Punta Gorda line Marion Avenue, 1 block south of Retta Esplanade. Walking tour guides are available at the chamber of commerce, located in the historic city hall building.

Babcock Wilderness Adventures (ages 4 to 13)
Route 31; 8000 State Rd.; (800) 500-5583; www.babcockwilderness.com. Admission is $19.95 for adults, $12.95 for kids ages 3 to 12, taxes not included.

East of town, wilderness still prevails. Rte. 31 is a tranquil drive along undeveloped lands. If you're planning on being in the area, call ahead to arrange a tour of Babcock. Prepare for a time warp back into Old Florida, naturally intact. Ninety-minute swamp buggy tours plow you through the farm country and wetlands of 90,000-acre Crescent B Ranch and Telegraph Cypress Swamp to see alligators, cattle, deer, turkeys, and wild pigs. The finale is winding through a maze hidden in the trees for a view of the rare and endangered Florida panthers. Bike tours lasting three hours are another mode of exploring. A prop shack chronicles the partial filming of the movie *Just Cause,* starring Sean Connery, at the site.

Charlotte County Historical Center (ages 4 to 10)
22959 Bayshore Rd., Charlotte Harbor; (941) 629-7278; www.charlottefl.com/historical. Open 10 a.m. to 5 p.m. Tues through Fri, 10 a.m. to 3 p.m. Sat. Closed Sun and Mon. Admission is $2 for adults, $1 for ages 12 and under.

This center's exhibits teach informally about local natural history, ecology, and history. One gallery is devoted to African animals, another holds dress-up costumes. Other exhibits rotate in and out.

Charlotte Harbor Environmental Center (ages 5 to 13)
10941 Burnt Store Rd.; (941) 575-5435; www.checflorida.org. Visitor Center at Alligator Creek is open Mon through Sat 9 a.m. to 3 p.m., Sun 11 a.m. to 3 p.m. Admission is free.

Guided tours (in season) around 4 miles of nature trails walk through pine and palmetto flatlands, hammocks, and marshes where alligators and bobcats live. Educational exhibits teach about local wildlife. Bring bug repellent. A smaller preserve, Cedar Point Park, at 2300 Placida Rd. in Englewood, adds a fishing pier on Oyster Creek to their nature walks.

On a **Budget**

- **Charlotte Harbor Environmental Center,** Punta Gorda, free admission
- **Manatee Park,** Fort Myers, $1 per hour parking
- **Naples Fishing Pier,** Naples, free admission
- **Collier County Museum,** Naples, admission free or by donation
- **Key Marco Museum,** Marco Island, free admission

King Fisher Fleet (ages 5 to 13)

Fishermen's Village shopping center, Maud Street, at 1200 West Retta Esplanade; (941) 639-0969; www.kingfisherfleet.com. Fares range from $10.95 to $25.95 for adults, half price for children under age 12.

With six cruises to choose from, it's the best place to go for nature-hunting and island-hopping boat excursions.

Muscle Car City Museum (ages 8 to 13)

3811 Tamiami Trail; (941) 575-5959, www.musclecarcity.net. Open 9 a.m. to 5 p.m. Tues through Sun, Diner open 7:30 a.m. to 4 p.m. Admission is $10 for adults, under 12 free with adult.

Chevy Corvettes, Pontiac GTOs, Camaros, and Oldsmobile Cutlass 442s are prominently featured among the almost 200 automobiles dating back to the 1920s in this new museum. A 1950s diner, the Filling Station, offers such old-time favorites as cheesesteak sandwiches, homemade ice cream, apple cobblers, and root beer floats. Owner Rick Treworgy, who has been collecting and restoring cars since the 1960s, plans to add a speed shop with parts and accessories for those who share his passion.

Peace River Wildlife Center (all ages)

3400 Ponce de Leon Parkway; (941) 637-3830. Open 11 a.m. to 4 p.m. daily for public tours; 8 a.m. to 5 p.m. daily, the center is open for people to bring in wildlife. A donation of $5 for adults and $3 for children is requested.

Adjacent to Ponce de Leon Historical Park (see below), the center conducts tours among cages of baby opossums, taped-together gopher tortoises, and other rescued and recovering animals.

Ponce de Leon Historical Park (all ages)

West end of Marion Avenue. Admission is free.

Here, supposedly, the infamous conqueror and seeker of eternal youth breached west coast shores in 1513. The monument for such a momentous event is humble, the centerpiece for a remote waterfront park that holds picnic facilities, a nature observation boardwalk, and a nature refuge.

Where to Eat

Harpoon Harry's. Fishermen's Village, 1200 West Retta Esplanade; (941) 637-1177; www.smugglers.com. River view, casual dining: sandwiches, seafood, steaks. Lunch and dinner daily. $–$$

Where to Stay

Fishermen's Village Villas. 1200 West Retta Esplanade #58; (941) 639-8721 or (800) 639-0020. Spacious time-share apartments above Fishermen's Village shopping arcade (well soundproofed). Swimming pool, clay tennis courts, bicycles, and full-service marina. $$

For More Information

Charlotte County Chamber of Commerce. 326 West Marion Ave., Suite 112, Punta Gorda 33950; (941) 639-2222; fax (941) 639-6330; 2702 Tamiami Trail, Port Charlotte 33952; www.charlottecountychamber.org.

North Fort Myers and Cape Coral

You can continue down Rte. 31 or take Hwy. 41 or I-75 South to reach North Fort Myers, about a half hour south of Babcock. Cape Coral lies to the west along Pine Island Road (Route 78).

Cape Coral Historical Museum (ages 6 to 13)

Off Pine Island Road at 544 Cultural Park Blvd., Cape Coral; (239) 772-7037. Open 1 to 4 p.m. Wed, Thurs, and Sun. Closed July and Aug. A donation of $1 per adult is requested.

Exhibits concentrate on the young town's social and natural history, including one devoted to the burrowing owl, something of a Cape Coral icon.

Fossil Expeditions (ages 7 to 13)

213 Lincoln Ave., Lehigh Acres; (239) 368-3252; www.fossilexpeditions.com. Four- to five-hour day trips with professional guides start at 9:30 or 10 a.m. depending on chosen site. $75 for adults, $65 for children ages 12 and under for a walk around; $100 if by kayak. Kayak, screen, and shovels provided.

Screen-wash for shark's teeth and bones of mammoths, camels, sabertooth cats, and other fossils at Peace River or Creek sites. Guides show how and where to look, and how to preserve finds to last another million years.

Greenwell's Bat-A-Ball and Family Fun Park (ages 4 to 13)

35 Northeast Pine Island Rd., Cape Coral; (239) 574-4386. Open 10 a.m. to 10 p.m. Sun through Thurs, 10 a.m. to midnight Fri and Sat, depending on action. Admission to the park is free; pay by the activity. Fee for minigolf is $6.50 for persons ages 12 and older, $5.50 for children ages 6 to 11 and seniors, $3.00 for ages 5 and younger. Second game is $3.00 for all ages. Race cars cost $4.00 to $6.50 for six minutes.

Named after the city's favorite sports son, Red Sox baseball player Mike Greenwell, it lets the kids spend some energy in the batting cages, at miniature golf (on a course in slightly shabby condition), in the video arcade, and on the go-karts.

Shell Factory (ages 4 to 13)

2787 North Tamiami Trail, North Fort Myers; (239) 995-2141 or (800) 282-5805; www.shell factory.com. Open 10 a.m. to 7 p.m. daily. Admission to Shell Factory is free; to bumper boat rides, $5 each; to nature park, $10 for adults, $8 for seniors, $6 for ages 4 to 12. Minigolf costs $5 for 18 holes.

Lee Island Coast

Lee Island Coast Visitor and Convention Bureau, 2180 West First St., Suite 100, Fort Myers 33901; (239) 338-3500 or (888) 231-6933; www.leeislandcoast .com.

A clever play on words, Lee County markets itself as the Lee Island Coast. Its visitor bureau handles a large territory, including North Fort Myers, Cape Coral, Pine Island and out-islands (and part of Gasparilla Island), Fort Myers, Sanibel and Captiva Islands, Fort Myers Beach, Estero, Bonita Beach, and Bonita Springs. Individual chambers of commerce are listed under each destination.

It comes by its "island" moniker honestly. Lee County contains more than one hundred barrier and coastal islands with 50 miles of white-sand beaches.

According to legend, this region was the kingdom of eighteenth-century pirate Gasparilla, attributed with good breeding and keen ransoming techniques. He is credited for naming Captiva Island after his kidnap victims and Gasparilla Island after himself.

Look for the gigantic conch shell. It marks a shopping and unusual entertainment complex that features Florida souvenirs, a small wild animal zoo, bumper boat rides for those 44 inches tall or taller; a stuffed African animal collection, and aquariums. The bazaar is filled with small gift shops, whose merchandise ranges from tacky to tasteful. Seashells are the focus.

Sun Splash Family Waterpark (all ages)

400 Santa Barbara Blvd., Cape Coral (go south off Pine Island Road); (239) 574-0557; www .sunsplashwaterpark.com. Admission is $16.95 for adults, $14.95 for children ages 3 to 12, $8.95 for seniors, and $3.95 for those 2 and under (tax not included). After 2 p.m. it is $13.95 for adults, $11.95 for children. From mid-Mar to the end of Sept, the park opens generally at 10 a.m. Hours and days of operation vary according to time of year. Closed Oct to June.

For cool refreshment on hot days, head to Sun Splash. There's something wet in store for all ages, from tot-size water slides to high-speed tube drops. The inner-tube river ride is fun for everyone. Snacks and lockers are available. No food or coolers are allowed inside the gates, but there are tables for picnics outside.

Where to Eat

Iguana Mia. 1027 Cape Coral Parkway, Cape Coral; (239) 945-7755. Mexican food in a fun atmosphere. Look for the unsightly green building. Kids' menu. $–$$

Where to Stay

Casa Loma Motel. 3608 Del Prado Blvd., Cape Coral; (239) 549-6000 or (877) 227-2566. If you're looking for an affordable place close to Cape Coral's family attractions, this one fits the bill. It sits on a canal and has a cheery pool waterside. $–$$

For More Information

Cape Coral Chamber of Commerce. 2051 Cape Coral Parkway, Cape Coral 33904; (239) 549-6900 or (800) 226-9609; www.capecoralfl .com.

North Fort Myers Chamber of Commerce. 3323 North Key Dr., Suite D-1, North Fort Myers 33903; (239) 997-9111; www .northfortmyerschamber.org.

Pine Island and Out-Islands

Follow Pine Island Road 15 miles west of Hwy. 41.

To poke into a fascinating pocket of untainted Florida island life, take Pine Island Road to the World's Most Fishingest Bridge, which crosses into the town of Matlacha (matt-la-SHAY) on Pine Island. You'll feel the difference in temperament as you continue through the town, past pastel Cracker-box guesthouses, ramshackle fish markets, teeny shops, and seafood restaurants. Next comes preserved mangrove forest, followed by a foray into tropical agriculture and the historic Cracker-shack world of Pineland, with its tiny post office and looming Indian mounds.

Cabbage Key Inn

Cabbage Key, accessible only by boat. P.O. Box 200, Pineland 33945; (239) 283-2278.

If you're out on the water, lunch on Cabbage Key is a must. It's served in a historic inn built by novelist Mary Roberts Rinehart in the 1930s as a wedding gift to her son. Some say Jimmy Buffett was inspired to write "Cheeseburger in Paradise" here. He's one of millions who have taped an autographed dollar bill to the inn's wall. After lunch, have a walk around the small island's short nature trail. The inn is open for lunch and dinner daily. $$–$$$$

Cayo Costa State Park (all ages)

P.O. Box 1150, Boca Grande 33921; (941) 964-0375. Accessible only by boat. Admission to the park is $2 per person.

This park is one of the most popular unbridged island destinations of southwest Florida. You'll love it if you favor secluded beaches. At the northern end, the almost entirely natural island provides a picnic ground for day-trippers and rustic cabins and tent sites for overnighters. There's no drinking water or electricity on the island. There are mosquitoes—lots of them. Avoid hot, still days if you plan on attacking the island's trails through subtropic jungle to historic sites such as a pioneer cemetery. Shuttles and boat rentals are also available from Captiva Island.

Gulf Coast Kayak Company (ages 6 to 13)

4530 Pine Island Rd., Matlacha; (239) 283-1125. Kayak rentals start at $30 for a half-day single. Three-hour nature tour is $45 per person; minimum two people. 24-hour advance reservations required.

To explore Pine Island's well-maintained natural pleasures, sign up here. It offers morning nature and manatee tours into the Matlacha Aquatic Preserve and other local natural areas. The tour guide is a naturalist and instructor.

Museum of the Islands (ages 5 to 13)

Stringfellow Road at 5728 Sesame Dr., Pine Island Center; (239) 283-1525; www.museum oftheislands.com. Open 11 a.m. to 3 p.m. Tues through Sat and 1 to 4 p.m. Sun, Nov 1 through Apr 30; 11 a.m. to 3 p.m. Tues, Thurs, and Sat, May 1 through Oct 31. Admission is $2 for adults, $1 for children. Group tours are available by appointment.

This museum enshrines eras past and present with vignettes portraying the Calusa Indians, pioneers, and fishermen.

Tropic Star Cruises (ages 5 to 13)

Pineland Marina, 13921 Waterfront Dr., Pineland; (239) 283-0015; www.tropicstarcruises .com. Fares for cruises that run from 9:30 a.m. to 4 p.m. are $30 for adults and $17 for children ages 7 and younger. Cabbage Key only, 9:30 a.m. to 2 p.m.: $25.

Board a fifty-nine-passenger boat that resembles the *African Queen* to cruise to exotic unbridged islands to the north. Lunch (extra) on Cabbage Key; sun and swim on Cayo Costa. Or charter a six-passenger water taxi at $150/an hour, captain and fuel included. Minimum 24-hour advance reservation required.

Where to Eat

Waterfront Restaurant. South end of Pine Island. 2131 Oleander St., St. James City; (239) 283-0592; www.waterfrontrestaurant .com. Casual, on the water, and the kids can play hangman on the butcher-paper tablecloths while waiting for their grouper fish sandwiches or foot-long Waterdoggies to arrive. Open daily for lunch and dinner. $–$$

Fort Myers

Across the river from North Fort Myers via Hwy. 41 or Business 41.

Across the river from Cape Coral, Fort Myers has a lot to offer family travelers in its museums and historic attractions. It serves as gateway to the coast's highly reputed island playgrounds.

Calusa Nature Center and Planetarium (ages 4 to 11)

3450 Ortiz Ave.; (239) 275-3435; www.calusanature.com. Museum and trails open 9 a.m. to 5 p.m. Mon through Sat, 11 a.m. to 5 p.m. Sun. Call for schedule at planetarium. Admission

to the museum is $9 for adults, $6 for children ages 3 to 12. Admission to the planetarium is included.

This center offers a 2-mile wildlife trail, Seminole Indian village, native bird aviary, and live animal exhibits. Staff demonstrate snake and alligator behaviors daily. The planetarium hosts a variety of presentations, using telescopes, laser lights, and astronomy shows.

Castle Miniature Golf (ages 5 to 13)
7400 Gladiolus Dr.; (239) 489-1999. Open 10 a.m. to 10 p.m. Mon through Thurs and Sun, 10 a.m. to 11 p.m. Fri and Sat. Admission is $10.49 for adults, $9.49 for children ages 12 and under, tax not included.

An eighteen-hole course located convenient to Lakes Park.

Centennial Park (all ages)
Downtown on Edwards Drive.

The park fronts the river with playgrounds, a fitness trail, picnic pavilions, and a fishing pier. It's the site of open-air concerts and special festivals.

City of Palms Park (ages 6 to 13)
Edison Avenue at Jackson Street; 2201 Edison Ave.; (239) 334-4700; www.redsox.com.

The Boston Red Sox play their spring exhibition season (March and April) here.

Edison-Ford Winter Estates (ages 6 to 13)
2350–2400 McGregor Blvd.; (239) 334-3614; www.edison-ford-estate.com. Continuous tours of both the Edison and Ford estates 9 a.m. to 5:30 p.m. daily. Admission to both homes and museum is $20 for adults, $11 for children ages 6 to 12.

Fort Myers's most venerable attraction sits right on the river and takes you into the home and workplace of a genius. The tour guides are enthusiastic and deliver fun anecdotes about the famed lightbulb inventor. On the ninety-minute walking tour, you'll be amazed at how many other things Edison invented. He owned 1,000 patents on everything from the phonograph to the movie camera. One of the best parts of the tour is the botanical gardens surrounding Edison's home. He was an avid botanist, and his outstanding collection of tropical plants proves it. Many he gathered looking for a cheaper way to produce

Recipe for **an Island**

Stick one torpedo-shaped mangrove pod into a sandbar. Bake in Florida sun for many years.

Mangroves are Florida's island builders. Their leggy, barnacle-crusted roots capture silt, sediment, leaves, and other muck, which eventually creates solid ground—and, in time, a new island.

Till the Cows Come Home

Fort Myers built itself as a cow town, where cow hunters such as Jake Summerlin became millionaires and legends. Today's lovely, royal-palm-lined McGregor Boulevard was once a dirt path that cows followed to the shipping port at Punta Rassa. The Thomas Edisons had to erect a picket fence to keep the free-roaming animals out of their garden. In 1886 the city widened the path as a gift to Edison. He later planted the boulevard's trademark palms.

City matron Tootie McGregor paid to have it paved in 1912 and requested that cattle be barred from the road. That, however, required a state law, which didn't pass—thanks to the powerful cattle lobby—until the 1950s.

rubber for his friend Harvey Firestone, who also wintered in Fort Myers. The tour continues on to the winter home of Edison's friend and next-door neighbor, none other than Henry Ford, whose estate is not quite as impressive because of the Fords' simple tastes. Thomas Edison, you'll soon discover, remains the patron saint of Fort Myers, with a college, mall, and all kinds of things named for him. Each year the town celebrates his legacy with the Edison Pageant of Light Festival, which culminates in a lighted night parade. The festival goes on for two weeks in early February.

Imaginarium: Hands-On Museum and Aquarium (all ages)

2000 Cranford Ave. (P.O. Box 2217), Fort Myers 33902; (239) 321-7420. Open 10 a.m. to 5 p.m. Mon through Sat, noon to 5 p.m. Sun. Admission is $12 for ages 13 and up, $10 for seniors, $8 for children ages 3 to 12 when accompanied by an adult.

The facility takes over the city's old waterworks and is clever in how it uses that as a theme. Everything is bright, colorful, and kid-fascinating (parent-fascinating, too). A Hurricane Experience chamber "blows 'em away," and a see-through mechanical body demonstrates how body parts work. Tots can crawl through a maze or play in a tiny house with cutaways showing building techniques. Older kids can "Be a Meteorologist" by selecting thunderstorm, hurricane, or tornado, then watching themselves broadcast on location via closed-circuit monitor. A movie theater shows animated features, aquariums and a touch tank display local and reef water life, a kid-size bank venue teaches about the world of financing, and an exhibit in the form of a car shows the effects of chemical abuse. Its gift shop sells a superb selection of child enrichment books and science-related games.

Lakes Regional Park (all ages)

7330 Gladiolus Dr.; (239) 533-7575 for park information; (239) 432-2017 for marina; (239) 267-1905 for train information. Open 7 a.m. to dusk daily. Parking is $1 an hour or $5 a day. Train rides run 10 a.m. to 2 p.m. Mon through Fri, 10 a.m. to 4 p.m. Sat, noon to 4 p.m. Sun. Cost is $4 for persons 6 years old and over, $1 for children ages 5 and under. $5 for adults and $2 for 5 and under on holidays

Outdoor days are well spent at this 277-acre complex of bike trails, playgrounds, picnic areas, food concessions, paddleboats, canoes, and a fitness trail. You can ride a model train for fifteen minutes around a village and the woods, a precursor of a railroad museum that's trying to grow there. The train runs daily. There's also a beach, but alligators and algae keep it from being a safe place to swim. Fishing is permitted.

Lee County Sports Complex (ages 6 to 13)

Near the intersection of Daniels Parkway; 14100 Six Mile Cypress Rd.; (941) 768-4270 or (800) 33-TWINS for Twins tickets; (941) 768-4210 for Miracles. Twins tickets range from $10 to $35; Miracles, $5 to $8.

Fort Myers is turning into Baseball Town, U.S.A., because, besides the Red Sox, it hosts the Minnesota Twins spring league here. Also, from April through August, the Miracle Professional Baseball team, a member of the Florida State League, competes here.

Manatee Park (ages 5 to 13)

10901 Rte. 80; (239) 694-3537. Park open 8 a.m. to 8 p.m.; visitor center open 9 a.m. to 4 p.m. daily, Nov through Mar. Parking is $1 per hour or $5 a day.

This is the place to take the kids in winter to spot manatees, the teddy bears of the water world. The sixteen-acre passive recreational park provides a manatee viewing area, interpretative exhibits, a nature boardwalk, a canoe and kayak launch, a fishing pier, and picnic facilities. It also serves as a rescue and release site for injured and rehabilitated manatees.

Six Mile Cypress Slough Preserve

Six Mile Cypress Parkway at Penzance Crossing; (239) 432-2004. Open daylight hours daily. Admission is free; parking costs $1 an hour, or $5 per day.

Boardwalks meander through 9 miles of wetlands ecology.

Top Family Beaches and Parks

1. **Delnor-Wiggins State Park,** Vanderbilt Beach

2. **Tigertail Beach,** Marco Island

3. **Lighthouse Beach,** Sanibel Island

4. **Barefoot Beach Preserve,** Bonita Beach

5. **Lover's Key State Park,** Bonita Beach

6. **Bowman's Beach,** Sanibel Island

7. **Cayo Costa State Park,** Cayo Costa

Top Family **Resorts**

1. **South Seas Plantation,** Captiva Island

2. **Best Western Pink Shell Resort,** Fort Myers Beach

3. **Sundial Beach Resort,** Sanibel Island

4. **Marriott's Marco Island Resort,** Marco Island

5. **Palm Island Resort,** Cape Haze

6. **Radisson Suite Beach Resort,** Marco Island

7. **Naples Beach Hotel & Golf Club,** Naples

Southwest Florida Museum of History (ages 5 to 13)

2300 Peck St. at Jackson Street; (239) 321-7430 Open 10 a.m. to 5 p.m. Tues through Sat. Admission is $9.50 for adults, $8.50 for seniors, $5.00 for children ages 3 to 12.

This museum holds forth in a historic railroad depot. Displays take you back to the days of the prehistoric Calusa Indians with scale models, vignettes, graphic depictions, and historical IQ games. Outdoors, you can tour an early-1900s replica of a local Cracker house and the world's last and longest Pullman private railcar, ca. 1930. Children will enjoy the hands-on switchboard and locomotive cab, the climb-aboard fire truck, and the baseball room.

Where to Eat

La Casita. 15185 McGregor Blvd.; (239) 415-1050. If your family values authentic Mexican cuisine, bring them to this adorable and Crayola-bright setting. Kids' menu. Open lunch and dinner hours daily; serves breakfast all day. $$

Where to Stay

Holiday Inn Historic District. 2431 Cleveland Ave., Fort Myers; (239) 332-3232 or (800) 315-2621. Near Edison-Ford winter homes. Pool and 122 completely renovated rooms. Kids under 10 **free.** $$–$$$

Sanibel Harbour Resort & Spa. East of the Sanibel Causeway at 17260 Harbour Pointe Dr.; (239) 466-4000 or (800) 767-7777. Mom and Dad can be coddled at the spa, while kids are cared for in the extensive Kids Klub program. Tennis facilities are world-class, and most of the rooms have a water view. $$$–$$$$

For More Information

Greater Fort Myers Chamber of Commerce. 2310 Edwards Dr., P.O. Box 9289, Fort Myers 33902; (239) 332-3624 or (800) 366–3622; fax (239) 332-7276; www.fort myers.org.

Sanibel and Captiva Islands

From Hwy. 41 or I-75's exit 131, head west on Daniels Parkway. Take a left on Summerlin Road (Route 867) and continue about twenty minutes to Sanibel Island (toll $3). To continue to Captiva, go right on Periwinkle Way once you reach Sanibel, then right on Tarpon Bay Road and left on Sanibel-Captiva Road.

At least a day on Sanibel Island is required visiting for those traveling through the area. It's among the most expensive of the area's destinations, but its beautiful shelling beaches and natural attractions make it worth the price. As you cross the causeway, watch for windsurfers, especially on breezy days. They put on a colorful show.

Tiny Captiva lies across a narrow, bridged pass from Sanibel. Twisty Captiva Drive runs scenically beneath vegetation canopies and along the sand-flounced, aquamarine Gulf of Mexico.

Adventures in Paradise (ages 5 to 12)

Port Sanibel Marina, Fort Myers; (239) 472-8443. Tues through Thurs and Sat, 9 a.m. to 3 p.m., cruise Sanibel Outer Islands with lunch at Cabbage Key (extra) for $55 for adults, $45 for children, and 3 and under free. Sea Life Encounter, 12:30 to 3 p.m. daily, $45 for adults, $35 for children.

You'll see dolphins, manatee, sea otters, and seahorses in the waters surrounding Sanibel and Captiva Islands on this cruise, and tour its private mangrove forest.

Lessons in the Sand

We looked like overzealous interior designers determined to duplicate Mother Nature's clever decorating scheme. Clenching paint swatches, we scanned the beach intently, picking up bits and shells and comparing them studiously with the color scale on our swatch. Regrouped, the six adults and two children exhibited our findings in an "art gallery" delineated in the sand and learned about the creatures connected with our beach-accessorized artifacts.

Participants filled the gallery with grasses, shells, fishing line, egg cases, debris, and other quizzical-looking objects. Emily, six, from Michigan, found a mermaid's purse. The naturalist showed the group turtle grass—salad, she said, for island tortoises. The animal that once lived in the reddish scallop shell, she explained, had a hundred eyes and could swim sideways.

Other fascinating facts and fun are part of SCCF's beach walk experience. It is geared to children and adults alike.

Bailey-Matthews Shell Museum (ages 3 to 13)

3075 Sanibel-Captiva Rd., Sanibel Island (south of the first mile marker); (239) 395-2233; www.shellmuseum.org. Open 10 a.m. to 5 p.m. daily. Admission is $7 for visitors age 17 and older, $4 for children ages 5 to 16; under 5 free.

After culling the beach for shells, your youngsters will enjoy learning more about their finds. Especially for them, a Children's Science Lab offers toddlers hands-on learning experiences in colorful reef-motif surroundings. But the touch table is under glass, so really it's just a "look table," and the museum eliminated the find-the-shell sticker game that kids loved. Kids under age seventeen get to pick two free shells. Other aesthetically arranged exhibits and vignettes examine the role of shells in natural and social history.

Billy's Rentals

1470 Periwinkle Way, Sanibel Island; (239) 472-5248.

Sanibel's 23 miles of bike paths provide an adventurous way to explore main streets and backwoods, where marsh rabbits scurry roadside. In-line skaters also favor the paved trail. Here's a good place to rent bicycles, surrey bikes, and other equipment for family biking, as well as scooters and beach gear. Rentals by hour, day, or week.

Bowman's Beach (all ages)

Bowman's Beach Road. Parking is $2 per hour.

The island's most secluded and shelly beach, it has picnic tables, restrooms, showers, and shady trees, but no lifeguards. Like all of Sanibel's beaches, it is maintained in its natural state.

Captiva Cruises (ages 5 to 13)

South Seas Resort Marina, Captiva; (239) 472-5300. Excursion fees range from $20.00 to $45.00, $12.50 to $25.00 for children ages 4 to 12.

The 150-passenger *Lady Chadwick* and other boats make dolphin, shelling, and luncheon excursions to the upper islands, with seating outdoors or in air-conditioned comfort. It's one of the few ways to see and dine on Useppa Island, where Zane Grey, Hedy LaMarr, and other illuminati of the 1920s reputedly recharged. It is now a private vacation club.

Crab Races (ages 4 to 13)

Crow's Nest Lounge, 'Tween Waters Resort, Captiva Drive, Captiva; (239) 472-5161. 6 p.m. Mon and Thurs.

These weekly events are a blast. For $3 you rent a hermit crab, which the kids can name, then cheer it on to victory. The announcer of eighteen-plus years is very funny, gives out prizes, and likes to joke with the kids. (There's an all-adult version later in the evening.) Half the pot goes to the United Way.

C.R.O.W. (Care and Rehabilitation of Wildlife) (ages 4 to 13)

3883 Sanibel-Captiva Rd., Sanibel Island; (239) 472-3644. Open 10 a.m. to 3 p.m. during the summer, starting at 11 a.m. Mon through Fri and 1 p.m. Sun, Nov through Apr. New Visitor Education Center requests a $5 per adult donation

This hospital complex duplicates natural habitat to rehabilitate sick and injured wildlife: birds, bobcats, raccoons, rabbits, and otters. Kids can play "Be the CROW Vet" at the Center. Visit by appointment or regularly scheduled tour in season.

J. N. "Ding" Darling National Wildlife Refuge (ages 5 to 13)

Off Sanibel-Captiva Road; 1 Wildlife Dr., Sanibel Island; (239) 472-1100. The refuge is open sunrise to sunset; the visitor center is open 9 a.m. to 4 p.m. May through Dec, 9 a.m. to 5 p.m. Jan through Apr. The visitor center is open Fri, but the refuge drive is not. Admission is $5 per car or $1 per cyclist or walk-in.

The refuge's visitor center teaches about local critters and the refuge's namesake—cartoonist and conservationist "Ding" Darling. The massive refuge encompasses more than 5,000 acres, but you don't really see that much if you simply drive through in your car. The best way to go is by canoe, kayak, or narrated tram (see below). Otherwise, get out and walk the short trails and climb the observation tower. You're likely to spot alligators, manatees, and lots of birds—some of them, like the roseate spoonbill, exquisitely rare. Best time to go is morning, low tide, and sunset, when birds are feeding. The still-developing visitor center contains exhibits on bird migration and mangroves.

Lighthouse Beach (all ages)

South end of Periwinkle Way; (239) 472-9075. Parking is $2 an hour.

Sanibel's beaches are maintained in a natural, low-impact state, meaning little development and facilities. This one is the most family accommodating with its nature trail, fishing pier, and historic site—the circa-1884 Sanibel lighthouse. The beach wraps around the island's south end to front both the Gulf and bay. Swimming is treacherous near the pass.

New Moon (ages 5 to 13)

'Tween Waters Marina, Captiva Drive, Captiva; (239) 395-1782; www.newmoonsailing.com.

Capt. Mick Gurley conducts sailing excursions and offers sailing classes for families and children (must be at least eight years old if not accompanied by parents). Lessons and extended sails to the Keys can be arranged. Advance reservations are requested.

Periwinkle Park (ages 2 to 7)

Periwinkle Way, Sanibel Island; (239) 472-1433. Open daily. Admission is free.

It has sites for tents and RVs, but you must reserve well in advance, especially for the winter-to-spring season. If you don't stay there, take a bike ride through and have a peek at the park's exotic bird aviaries. Some 600 feathered friends live here, including flamingos and toucans.

Sanibel-Captiva Conservation Foundation (SCCF) (all ages)

3333 Sanibel-Captiva Rd. (P.O. Box 839), Sanibel Island 33957; (239) 472-2329; www.sccf.org. Mid-Oct through mid-May the center opens Mon through Fri 8:30 a.m. to 4 p.m., closed Sat; June through Sept 8:30 a.m. to 3 p.m.; 10 a.m. to 3 p.m. Sat, Dec through Apr. Admission is $3 adult, children under 17 free.

The center has a touch tank in its visitors gallery, a soft, life-size manatee that children can climb, an alligator's jawbone, and wildlife blocks—a great place for preschoolers. Outside, take an easy walk to the bird observation tower and butterfly house to discover more about the local environment. The foundation hosts guided tours, interpretive beach walks, wildlife boat tours, and special children's programs.

Sanibel Historical Village (ages 4 to 13)

950 Dunlop Rd., Sanibel Island; (239) 472-4648. Open 10 a.m. to 4 p.m. Tues through Sat. Closed mid-Aug to Nov. A donation of $2 per adult is requested.

This makes for a fun, lightly educational pause from the sun and sand. The village huddles together a pioneer Cracker house-turned-museum, 1920s post office, historic general store, another vintage home, and teahouse.

Sweet Water Boat Rentals (ages 3 to 13)

'Tween Waters Marina, Captiva Drive, Captiva; (239) 472-6336. Rental rates begin at $200 a half day, $300 a full day for a 19-foot boat. Add $50 more for a 23–24 footer. Tax and fuel are additional.

To explore the upper islands or go out fishing on your own, rent a boat for the day.

Tarpon Bay Explorers (ages 5 to 13)

900 Tarpon Bay Rd., Sanibel Island; (239) 472-8900; www.tarponbay.com. Open 8 a.m. to 6 p.m. daily. Last rentals go out two hours before closing. Canoe and kayak rentals start at $30 for the first two hours for a double. Call ahead for tram schedule. Two-hour tram tours cost $13 for adults, $8 for children ages 12 and under.

It rents canoes and kayaks for paddling through "Ding" Darling Refuge (see above). You can also catch an interpretive tram or guided on-water tour of the refuge from here.

Where to Eat

Island restaurants, including the very finest, welcome children. Some, such as those listed here, make a more concerted effort to attract families than others.

expensive for dinner and touristy. Go have lunch or one of their sinful desserts and a look at the childhood-nostalgic decorations. $$$

The Bubble Room. 15001 Captiva Dr., Captiva; (239) 472-5558. Fun and whimsical but

Hungry Heron Restaurant. 2330 Palm Ridge Rd., Sanibel; (239) 395-2300. A favorite of locals, especially those with kids, because it shows cartoons, and lists a long selection of dishes for preteenagers. Service can be slow. Open for lunch and dinner daily and breakfast Sat and Sun. $$

Mucky Duck. 11546 Andy Rosse Lane, Captiva; (239) 472-3434; www.muckyduck.com. Popular, fun beachside eatery. Go early, put your name in, and spend the hour or so wait on the beach right outside the door, where sunsets are spectacular. Lunch and dinner Mon through Sat. $$–$$$

Where to Stay

Jensen's Twin Palm Cottages & Marina. Captiva Drive (P.O. Box 191), Captiva Island 33924; (239) 472-5800; www.gocaptiva.com. One- and two-bedroom cottages on the water with a focus on fishing lifestyles. $$–$$$

South Seas Island Resort. North end of Captiva; 5400 Plantation Rd., Captiva; (239) 472-5111 or (866) 565-5089; www.southseas .com. Spacious beach resort perfect for families. Hotel rooms, suites, villas, cottages, homes. Recreational opportunities include nine-hole golf course and excellent kids' program. A **free** resort trolley transports you around the 330-acre property. $$$–$$$$

Sundial Beach & Golf Resort. 1451 Middle Gulf Dr., Sanibel; (239) 472-4151 or (800) 552-5552; www.sundialresort.com. It has the best programs for and attitude about "age-challenged" guests. Touch tank on-site in the environmental center. Kids can dial a bedtime story, go on nature beach walks, or choose from dozens of scheduled activities. Full kitchens, water-sports equipment rentals. $$$–$$$$

For More Information

Sanibel-Captiva Islands Chamber of Commerce. 1159 Causeway Rd., Sanibel Island 33957; (239) 472-1080; www.sanibel-captiva.org.

Fort Myers Beach

From Sanibel Island, follow Summerlin Road (Route 867) about five minutes to San Carlos Boulevard and turn right (west). Cross the high bridge to Estero Boulevard (Route 865), Fort Myers Beach's main drag.

This beach town, situated on Estero Island, is trying to change its image from a spring-break party place to a family destination. Playgrounds are appearing on beaches, and resorts heartily welcome kids. Still, in March and April the college gang swarms in. Fort Myers Beach is water-sports heaven. You can book a Jet Ski tour to see dolphins or head skyward by parasail.

Bowditch Point Regional Park (all ages)

North end of Estero Boulevard; (239) 461-7400. Parking costs $1 per hour.

A lovely beach, it fronts Estero Bay and the Gulf. This is a nice beach for the family, with playground equipment, picnic tables, grills, hiking paths, and distance from the beach bar scene at so-called Times Square, where the bridge connects to the island.

Southwestern **Climes**

Southwest Florida feels the most tropical of Gulf Coast regions. Winter temperatures rarely dip below 70 degrees in the daytime and require little more than sweatshirts (unless you plan on boating; bring warm-weather gear). Summers are sticky and hot, normally showered each afternoon by thunderstorms. Plan to spend a lot of time in the water. On the islands, insulated by water, temperatures stay lower in the summer and higher in the winter.

Fish-Tale Marina (all ages)

7225 Estero Blvd.; (239) 463-3600. Open 8 a.m. to 5 p.m. daily. Rental fees begin at $135 for a half day, $215 for a full day. Refueling, collision waiver, and tax are extra.

Rent a fishing or pontoon boat for a self-guided family water adventure.

Getaway Deep Sea Fishing (ages 4 to 13)

Getaway Marina, 18400 San Carlos Blvd.; (239) 466-3600. Half-day trip (9:30 a.m. to 3:30 p.m.) is $55 for adults, $30 for children 12 and under, and $20 for those not fishing; no reservations necessary.

Party boat excursions take you into deep waters aboard a 90-foot craft to hook into grouper, shark, mackerel, and other prize catches.

Lovers Key State Park (all ages)

South of Estero Island on Rte. 865; 8700 Estero Blvd.; (239) 463-4588. Open 8 a.m. to sunset daily. Park entrance is $8 per vehicle with up to eight passengers, $4 for a single passenger, and $2 for extra passengers, bicyclists, and pedestrians.

It makes a great getaway beach destination while offering the convenience of picnicking facilities and nature activities. A tram or footbridge takes you to the beach and over a mangrove estuary. Kayak and bike rentals are available, plus there are camping and food concessions. This is a good place to spot ospreys, collect shells, and have a picnic.

Where to Eat

As headquarters for a major shrimp fleet, Fort Myers Beach serves the freshest of seafood. Every March it celebrates its briny harvest with the Fort Myers Beach Shrimp Festival. Festivities include a blessing of the fleet, parade, and shrimp boil. For more information call (239) 454-7500.

Snug Harbor. 645 San Carlos Blvd.; (239) 463-4343; www.snugharborrestaurant.com.

Waterfront dining indoors or out with seafood, salad, and pasta specialties. Lunch and dinner daily. $$–$$$

Where to Stay

Fort Myers Beach's resorts are generally less expensive than those on neighboring islands.

Pink Shell Beach & Bay Resort. 275 Estero Blvd.; (239) 463-6181; www.pinkshell

.com. At the island's quieter north end, with modern upscale condos. Twelve acres Gulf to bay, with marina, restaurant, boat tours, a kids' activity program, water-sports rentals, swimming pools, and tennis courts. $$–$$$$

For More Information

Greater Fort Myers Beach Chamber of Commerce. 17200 San Carlos Blvd., Fort Myers Beach 33931; (239) 454-7500; fax (239) 454-7910; www.fmbchamber.com.

Bonita Beach and Bonita Springs

Follow Rte. 865 for about ten minutes south of Lovers Key.

Route 865, which transports you the 15 miles from Estero Island to Little Hickory Island, passes undeveloped barrier island territory and the key-clotted Estero Bay Aquatic Preserve. The town of Bonita Beach on Little Hickory Island marks the beginning of more developed beachfront. On the mainland, Bonita Springs is metamorphosing from a tomato-growing town to a golfing development mecca between Fort Myers and Naples.

Barefoot Beach Preserve (all ages)

Entrance at Hickory Boulevard and Bonita Beach Road; (239) 353-0404. Open 8 a.m. to sunset daily. Parking is $4 a day.

Food concessions, picnic areas, and a brush with nature mean your family is going to love this 342-acre park.

Smart Travel

- There are plenty of fast-food places in southwest Florida, but if you're looking for something that pleases parents and kids alike, you're in luck here. Few restaurants do not accommodate children in southwest Florida. Naples restaurants as a whole are least conducive to families.

- Call ahead to a restaurant to discover the house policy. Some that do not actually have a kids' menu will fix hamburgers, pasta, or PBJs for small visitors. Ask about high chairs and booster seats.

- Almost any restaurant can be a family restaurant if you're prepared. Bring crackers, straw-sip containers of milk or juice, coloring books and crayons, electronic games—whatever it takes to keep them fed and occupied while you try to act like a normal person out for dinner.

- Although children under age sixteen can fish free in Florida, adults must purchase separate salt- and freshwater licenses.

Bonita Beach Public Beach (all ages)

South end of Hickory Boulevard; (239) 461-7400. Parking is $1 per hour.

Older kids especially will like all the fun, games, and excitement—volleyball, windsurfing, hot dog stands, loud music. Lifeguards are on duty.

Little Hickory Island (all ages)

26082 North Hickory Blvd./Route 865, Fort Myers Beach. Open sunrise to sunset. Admission is free; parking is $1 per hour.

Located in southern Lee County near Bonita Beach, a shelly, white-sand beach combined with a feeling of seclusion is the main attraction at this beachfront park. A ramp runs from the parking lot to the sand, allowing wheelchair access, and the shore is wide and clean. Surf fishing is a favorite pastime for visitors here, with locals and tourists alike raving about abundant catches. The beach offers restrooms, picnic tables, and showers.

Where to Eat

Anthony's Trattoria. 8951 Bonita Beach Rd. (Springs Plaza), Bonita Springs; (239) 947-2202. For good Italian food in a family-friendly setting. Kids' menu. Lunch every day except Sun; dinner daily. $$–$$$

Doc's Beach House. 27980 Hickory Blvd., Bonita Beach; (239) 992-6444. You barely have to leave the beach to eat here. Downstairs is ultracasual, with outdoor seating; upstairs, enjoy a beach view with air-conditioning. Burgers, hot dogs, chili, and finger foods. Open for breakfast, lunch, and dinner daily. $–$$

For More Information

Bonita Springs Area Chamber of Commerce. 25071 Chamber of Commerce Dr., Bonita Springs 34135; (239) 992-2943; fax (239) 992-5011; www.bonitaspringschamber .com.

Estero

North of Bonita Springs on Hwy. 41 about 15 miles.

Beachcomber Tours (all ages)

4765 Estero Blvd., Fort Myers Beach; (239) 443-7456; www.beachcombertoursinc.com. Call for reservations and directions to the Gulf Star Marina; pickups also available by arrangement at Koreshan State Park and Lovers Key Resort. All trips cost $30 for adults and $20 for children 12 and under. $20 for all on sunset cruise.

Offers dolphin watch and shelling trips, sunset cruises, Estero River nature tours, and trips to Mound Key.

Estero River Tackle and Canoe Outfitters (ages 6 to 13)

20991 South Tamiami Trail; (239) 992-4050. Open 7 a.m. to 6 p.m. daily. Three-hour rentals cost $22.50 and up for canoes, $17.50 and up per person for kayaks.

Amazing
Florida Facts

Cuban fishermen set up "pescadero rancheros" fish camps when the 9-mile strip of Cayo Costa was known as La Costa Island. They caught, dried, and salted fish for the Key West markets after the first settler, Trevio Padilla, lost his trading fleet in Cuba during the Spanish-American War. The families lived in windowless, dirt-floor "cabbage huts" made of palm fronds, until plank houses and a one-room schoolhouse were built. Eventually they moved to the mainland, but many of the early settlers names are found in the pioneer cemetery.

Across the street from Koreshan, you can rent a canoe for the 4-mile trip into the park's wildlife asylum. It has a boat ramp on the river and also sells bait and tackle.

Koreshan State Historic Site (ages 5 to 13)

Hwy. 41 and Corkscrew Road (P.O. Box 7), Estero 33928; (239) 992-0311. Open 8 a.m. to sunset daily. Park entrance is $5 per vehicle of eight persons or fewer, $2 per extra passenger, cyclist, or pedestrian.

For an unusual journey to times past, make a northward side trip on Hwy. 41 to Estero. This historic site commemorates a turn-of-the-twentieth-century religious cult that settled the banks of the Estero River. Koreshans were preoccupied with science and the arts. They theorized that the earth clung to the inside of the world's sphere, and they also planted experimental tropical gardens. You can camp in the grounds where they once made their home. Many of their buildings have been reconstructed, and the rare gardens still flourish.

Naples

South of Bonita Springs on Hwy. 41.

A city of contrasts, Naples balances wild and natural attractions with ultra-civilized culture and wealth. Naples sits on the doorstep to the Florida Everglades, and its southern neighborhoods most reflect this rugged aspect of its personality.

Collier County Museum (ages 4 to 13)

3301 Tamiami Trail East; (239) 252-8476. Open 9 a.m. to 5 p.m. Mon through Fri, 9 a.m. to 4 p.m. Sat. Admission is free or by donation.

In a lush park setting, the museum displays a Seminole Indian village, classic swamp buggy, archaeological lab, skeleton of an Ice Age giant ground sloth, re-created nineteenth-century trading post, and steam locomotive from the county's cypress logging era, as well as indoor prehistoric artifacts.

The Conservancy of Southwest Florida (all ages)

Merrihue Drive at 1450 Fourteenth Ave. North; 1 block east of Goodlette Road; (239) 262-0304; www.conservancy.org. Open 9 a.m. to 4:30 p.m. Mon through Sat. Museum admission is $9 for adults and $4 for children ages 3 to 12. Canoe rentals start at $15, $20 kayak, single; $35 tandem kayak or canoe.

Stroke a snake. Watch a turtle chow down. Name that tree. The Discovery Center exhibits, serpentarium, trail walks, and discovery experiences are a natural for kids. They can watch injured and sick animals rehabilitating or sign up for a special hiking, canoe, or boat trip (minimum age six). Canoe and kayak rentals are available. A **free** boat ride takes you through the thirteen-acre Conservancy's mangrove estuary to the Gordon River and a canal where nature suffers at the hands of progress. The center is associated with the Rookery Bay Estuarine Reserve and its programs.

Corkscrew Swamp Sanctuary (ages 5 to 13)

21 miles east of Hwy. 41 off Immokalee Road; 375 Sanctuary Rd.; (239) 348-9151. Open 7 a.m. to 5:30 p.m. Oct 1 to Apr 10, 7 a.m. to 7:30 p.m. Apr 11 to Sept 30. Admission is $10 for adults, $6 for college students, $4 for children ages 6 to 18, 5 and under free.

In Naples's northern reaches, nesting wood storks and some of the nation's oldest bald cypress trees are the star attractions. The 11,000-acre preserve, operated by the National Audubon Society, features a 2-mile boardwalk that crosses swampland inhabited by rich plant and marine life. You can usually spot an alligator or two and sometimes deer, otters, and wild hogs. A new interactive Audubon visitor center sensitizes guests to the unusual ecosystem.

Delnor-Wiggins State Park (ages 4 to 13)

Route 846 at 11100 Gulf Shore Dr. North, Naples Park; (239) 597-6196. Open 8 a.m. to sunset daily. Park entrance is $6 per vehicle with up to eight persons, $4 for a single passenger, and $2 for extra passengers, bicyclists, and pedestrians.

If your family favors beach seclusion and nature over water sports and crowds, spend the day here, just north of Naples. Fishing in the swift pass waters is as rowdy as it gets. Climb the observation tower for excitement. Bring a picnic; tables and grills are provided. Lifeguards are on duty, and beach and kayak rentals and food concessions are available.

Florida Sports Park (ages 7 to 13)

Route 951, less than 4 miles south of I-75's exit 101; P.O. Box 990010, Naples 34116; (239) 774-2701 or (800) 897-2701. Call for prices and dates.

Three times yearly the nationally televised Swamp Buggy Races take place here. Swamp buggies are vehicles adapted to the Everglades' marshy terrain; these are speedy, souped-up versions. The races in October feature a downtown parade. The year's Swamp Buggy

Queen makes her first appearance at the March race and gets dunked in the mud at every race. (The third race is in May.)

King Richard's Family Fun Park (ages 3 to 13)

North of Pine Ridge Road (exit 107 off I-75), 6780 North Airport Rd.; (239) 598-1666. Open 11 a.m. to 9 p.m. Mon through Thurs, 11 a.m. to 10 p.m. Fri and Sat, noon to 9 p.m. Sun. Admission is $5.50 per ticket to each attraction, $31.50 for 6 tickets.

Pick your fun: water sports (for children up to age ten), laser tag, a rock wall, and extreme go-karts (for persons eighteen and older).

Lowdermilk Park (all ages)

Gulf Shore Boulevard at Banyan Boulevard. Open 7 a.m. to dusk. Parking is metered.

Families are likely to find entertainment at Lowdermilk, where there's volleyball, playgrounds, picnicking, and concessions.

Naples Fishing Pier (all ages)

Twelfth Avenue South; (239) 213-3062. Open 9 a.m. to sunset. Free, but parking is metered and limited.

Gorgeous white beaches run the length of Naples. The beach around the historic pier is a popular spot, especially for anglers and sunset-gazers. It comes equipped with a bait shop, snack bar, restrooms, and showers. There's no charge, which makes it Florida's largest free fishing pier.

Palm Cottage and Norris Gardens (ages 8 to 13)

137 Twelfth Ave. South; (239) 261-8164. www.napleshistoricalsociety.org. Open 1 to 4 p.m. Tues through Sat, Nov through Apr; Wed and Sat only May through Oct. Admission is $8 for adults and $5 for children under 12.

A speck of local history resides here. Built in the 1880s of tabby mortar and Florida mahogany, it was one of the first buildings in southwest Florida to be constructed of local materials. Alternately a home and part of the Naples Hotel, today it houses the Collier County Historical Society and remembers lifestyles of the rich and acclaimed who once visited.

Sweet Liberty Sailing Catamaran (all ages)

City Dock, 880 Twelfth Ave. South, Naples; (239) 793-3523; www.sweetliberty.com. Reservations required. Sunset cruise each evening departs one and a half hours prior to sunset and is $29.50 for adults, $15 for children ages 12 and under. Shelling trips (9:30 a.m. to 12:30 p.m.) are $40 for adults, $15 for children ages 12 and under. Sightseeing Naples waterfront (1:30 to 3:30 p.m.) is $29.50 for adults and $15 for children ages 12 and under.

Enjoy a quiet, smooth, relaxing tour aboard a 53-foot sailing catamaran. There is plenty of room to walk around, inside and outside seating, and two restrooms on board.

The Zoo at Caribbean Gardens (all ages)

1590 Goodlette Rd.; (239) 262-5409; www.napleszoo.com. Open 9 a.m. to 5 p.m. daily (ticket office closes at 4:30 p.m.). Admission is $19.95 for adults, $18.95 for seniors, $11.95 for children ages 3 to 15, plus tax.

A boat tour, animal shows, and tropical gardens add to the allure of this small zoo. Favorite spots for the kids include Young Explorers Playground Forest. "Meet the Keeper" and multimedia animal shows (video and live) feature Bengal tigers, lions, alligators, dingoes, monitor lizards, and leaping lemurs.

Where to Eat

Naples is known for its chichi restaurants and daring cuisine. Families are not discouraged, but these places often have no specific kids' menu or other accommodations, especially for the high-chair crowd. Those below have a more relaxed, family atmosphere.

Remy's Neighborhood Bistro. 2300 Pine Ridge Rd. (Target center), Naples; (239) 403-9922. American cuisine with a French twist. Open for lunch Mon-Fri and dinner daily. $

Riverwalk Fish & Ale House. Tin City, 1200 Fifth Ave. South; (239) 263-2734. Casual, shanty-style waterfront dining with emphasis on seafood. Kids' menu. Lunch and dinner daily. $$

Where to Stay

Staying in Naples with a family can be a pricey venture. Yet even its storied luxury resorts are kid friendly.

Naples Beach Hotel & Golf Club. 851 Gulf Shore Blvd. North; (239) 261-2222 or (800) 237-7600; www.naplesbeachhotel.com. Fifty-year-old property with eighteen-hole golf course, spa and fitness center, beachfront and water-sports rentals, tennis courts, pool, kids' club, and dining room. There are 315 rooms and efficiencies. $$$–$$$$

The Ritz-Carlton. 280 Vanderbilt Beach Rd. in north Naples; (239) 598-3300 for information; (800) 241-3333 for reservations; www.ritz-carlton.com. Great beach and a commitment to family travelers. Try booking on the club floor, where all-day complimentary munchies can save on restaurant bills. Kids' programs. $$$$

Trianon Old Naples. 955 Seventh Ave. South; (239) 435-9600. Located in a residential area within walking distance of the waterfront and shopping district; 55 guest rooms, 3 large one-bedroom suites, pool, off-street parking. Continental breakfast in the lobby. Gulf beaches are just five minutes away. $$$

For More Information

Chamber Center. 3620 Tamiami Trail North, Naples 34103-3724; (239) 262-6367; www.napleschamber.org.

Visitor Information Center. 895 Fifth Ave. South, Naples 34102-6605; (239) 262-6141.

Marco Island

South of Naples along Rte. 951 about thirty minutes.

The northernmost of the Everglades' Ten Thousand Islands, Marco Island is nonetheless highly developed. Its golden crescent beach is lined with high-rises and resorts. To get away from all the high-rise glitz, go to the fishing village of Goodland, on the island's northeast side. It's a fun place for lunch and a great place to buy seafood.

Captain's John and Pam Stop

Calusa Island Marina, Goodland; (239) 394-8000; www.stopsmarinecharters.com. Rate is $55 plus tax per person for three hours. Open daily 8:30 a.m.

Take a backwater ecotour fishing or shelling from the local fishing capital into Ten Thousand Islands and thereabouts. Modes of transportation include a 26-foot luxury vessel and a 25-foot center console.

A Birder's **Paradise**

Whether snowbirds (migratory) or permanent residents, our feathered friends love warm weather. So much so, the state has established a 2,000-mile Great Florida Birding Trail for self-guided hikes: http://myfwc.com/gfbt. Many different species can be seen in the wildlife refuge locations scattered throughout the state, but can you spot one that visitors seldom see? Like the

Limpkin—this brown bird splattered with white spots likes to hide in marsh grasses. Because apple snails are its favorite food, it has to live in Florida or southern Georgia where there's plenty of them to eat

Roseate Spoonbill—once close to extinction, the big pink bird with the wide flat bill is slowly moving from the Everglades as far north as the Tampa Bay area.

Wood Stork—formerly called a wood ibis, this large (over 3 feet tall) bird is a striking sight with its white wings banded in black and naked head. On the Gulf coast you might find nesting colonies in the Corkscrew Swamp Sanctuary.

Florida Scrub Jay—Preferring isolated patches of scrub oak in the state, this cousin of the common blue jay has been rapidly losing its habitat to developers. A friendly little bird, it mates for life, and the juveniles help their parents raise the next generation. They love peanuts, so if you see a protected scrub jay in Oscar Scherer State Park, it may even take one out of your hand.

Key Marco Museum (ages 7 to 13)

Corner of Bald Eagle Drive and Waterway Drive in the Association of Realtors building; 140 Waterway Dr.. Open 9 a.m. to 4 p.m. Mon through Fri. Admission is free.

Marco Island has a proud archaeological history, and digs have unearthed important ancient finds. This museum displays some of the artifacts, as well as photographs and other memorabilia of more modern times.

Marco Island Trolley (ages 4 to 13)

Park at the chamber of commerce, near the island's north bridge on Collier Boulevard, or catch it at any of its stops; (239) 394-1600. Admission is $25 for adults, $12 for children under age 12.

This is a great tour of the island. You can get off and reboard as often as you like. One highlight is driving up the steep Indian Hill on the island's north end. You'll learn about the area's history from the drivers, who are generally fun characters.

Tigertail Beach (all ages)

Hernando Drive (take Tigertail Court north off Collier Boulevard). Open 7 a.m. to dusk daily. Parking is $3 a day.

Marco Island's main public access often fills up early. Offshore, a sandbar known as Sand Dollar Island surfaces in low tide. Between it and the beach, tidal pools fill with fish, small shells, and the shorebirds that feed upon them. Behind the beach, a restricted nesting area assures good bird-watching. The park has picnic facilities, food concessions, volleyball, a cool playground divided for two different age ranges, and water-sports rentals.

Where to Eat

Snook Inn. 1215 Bald Eagle Dr.; (239) 394-3313. Waterfront seafood house with twice-weekly seafood buffets, open daily. $$$

Stan's Idle Hour Seafood Restaurant. 221 West Goodland Dr., Goodland; (239) 394-3041. A favorite stop for waterfront dining and local color. You shouldn't miss Sun's goings-on. Country music accompanies a strange dance ritual invented here and known as the Buzzard Lope. In January, Stan's hosts the Mullet Festival, a small-town hoedown. Closed Mon year-round and in late summer, otherwise it's open for lunch and dinner. $$

Where to Stay

Marco Island Lakeside Inn. 155 First Ave., Marco Island; (239) 394-1161 or (800) 729-0216; www.marcoislandlakeside.com. Located just 1 mile from the Marco Island beaches. On-site restaurant (sushi and steaks), heated pool. $$$–$$$$

Marriott's Marco Island Resort Golf Club & Spa. 400 South Collier Blvd.; (239) 394-2511 or (800) 438-4373; www.marcomarriottresort .com. Two playgrounds, kids' pool, wide beach, recreation program, shopping arcade, pizza parlor, and restaurants. Each room has a microwave oven, refrigerator, toaster, iron, and ironing board. $$$–$$$$

For More Information

Marco Island Area Chamber of Commerce. 1102 North Collier Blvd. (P.O. Box 913), Marco Island 34145; (239) 394-7549 or (800) 788-MARCO; www.marcoisland chamber.org.

Everglades City and Chokoloskee Island

From Goodland, take Rte. 92 off the island to Hwy. 41. Turn right. Take Rte. 29 from Hwy. 41 to reach Everglades City.

East of Marco Island, the wilderness of the Everglades and various surrounding national and state parks and refuges begins.

If you're serious about exploring the vast maze land of the Everglades, Everglades City is a good place to set up base camp. From Everglades City, a causeway takes you to Chokoloskee Island, a throwback to frontier days.

Collier-Seminole State Park (ages 5 to 13)

20200 East Tamiami Trail at Rte. 92, Naples; (239) 394-3397. Open 8 a.m. to sunset daily. Park entrance is $5 per vehicle of eight persons or fewer, $2 per extra passenger, cyclist, or pedestrian.

Come here to camp and canoe in winter. In warm weather the mosquitoes will drive you away, or crazy. For the kids, the 6,400-acre park also holds a nice playground, nature trails, and one of the dredges used to forge Tamiami Trail out of the swamps. If you're not up to canoeing, you can hop on a boat tour (239-642-8898) down the Blackwater River and into the Ten Thousand Islands.

Everglades National Park Boat Tours (ages 5 to 13)

National Park Ranger Station, Chokoloskee Causeway, Rte. 29; (239) 695-2591 or (800) 445-7724. Tours depart daily every thirty minutes, beginning at 9 a.m., until 4:30 or 5 p.m., depending on what time the sun sets. Tours last about an hour and a half. Cost is $26.50 for adults, $13.25 for kids ages 5 to 12. Canoe rentals are $25.44 a day.

The national park conducts naturalist-narrated tours through the maze of Ten Thousand Islands and its teeming bird, alligator, and aquatic life. The facility also rents canoes. In season, rangers lead guided canoe tours.

Everglades National Park Wilderness Waterway (ages 7 to 13)

Everglades National Park is accessible from the east (see Southeast chapter) as well as from the west, via Hwy. 41.

Avid outdoor types can explore the eerily lonesome terrain of the Ten Thousand Islands via the 98-mile Wilderness Waterway canoe trail. (Do this in cool weather.) Canoeists must register with park rangers. You can paddle portions of the trail; the entire length takes at least eight days. Chickee (Indian-thatched) hut landings provide rustic shelter for campers. Several outfitters run guided tours within the park. Canoeists must bring all of their own gear unless outfitted by one of these businesses. A list of canoe rentals, outfitters, and recommended gear, plus necessary charts, guidebooks, and complete information are available from the U.S. Department of the Interior, National Park Service, Everglades National Park, P.O. Box 279, Homestead 33030.

Gator Trivia

- Alligators can live a year without food.
- Alligators are born without a predetermined sex. Incubation temperature differences determine the sex of the babies.
- Feeding alligators causes them to lose fear of humans.
- Fine for feeding an alligator: up to $500 and sixty days in jail.

Ted Smallwood's Store and Museum (ages 7 to 13)

360 Mamie St., Chokoloskee Island; (239) 695-2989. Open 10 a.m. to 5 p.m. daily Dec through Apr, 11 a.m. to 5 p.m. May through Nov. Admission is $3.00 for adults, $2.50 for seniors, free for children under age 12 when accompanied by an adult.

Explore the Everglades' wild and woolly era at this old Indian trading post of the early 1900s. Learn how Smallwood's was the site of an outlaw gun-down in 1910 and all about frontier life in the 'Glades through simple vignettes and antique general store products. The view from the back porch may be the best part; the rest is somewhat gloomy and dusty.

Wooten's Everglades Tours (ages 7 to 13)

East of Everglades City, 32330 Tamiami Trail East (Star Route, Box 120), Ochopee; (800) 282-2781.

In the vicinity you'll find any number of swamp buggy and airboat (another craft born of Everglades ingenuity—but noisy) tours, fishing charters, and such. Wooten's is one of the more well-respected names in the business.

Where to Eat

Rod & Gun Club. 200 Broadway, Everglades City; (239) 695-2101. A historic lodge with walls covered in trophy catches and alligator hides, serving Everglades fare—fish, frog's legs, peanut butter pie, and Southern-fried specialties. Lunch and dinner daily; Dinner weekends only, July and Aug. $$–$$$

Where to Stay

Ivey House. 107 Camellia St., Everglades City; (239) 695-3299; www.iveyhouse.com. Not only a casual inn but also headquarters of North American Canoe Tours, which provides a variety of backcountry trips into the Ten Thousand Islands and the Everglades Wilderness Waterway. Lodging and canoe trip prices vary with the details and the season, and lodging is higher during the Seafood Festival (first weekend in February). $–$$

For More Information

Everglades Area Chamber of Commerce. Corner of Hwy. 41 and Rte. 29 (P.O. Box 130), Everglades City 34139; (239) 695-3941 or (800) 914-6355.

Annual Events

Edison Pageant of Light. Fort Myers; (239) 334-2999. Taking place late January to early February, it honors former winter resident Thomas Edison with events culminating in

More Things to See and Do
in Southwest Florida

- **Big Cypress National Preserve,** Naples; (239) 695-4111, ext. 0
- **Coral Cay Adventure Golf,** Naples; (239) 793-4999
- **C.R.E.W. Marsh Trail System,** Naples; (239) 657-2253
- **Everglades Wonder Gardens,** Bonita Springs; (239) 992-2591
- **Fakahatchee Strand State Preserve,** Naples; (239) 695-4593
- **Golden Gate Aquatic Complex,** Naples; (239) 353-7128
- **Golf Safari,** Bonita Springs; (239) 947-1377
- **Gulf Coast Skimmers Water Ski Show,** Naples; (239) 732-0570
- **Gulfside Park,** Sanibel; (239) 472-9075
- **Museum of the Everglades,** Everglades City; (239) 695-0008
- **Ostego Bay Foundation,** Fort Myers Beach; (239) 765-8101

a lighted night parade. Miles of light strings electrify the historic homes, decorated in special holiday garb. **Free.**

Everglades Seafood Festival. Everglades City; (239) 695-4100. Three days of music, an artisan fair, and seafood the end of January and first weekend of February. **Free.**

Native American & Pioneer Heritage Days. Collier-Seminole State Park, Naples; (239) 394-3397. For three days in late February, the park celebrates the culture of local and nationwide tribes and early Everglades settlers.

Sanibel Shell Fair and Show. Sanibel Island; (239) 472-2155. A four-day exhibit early in March that features sea life displays, specimen shells, and shell art.

Fourth of July Freedom Swim. Punta Gorda. Participants swim the half-mile stretch across the mouth of the Peace River from Charlotte Harbor to Fishermen's Village while boaters accompany them. Entertainment and fireworks follow.

Kids Fishing Tournament. Fishermen's Village, Punta Gorda. Takes place one Saturday in July.

Old Florida Festival. Naples; (239) 774-8476. Music, Seminole War reenactments, history camps, and traditional arts and crafts the first weekend of November.

Sandsculpting Contest. Fort Myers Beach; (239) 454-7500. One weekend early in November, masters, amateurs, and spectators gather. **Free.**

Teddy Bear Teas. Naples; (239) 598-6644. A whimsical December holiday date with stuffed toys.

Southeast
Florida

outheast Florida—home of Miami Beach, Fort Lauderdale, Palm Beach, and other giant resort towns—is the first Florida many get to know. From the north, you first enter Palm Beach County, stretched long and lean along the coast. At northern extremes, this foray into the state's most populated, metropolitan area meets with lightly trodden wilderness. Then the city life begins and doesn't end until 100 miles later, when you've left the Fort Lauderdale–Miami area for the eccentricities of the Florida Keys.

Despite its urban sprawl, however, the south coast's traffic and development are easily left behind with a short drive away from the coast. In the West Palm Beach environs, a westward trek takes you to big and fishy Lake Okeechobee and the Loxahatchee National Wildlife Refuge. From Fort Lauderdale and Miami, a half hour gets you to the Everglades and Seminole and Miccosukee Indian territory. This tour will guide you to side trips into Florida's most profound wilderness as it heads to the very last speck of land in the state, Key West.

Jupiter Island

From Hwy. 1 or Rte. A1A in Hobe Sound, turn east on Rte. 707 (Bridge Road).

Jupiter Island hides its privileged residents from the noisy, fun resort world around it. (It's Palm Beach without the reputation. In fact, some say Palm Beach is where people live who cannot afford Jupiter Island.) The drive down Beach Road (Route 707) affords a vision of natural and wealth-driven beauty. Just don't expect to catch more than a glimpse of the mansions; money can buy a lot of shrubbery.

Canoe Outfitters of Florida (ages 7 to 13)

Riverbend County Park, on Rte. 706 (Indiantown Road), about 9 miles west of Hwy. 1; 9060 West Indiantown Rd., Jupiter; (561) 746-7053; www.canoeskayaksflorida.com. Open Thurs through Mon. Package rate for the full trip is $50 for two and $60 for a three-person canoe.

SOUTHEAST FLORIDA

Okeechobee

Lake
Okeechobee

Jupiter
Island

Juno Beach

North Palm Beach
Palm Beach
Shores

West Palm Beach

Florida Turnpike

Delray Beach

Boca Raton

Coconut Creek

Fort
Lauderdale

Davie
Dania
Hollywood

North Miami

Miami Beach

Miami
Key
Biscayne

Everglades
National
Park

Homestead

Key Largo

Long Key
Islamorada

Marathon

Key West
Big
Pine
Key

For a slower waterborne pace, take a leisurely canoe or kayak trip on the wild and scenic Loxahatchee River, along with the gators and multitude of birds.

Carlin Park (all ages)

Off Rte. A1A on Jupiter Beach Road, just north of Rte. 706.

This is Jupiter Island's most spectacular and popular recreational area, with food concessions, playgrounds, lots of picnic shelters with grills, lifeguards, and a wide apron of clean sand. Concerts and other special events are held outdoors and in its civic center. North of the Carlin Park access, at Jupiter Beach Park, jetties reaching into the pass make for great fishing.

Hibel Museum of Art (ages 6 to 13)

On the MacArthur campus of Florida Atlantic University in Jupiter, Florida; (561) 622-5560; www.hibel.com/museum.htm. Open 11 a.m. to 4 p.m. Tues through Fri. Admission is free.

Amid the community's renowned art scene, you'll find the Hibel, dedicated to the paintings, lithographs, porcelains, and sculptures of American artist Edna Hibel, an artist for over eighty years.

TopPicks for Family Fun in Southeast Florida

1. Driving through Lion Country Safari, West Palm Beach

2. Playing weird science at Museum of Discovery and Science, Fort Lauderdale

3. Watching the primates swing free at Monkey Jungle, Miami

4. Swimming the caves and crannies of Venetian Pool, Coral Gables

5. Biking Shark Valley, Everglades National Park (don't do this in the summer).

6. Spending the whole day beached at Crandon Park, Key Biscayne

7. Counting angelfish on the glass-bottom boat ride, Biscayne National Underwater Park

8. Seeing deer in miniature at National Key Deer Refuge, Big Pine Key

9. Celebrating day's end at the bottom of the United States at Mallory Square pier, Key West

Road Markers

Route A1A and Hwy. 1 thread together coastal communities with increasing tightness as you head south. I-95 and the Florida Turnpike offer quicker access. The turnpike is best for avoiding rush-hour traffic snarls.

South of Miami, expect slow traffic en route to the Keys, especially on a Friday afternoon, when it seems as if all of Miami is headed there for the weekend.

Jupiter Inlet Lighthouse (ages 7 to 13)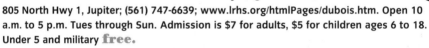

Near the intersection of Hwy. 1 and Alternate Rte. 707, Jupiter; (561) 747-6639; www .jupiterlighthouse.org. Open 10 a.m. to 5 p.m. Tues through Sun; last tour leaves at 4 p.m. Admission is $7 for adults, $5 for children ages 6 to 18.

This stands as one of Florida's most scenic lighthouses, built in 1860. Visit the small museum at the base and climb to the top (must be 48 inches or taller) by tour only.

Loxahatchee River Historical Society (ages 6 to 13)

805 North Hwy 1, Jupiter; (561) 747-6639; www.lrhs.org/htmlPages/dubois.htm. Open 10 a.m. to 5 p.m. Tues through Sun. Admission is $7 for adults, $5 for children ages 6 to 18. Under 5 and military free.

The society occupies a Cracker-style building in Burt Reynolds Park and relates how nature shaped the land's history. Other exhibits the kids will enjoy include pioneer toys, an outdoor Seminole Indian Living History Village, Spanish silver coins, and an 1892 Cracker shack that's being restored.

Where to Eat

The Crab House. 1065 Rte. A1A, Jupiter; (561) 744-1300. View of the Intracoastal Waterway and Jupiter Lighthouse. Crab, seafood, prime rib, and pasta. Kids' menu. Lunch and dinner daily. $$$

Where to Stay

See nearby North Palm Beach for lodging suggestions.

For More Information

Jupiter–Tequesta–Juno Beach Chamber of Commerce. 800 North Hwy 1, Jupiter 33477; (561) 746-7111; www.jupiterfl.org.

Juno Beach

Just south of Jupiter on Hwy. 1 or Rte. A1A.

To the south, the beaches are bluff lined, necessitating steep stairways to get from Rte. A1A parking to sea level. The tall dunes successfully cloister the beach from the reality shock inherent in developed areas.

Loggerhead Park and Marinelife Center of Juno Beach
(all ages)

14200 Hwy 1; (561) 627-8280 (Marinelife Center); www.marinelife.org. The center is open 10 a.m. to 5 p.m. Mon through Sat, noon to 4 p.m. Sun, and there is Storytime for kids on Wed at 10:30 a.m.

Loggerhead Beach has the most to offer among the local beaches. Across the street from the beach access, a nicely groomed park provides tennis, picnicking, a playground area, and the Marinelife Center of Juno Beach. The latter introduces you to maritime fauna and flora with a nature trail and indoor displays on shells, crabs, sharks, and sea turtles. During turtle nesting season (June and July), the center conducts nighttime Turtle Walks. In May, it hosts Turtle Time Festival on the beach to promote conservation, with music, food, and children's entertainment.

North Palm Beach County

Just south of Juno Beach on Hwy. 1.

John D. MacArthur Beach State Park (ages 4 to 13)

10900 State Road 703, North Palm Beach; (561) 624-6950; www.floridastateparks.org/mac arthurbeach. Open 8 a.m. to sunset daily. Park entrance is $5 per vehicle of eight persons or fewer, $1 per extra passenger, cyclist, or pedestrian. The nature center, free with park admission, is open 9 a.m. to 5 p.m. daily.

The area's most naturally intact beach runs for an 8,000-foot stretch on the north end of Singer Island. But there's more than beach to see here. The adventure begins at the nature center, near the park's entrance. You'll find aquariums, wildlife exhibits, historical documents, and an interpretive video. Outside, you walk around a butterfly garden and picnic pavilions, then across a 1,600-foot boardwalk (tram service available) to a nature trail that finally leads to the remote beach known for great snorkeling. Saturday and summer programs teach families about the environment.

Sailfish Marina and Resort (ages 4 to 13)

Sailfish Marina, 98 Lake Dr., Palm Beach Shores; resort desk (561) 844-1724, water taxi reservations (561) 472-1252; www.sailfishmarina.com. Open daily. Ninety-minute water-taxi tours (at 10 a.m., noon, and 2 and 4 p.m.) run $28 for adults, $14 for children under 12.

Palm Beach Water Taxi conducts narrated tours of Palm Beach mansions and yachts and Peanut Island, an Intracoastal island containing a recreational park and maritime museum. Sailing and fishing charters specializing in kingfish, dolphinfish, and sailfish also depart daily from its docks. Families can observe and feed tropical fish in the marina's aquarium. Thurs nights bring local artists and artisans with their marine-themed wares for Sunset at Sailfish. Ask about summer Camp Sailfish. Rooms, efficiencies, and kids' program available. $–$$

Where to Eat

Little Moir's Food Shack. 103 South U.S. 1, Jupiter; (561) 741-3626; www.littlemoirs-foodshack.com. A local favorite hidden in a strip shopping center. Funky, Caribbean, noisy. Great if you don't mind eating fabulous fish while being bumped by the next diner over. $–$$

Solu. Inside The Resort at Singer Island, 3800 N. Ocean Dr., Singer Island; (561) 340-1700; www.solurestaurant.com. Open every day 7 a.m. to 10:30 p.m. Upscale, Asian/Caribbean. The ocean view is to die for. $$$$

Where to Stay

Palm Beach Shores Resort. South end of Singer Island, 181 Ocean Ave. (Route A1A), Palm Beach Shores; (561) 863-4000 or (800) 328-2289. Its Beach Buddies club tantalizes tiny tots with lots of games and toys, plus the program sponsors nighttime parties and off-campus field trips. Tennis, water sports, fishing charters, and a less-traveled beachfront add to the amenities; 257 two-room suites. $$$–$$$$

PGA National Resort & Spa. 400 Avenue of Champions, Palm Beach Gardens; (561) 627-2000 or (800) 633-9150. Golf focus. Five eighteen-hole courses, a lake beach, nineteen tennis courts, a European spa, five restaurants, summer tennis and golf programs for kids, and 459 rooms, suites, and villas. $$$–$$$$

For More Information

Northern Palm Beaches Chamber of Commerce. 1983 PGA Blvd., Suite 104, Palm Beach Gardens 33408; (561) 694-2300; www .npbchamber.com. Open 8 a.m. to 5 p.m. Mon through Fri.

Palm Beach

From Singer Island, head south on Hwy. 1 or take scenic Flagler Drive for about ten minutes to West Palm Beach. Cross the Rte. A1A bridge (Royal Palm Way) into the moneyed world of the nation's social register.

If for no other reason, go to Palm Beach to gawk at the estates on a gold-paved drive down Ocean Boulevard. Hang out at Chuck & Harold's restaurant and see what celebrities you can spy. Stop in at the bookstore next door for a great selection of kids' reads. Window-shop as if price were no object along Worth Avenue. (Many shops are closed in the summer as they open their shops in Newport or The Hamptons.)

While the *hoi polloi* park and window-shop on Worth Avenue, the People of Quality arrive by appointment in their limos. Worth Avenue is the only place where I have seen a traffic jam of Rolls Royces.

Patriotic Palm Beach

Well-heeled Palm Beach dressed in khaki to do its civil duty during World War II. While German U-boats scoured local shores, torpedoing tankers and sometimes sending spies ashore, the ornate Breakers was dressed down to serve as a hospital for servicemen. Lights-out orders were issued to the island's coastal residents.

Flagler Museum (ages 9 to 13)
1 Whitehall Way at Cocoanut Row (P.O. Box 969), Palm Beach 33480; (561) 655-2833; www .flagler.org. Open 10 a.m. to 5 p.m. Tues through Sat, noon to 5 p.m. Sun. Admission is $15 for adults, $8 for children ages 13 to 18, $3 for children ages 6 to 12; under 6 free.

Lots of glittery, gilded stuff. Kids and adults love looking at the ornate Whitehall, palatial home of Henry Flagler. Flagler is credited with settling the east coast by improving and building railroads from St. Augustine to Key West. Children are especially impressed with the railway car out back. You can see the home by guided or self tour.

Where to Eat

Green's Pharmacy. 151 North County Rd.; (561) 832-0304. Locals and wealthy winterers meet at the luncheonette counter or tables. All-American food, hearty breakfasts. Breakfast and lunch daily. $

Hamburger Heaven. 314 South County Rd., Palm Beach. (561) 655-5277. 7:30 a.m. to 4 p.m. every day, dinner to 8 p.m. Mon through Thurs in the summer season. Since 1946 Hamburger Heaven has been the place to see and be seen for casual dining on Palm Beach. The waitstaff, utterly unimpressed by the rich and famous, do their best but the small joint can be very crowded at times. $$

Where to Stay

The Breakers. 1 South County Rd.; (561) 655-6611 or (800) 833-3141; www.thebreak ers.com. A posh old dame of a resort on the beach, with complete amenities. If your bank account can take it, you may want to check into its summer kids' camps. Year-round it holds youth programs. $$$–$$$$

For More Information

Palm Beach County Convention and Visitors Bureau. 1555 Palm Beach Lakes Blvd., Suite 800, West Palm Beach 33401; (561) 471-3995 or (800) 833-5733; www.palm beachfl.com. Open 8:30 a.m. to 5:30 p.m. Mon through Fri.

West Palm Beach

Downtown West Palm Beach is a happening place for shoppers and diners, especially in the stylish Clematis Shopping and Entertainment District along Clematis Street (between Flagler Drive and Rosemary Avenue).

Drift and wreck diving attracts the scuba crowd to these parts. You'll have no problems finding outfitting and certification operations throughout the Palm Beach area.

KOA Kampground (ages 5 to 13)

Next door to Lion Country Safari; 2000 Lion Country Safari Rd., Loxahatchee; (561) 793-9797 or (800) 562-9115.

A full-service campground, it has a swimming pool, playground, sports facilities, and general store. Campers receive a discount to Safari World. Cabins are also available.

Lion Country Safari (all ages)

Off Southern Boulevard (Hwy. 441/98), west of Hwy. 1 about 20 miles; 2003 Lion Country Safari Rd., Loxahatchee; (561) 793-1084; www.lioncountrysafari.com. Open 10 a.m. to 5:00 p.m. daily (no admissions after 4:00 p.m., slightly longer hours at times). Admission is $24 plus tax for adults, $22 for seniors, and $18 for children ages 3 to 9.

One of the best wildlife experiences your child can have in Florida: Your car becomes a safari jeep as you leisurely wend your way past lions lolling on the roadside, as well as giraffes, rhinoceroses, zebras, chimps, bison, elephants, ostriches, and wildebeest, through 500 acres of animals large and larger. At the end of the ride, Safari World entertains with rides, a petting zoo, miniature golf, dinosaur models, a free-flight feeding aviary, and other adventures. It's definitely worth the trip from the beach. Your car must have a hard-top roof or you must trade it in for a rental. Ask about the weeklong summer day camps for kids ages six to thirteen.

Palm Beach Polo & Country Club (ages 9 to 13)

Forest Hill and South Shore Boulevards, west of Hwy. 441 South, 11199 Polo Club Rd., Wellington; (561) 204-5687; www.palmbeachpolo.com. Public matches begin 3 p.m. Sun, Jan through mid-Apr. Admission is $15.

Polo and croquet are two trademark Palm Beach–area sports. To catch a polo match, attend Palm Beach Polo & Country Club's Sunday events. At halftime, join the stompers, who go onto the field to stamp down divots made by the horses' hooves. And remember the polo patron rule: never stomp on the steaming divots.

Palm Beach Zoo at Dreher Park (all ages)

1301 Summit Blvd.; between Southern and Forest Hills Boulevards; (561) 547-WILD; www .palmbeachzoo.org. Open 9 a.m. to 5 p.m. daily, last entry 4:15 p.m. Admission is $12.95 for adults, $9.95 for seniors, $8.95 for children ages 3 to 12.

The twenty-three-acre zoo provides home to more than 1,700 animals of native and exotic species, some of which are endangered. The reptile exhibit and petting zoo fascinate kids. Enjoy the new Tropics of the Americas exhibit.

Rapids Water Park (ages 4 to 13)

6566 North Military Trail; (561) 842–8756; www.rapidswaterpark.com. Open daily 10 a.m. to 7 p.m. late Mar through early Sept. Admission is $31.95 plus tax for ages 3 and older.

Cool off and splash down at Rapids Water Park. It soothes summer swelter with giant water slides, a wave pool, a lazy river, and a rain forest. Separate pools are designed for kids and adults.

South Florida Science Museum (ages 6 to 13)

In Dreher Park at 4801 Dreher Trail North; (561) 832-1988; www.sfsm.org. Open 10 a.m. to 5 p.m. Mon through Fri, 10 a.m. to 6 p.m. Sat, and noon to 6 p.m. Sun. Admission is $9.00 for adults, $7.50 for seniors, and $6.00 for children ages 3 to 12. Call for planetarium and science theater hours. Planetarium admission is $4 extra per adult, $2 extra per child.

Family oriented, the museum has the usual bubble, electricity, sound, energy, and hand-manipulative gadgets found in today's interactive science museums, but with more extensive aquariums. They hold marine life from the Pacific, Atlantic, coral reefs, and mangroves. The jawbone of a sperm whale reaches floor to ceiling.

SunFest (ages 5 to 13)

Flagler Drive between Banyan Street and Lakeview Avenue (mailing address: 525 Clematis St., West Palm Beach 33401); (561) 659-5980 or (800) SUN-FEST; www.sunfest.org. Admission at the gate is $31 per person over age 12; $10 children ages 6 to 12; under 6 free. Multiday and other options are available online only.

Begun as a jazz festival in 1982, it has grown into a well-known, well-attended extravaganza of music in all genres, plus an art and crafts show, a youth park, food, and fireworks. It takes place late April through early May.

Weekend Jaunt: Lake Okeechobee

Continue heading west on Hwy. 98/441 to escape the metropolis for the rural. Turn north on Hwy. 98 to reach the town of Okeechobee on Lake Okeechobee's north shore, or north on Hwy. 27 to get to Clewiston on the south shore.

As distant as ritzy Palm Beach County may seem from the lifestyles and wilderness of the Florida Everglades, it is tied into the same ecosystem, which includes Lake Okeechobee some 20 miles to the west.

Lake Okeechobee, known also as Florida's Inland Sea, is the second-largest freshwater lake entirely within U.S. boundaries. Problem is, you can't see it unless you are in or atop it. That's because in 1928, following a devastating hurricane flood, President Herbert Hoover mandated the construction of a 35-foot-high dike now bearing his name.

If you want to show the kids how sugar grows, drive around the south end of the lake to Clewiston, site of the annual Sugar Festival in April.

On a **Budget**

- **Hoffman's Chocolate Shoppe,** Greenacres City, free admission

- **Gumbo Limbo Environmental Complex,** Boca Raton, free admission

- **Holocaust Memorial,** Miami Beach, free admission

- **Miami Museum of Science and Planetarium,** Miami, free planetarium show first Friday of the month

- **National Key Deer Refuge,** Big Pine Key, free admission

Arthur R. Marshall Loxahatchee National Wildlife Refuge
(ages 8 to 13)

A couple of minutes west of Lion Country Safari, 10216 Lee Rd., Boynton Beach; (561) 734-8303; www.fws.gov/Loxahatchee. The visitor center is open 9 a.m. to 4 p.m. weekdays, 9 a.m. to 4:30 p.m. weekends, except in summer (May through Oct), when it closes Mon and Tues. The park is open sunrise to sunset daily. Admission is $5 per vehicle.

This is the nearest access to the raw, wet nature that Florida struggles to keep in its grasp. Vast and often forbidding, the 146,000-acre preserve is best seen by guided tour. Stop first at the visitor center at the refuge's south end and experience its audiovisual programs. Walking and canoe trails introduce you to its rare ecology.

Hoffman's Chocolate Shoppe   (ages 2 to 10)

5190 Lake Worth Rd. (Route 802), Greenacres; south of Hwy. 98 via Hwy. 441; (561) 967-2213; www.hoffmans.com. Open 9 a.m. to 8 p.m. Mon through Sat, 11 a.m. to 6 p.m. Sun. Admission is free.

On the return trip to the coast, watch the modern-day candy-making process at Hoffman's, seated in a Bavarian Tudor building you can watch the kitchen through a glass wall. Everyone gets a free sample. During the holidays (beginning the weekend before Thanksgiving), the site turns magical with lights, music, Santa, and performances by local artists and schools.

Lake Okeechobee Guide Association   (ages 6 to 13)

5286 SW 16th Ave., Okeechobee; 863) 763-2248 or (800) 284-BIG-O; fishokeechobee.com. Cost for a full day (one or two people) is $325 or $250 for a half day, which includes tackle. Extra person for $50. Bait is extra. Freshwater fishing license ($17) is required.

Bass and speckled perch fishing is Lake Okeechobee's lure. For a charter, contact this association.

Lake Okeechobee Scenic Trail   (ages 8 to 10)

(863) 983-8101; www.dep.state.fl.us/gwt/state/lakeotrail/default.htm.

You can walk along the lake's dike. Bike riding is a great way to get an elevated view of the waters, the surrounding landscape, and its abundant wildlife. You can enter this hiking-biking-horseback riding trail, 100 miles long, from any major highway.

Okeechobee Airboat Rides (ages 5 to 13)

900 Hwy 78 W. Okeechobee; (863) 824-0500; www.okeechobeeairboat.com. Call for an appointment. $25 adults, $15 kids 12 and under.

Kids and adults alike will love taking an airboat ride on Florida's Lake Okeechobee, headwaters of the Florida Everglades and home to hundreds of endangered and protected species of wildlife.

Where to Eat

Clewiston Inn. 108 Royal Palm Ave., Clewiston; (863) 983-8151 or (800) 749-4466; www.clewistoninn.com. This historic setting may seem like a formal place to take the kids, but it's quite family friendly and affordable. Home-cooked Southern-style fare is served in a colonial setting. Breakfast, lunch, and dinner Mon through Sat; Sun brunch 11:30 a.m. to 3 p.m. $–$$

Where to Stay

Roland Martin's Marina and Resort. 920 East Del Monte Ave. (off Hwy. 27), Clewiston; (863) 983-3151 or (800) 473-6766; www.rolandmartinmarina.com. Tailor-made for fishing fanatics. Pool, marina store, cafe, and full-service marina. RV parking, rooms, efficiencies, and bungalows. $–$$

For More Information

Clewiston Chamber of Commerce. P.O. Box 275, Clewiston 33440; (863) 983-7979; www.clewiston.org.

Okeechobee County Chamber of Commerce. 55 South Parrott Ave., Okeechobee 34972; (863) 763-6464.

Boca Raton

Take Rte. 802 east to I-95 and head south to exits 48, 45, or 44.

Back to the coast, and on to another of southeast Florida's most chichi neighborhoods: Boca Raton has nice beaches and assorted attractions to offer families (and, yes, Florida really has an upscale community named "Rat's Mouth").

Boomer's Family Recreation Center (ages 4 to 13)

3100 Airport Rd.; (561) 347-1888; www.boomersparks.com. Indoor play is open 10 a.m. to 10 p.m. Mon through Thurs, 10 a.m. to midnight Fri and Sat, 11 a.m. to 10 p.m. Sun. Outdoor activities are open 1 to 10 p.m. Mon through Thurs, 10 a.m. to midnight Fri and Sat, 10 a.m. to 10 p.m. Sun. Major attractions cost $3.49 to $24.49. Family packages available. Online discounts.

Games, bumper boats and cars, laser tag, a rock-climbing wall, miniature golf, go-karts, junior (under age ten) play area, and a play center all have an Australian theme.

Butterfly World (all ages)

Tradewinds Park South, 3600 West Sample Rd., Coconut Creek; (954) 977-4400; www.butterflyworld.com. Open Mon through Sat 9 a.m. to 5 p.m. and 11 a.m. to 5 p.m. Sun (ticket sales end at 4 p.m.). Admission is $24.95 for adults, $19.95 for children ages 3 to 11.

Watch their eyes light up with the natural magic of three acres of waterfalls and gardens all aflutter with beautiful butterflies. You'll also see other insects, plus fish and birds, including lorikeets.

Children's Museum (ages 2 to 10)

498 Crawford Blvd.; (561) 368-6875; www.cmboca.org. Open noon to 4 p.m. Tues through Sat. Admission is $3 per person. Infants are free.

Hands-on permanent exhibits here include a minimart, bank, Dr. Dig's Backporch, a pioneer kitchen, and Faces: A Celebration of Florida Cultures. It hosts workshops, story times, and special events such as KidsFest every April.

Gumbo Limbo Nature Center (all ages)

1801 North Ocean Blvd. (Route A1A), across from Red Reef Park; (561) 338-1473; www.gumbo limbo.org. Open 9 a.m. to 4 p.m. Mon through Sat and noon to 4 p.m. Sun. Suggested donation $3.

The center educates children through nature trails, interpretive displays, aquariums, an observation tower, seminars, field trips, and other programs. Outdoor marine tanks hold baby loggerhead turtles, local fish, tide pool inhabitants, and touchables. Visitors can often observe rare and endangered species—such as manatees, ospreys, sea turtles, and brown pelicans—in the wilds.

Morikami Museum and Japanese Gardens (ages 6 and up)

4000 Morikami Park Rd., Delray Beach; (561) 495-0233; www.morikami.org. Museum and gardens open 10 a.m. to 5 p.m. Tues through Sun. Admission is $10.65 for adults, $9.59 for seniors, and $6.39 for college students and children ages 6 to 18.

The museum houses 5,000 Japanese art objects and artifacts. The 200-acre gardens reflect major periods of Japanese garden design, from the eighth to the twentieth centuries.

South Beach Park (all ages)

400 North Ocean Blvd. (Route A1A); (561) 393-7973; www.ci.bocaraton.fl.us/rec/parks/southbeach.shtm. Open 8 a.m. to sunset. Parking costs $17 weekends and holidays, $15 weekdays.

A series of well-maintained, nicely landscaped public beach accesses with paid parking stretch along Rte. A1A. This one is a favorite and provides lifeguards and showers.

Florida Trivia

Stately Butterfly Most states have a state tree and flower. But did you know Florida has a state butterfly? In 1996 the zebra long wing—named for its black stripes—was so declared.

Where to Eat

Tom's Place. 1225 Palm Beach Lakes Blvd., West Palm Beach; (561) 997-0920; www.tomsplaceforribs.com. Tues to Thurs 11:30 a.m. to 9:30 p.m., Fri 11:30 a.m. to 10 p.m., Sat noon to 10 p.m. Closed Sun and Mon. Barbeque, down-home and good for the soul (if not the heart). Lunch and dinner Tues through Sat. $–$$$

Where to Stay

Boca Raton Resort & Club. 501 East Camino Real; (561) 447-3000 or (888) 543-1277; www.bocaresort.com. Historic landmark on the Intracoastal Waterway, with a marina, sports facilities, shops, and several restaurants. Boca Baby takes care of guests age two and under; Boca Tots ages three to five; Boca Bunch ages six to eleven; and tweens and teens ages twelve to seventeen. Parents can order gourmet baby food from the restaurant's menu. Security gates. $$$$

For More Information

Greater Boca Raton Chamber of Commerce. 1800 North Dixie Hwy, Boca Raton 33432-1892; (561) 395-4433; www.bocaratonchamber.com.

Fort Lauderdale

About 15 miles south of Boca Raton along Rte. A1A or Hwy. 41.

Fort Lauderdale has outgrown its *Where the Boys Are* reputation to become a mecca for families instead of party animals. Its attractions sample history, nature, science, and sports.

One of the world's most famous beaches, Fort Lauderdale Beach is also one of the most developed. It has been restyled with a wavy wall that separates beach from a paver-brick walk for strollers, bikers, and in-line skaters. Across the street, sidewalk cafes line up with shops, bars, and motels. The central hub of the beach lies at the intersection of Las Olas and Ocean Boulevards. You'll find water-sports rentals on the beach and in nearby shops.

Bonnet House Museum & Gardens (ages 5 to 13)

900 North Birch Rd., (954) 563-5393; www.bonnethouse.org. From Dec to Apr, tours are 10 a.m. to 4 p.m. Tues through Sat, last tour at 2:30 p.m.; from May to Nov, tours are 10 a.m. to 3 p.m. Wed through Fri; Sun, tours are noon to 4 p.m. with the last one at 2:30 p.m. The museum is closed Mon. Tours are $20 for adults, $18 for seniors, $16 for children ages 6 to 12; children 5 and under free. Admission to grounds only, $10.

This is more than a historic attraction. Built by two artists in the 1920s between the sea and a small lake, the ninety-five-acre estate holds lush grounds beautified by swans, orchids, and monkeys. Its beach is located across the street. Visitors can see the house by seventy-five-minute tour only but can walk the nature trail on their own. In April, the property is the site of Bonnet House Jazzfest on the Green.

Brian Piccolo Park (ages 6 to 12)

9501 Sheridan St., Cooper City; (954) 437-2626; www.broward.org/parks/bp.htm. Admission to the skate park is $8 per person for two hours; velodrome admission is $2 to $4 per person. Park entrance fee on weekends only. Hours for skate park and velodrome vary.

Named for the football star who died at age 26 of cancer, inspiring the movie *Brian's Song*. Pack a picnic lunch and head out of town to Brian Piccolo Park—or eat at its Snack Attack stand. Just don't forget your wheels. The best parts of Brian Piccolo are its skate park and velodrome (bike racing track). You can rent skates, skateboards, and race bikes. The facilities stay open in the evening. Lessons and classes are available.

Everglades Day Safari (ages 4 to 18)

Call (239) 472-1559 or (800) 472-3069 for reservations and to arrange pickup location; www.ecosafari.com. Departs Fort Lauderdale each morning at 7:45 a.m. and returns about 5:30 p.m. Fee is $140 for adults and $104 for children ages 6 to 11.

This guided trip through the Everglades includes a jungle cruise, nature walk, lunch, wildlife drive, and an airboat ride.

Fort Lauderdale Stadium (ages 6 to 13)

1301 Northwest Fifty-fifth St., off Commercial Boulevard; (954) 776-1921. Tickets cost $5 to $20.

The excitement of major league baseball visits Fort Lauderdale each March when the Baltimore Orioles train preseason here.

Hugh Taylor Birch State Park (ages 5 to 13)

Off Ocean Boulevard at 3109 East Sunrise Blvd.; (954) 564-4521; www.floridastateparks.org/hughtaylorbirch. Park is open 8 a.m. to sunset daily. Beach gate is open 9 a.m. to 5 p.m. Park entrance is $6 per vehicle of eight persons or fewer, $1 per extra passenger, cyclist, or pedestrian.

This park accommodates four biological habitats as well as recreationers. Within its 180 acres between ocean and Intracoastal, it has canoe rentals and a 1.7-mile exercise course for hikers and runners. The beach lies across the street from the entrance.

Museum of Discovery and Science (all ages)

401 S.W. Second St.; (954) 467-6637 or (954) 463-IMAX; www.mods.org. Open 10 a.m. to 5 p.m. Mon through Sat, noon to 6 p.m. Sun. Admission to the museum, including one IMAX film, is $15 for adults, $14 for seniors and students, and $12 for children ages 2 to 12.

The best the city has to offer families occupies two floors packed with exciting curiosity sparkers. Kids love Virtual Volleyball, the space flight simulator, and the nature section with its fascinating aquariums, spiders, snakes, and enchanted Florida forest. Games slyly teach about fitness, health, physics, and other scientific phenomena. Stop in the gift shop for learning tools of the painless variety. Ecofloat environmental boat tours showcase the beaches, barrier islands, mangrove estuaries, sinkholes, and other diverse local habitat during the summer. Part of the complex, Blockbuster 3-D IMAX Theater shows sky-high discovery films about nature and science.

Old Dillard Museum (ages 5 to 13)

1009 N.W. Fourth St.; (754) 322-8828; www.broward.k12.fl.us/olddillardmuseum . Open 10 a.m. to 4 p.m. Mon through Thurs in the summers and 11 a.m. to 4 p.m. Mon through Fri during the school year (mid-Aug to mid June). Admission is free.

Housed in what was the first local public school for African Americans, it today holds three permanent displays: a hands-on, minds-on exhibit; the Jazz Gallery; and a replica of the 1920s classroom.

Parker Playhouse (ages 3 to 13)

707 Northeast Eighth St.; off Hwy. 1; (954) 468-3285; box office (954) 462-0222; www.parker playhouse.com. Ticket prices vary.

Bringing children's classics to the stage, professional performances run daily October through April.

Smart Travel

- Big cities call for big precautions. Always keep car doors locked and drive on main thoroughfares.

- Getting lost in Miami, where even the street signs can be bilingual, can mean speaking a different language to get directions back on track. It wouldn't hurt to brush up on your Spanish and bring along a phrase book.

- You cannot fully enjoy the Florida Keys without getting into the water. The best way to understand its treasures is by snorkeling. Children can snorkel as early as age four. If they're afraid of the water, have them stand at the beach's edge and just stick their head in the water with you holding the mask to their eyes. Chances are they'll be fascinated.

- For your own safety and the health of the reefs, never touch or stand on coral.

Riverwalk Park (all ages)

20 North New River Dr.; (954) 828-5346.

Across the street from the museum, this linear recreational area prettily follows New River to Las Olas Boulevard and features educational stations like the one that lets you play with marine navigational instruments. Sunday jazz brunches feature top artists.

South Beach Park (all ages)

South of the Rte. A1A (Southeast Seventeenth Street) Causeway.

Here the crowds are thinner and the development less intrusive. For families, there are picnic tables and a playground. Street parking is metered. Lifeguards supervise.

Stranahan House (ages 7 to 13)

335 S.E. Sixth Ave. at Las Olas Boulevard; (954) 524-4736; www.stranahanhouse.org. Tours given each day at 1, 2, and 3 p.m. Admission is $12 for adults, $11 for seniors, and $7 for children under age 12.

The area's oldest home, ca. 1901, is lavishly furnished with period antiques. Docents gear the tour toward any children in the group.

Water Taxi (all ages)

651 Seabreeze Blvd.; (954) 467-6677; www.watertaxi.com. Taxis run 9 a.m. until midnight daily, sometimes later. An all-day pass costs $13, $10 for seniors and 12 and under. Family pack ($48) covers 2 adults and 3 youth or seniors.

Getting around by boat is the best way to go in Fort Lauderdale. If you don't have one, you can jump aboard the Water Taxi and get a lift to shopping, restaurants, and other attractions. Reserve in advance or wait (for up to thirty minutes) at a scheduled stop.

Winterfest (ages 4 to 13)

(954) 767-0686; www.waterfantaseas.com/winterfest_boatparade.asp.

Lighted boat processions are common throughout Florida at Christmastime. One of the first and grandest illuminates the waterway during a monthlong celebration.

Where to Eat

Mai-Kai. 3599 North Federal Hwy; (954) 563-3272; www3.maikai.com. Polynesian decor and dance performance. Special kids' performance Sunday (kids under age twelve admitted to show **free** every night). Dinner only. Show is extra. $$–$$$

Where to Stay

Embassy Suites Fort Lauderdale. 1100 SE 17th St.; (954) 527-2700 or (800) EMBASSY for reservations; www.embassysuitesftl.com. Close to the beach and local attractions. Great pool with splashy waterfalls and lush tropical setting; **free** breakfast buffet. $$–$$$$

Harbor Beach Marriott Resort & Spa. 3030 Holiday Dr.; (954) 525-4000 or (800) 222-6543; www.marriottharborbeach.com. A beach, water-sports rentals, a large free-form pool, and a kids' recreational program give families all they need in a Fort Lauderdale resort; away from the beach crowds. Mom and Dad will appreciate the $8 million, 20,000-square-foot spa. $$–$$$$

For More Information

Greater Fort Lauderdale Convention and Visitors Bureau. 100 East Broward Blvd., Suite 200, Fort Lauderdale 33301; (954) 765-4466; www.sunny.org.

Weekend Jaunt: Miccosukee Country

Follow I-595 west to I-75 (alligator Alley). Detours off the interstates take you to the natural and other attractions on Fort Lauderdale's other side.

Billie Swamp Safari & Camping Village (ages 3 to 13)

19 miles north of I-75 off exit 49; 12261 Southwest 251st St., Princeton; (954) 966-6300 (800) 949-6101; www.seminoletribe.com. Open 10 a.m. to 5 p.m. daily. Prices vary with the options chosen.

To see the Everglades through the eyes of a Native American, stop here. There is also a gift shop, wildlife shows, and the Swamp Water Cafe. Tours include the wildlife show and an hour-and-a-half swamp buggy tour into the wetlands of the Everglades. Guided hikes and night swamp buggy safaris are also available. Ask about family and overnight packages.

Flamingo Gardens and Arboretum (ages 5 to 12)

3750 South Flamingo Rd., Davie; 3 miles south of I-595; (954) 473-2955; www.flamingo gardens.org. Open 9:30 a.m. to 5:00 p.m. daily. Closed Mon June through Nov but open Labor Day. Admission is $17.00 for adults, $8.50 for children ages 4 to 11. Twenty percent discount for seniors and military, 30 percent for students. Optional tram tour $4.00 for adults, $3.00 for children.

A tram takes you through the sixty acres of citrus groves, botanical gardens, free-flight aviary, and habitat for flamingos, alligators, hummingbirds, and other fauna. Centerpiece is the 1933 Wray estate, framed by 200-year-old oaks. The gardens specialize in the cultivation of endangered heliconia plants and the protection of wood storks and roseate spoonbills.

Sawgrass Recreation Park (ages 4 to 13)

2 miles north of I-75 at 1006 North Hwy 27, Weston; (954) 389-0202 or (800) 457-0788; www .evergladestours.com. Admission to thirty-minute airboat tour and exhibits is $19.50 for adults and $10.00 for children ages 4 to 12. Tax is additional.

An eighteenth-century Indian village is the main attraction here. Spend the day exploring, airboating, and fishing. Spend the night camping. You'll also find alligator and reptile shows, fishing boat rentals, a birds of prey exhibit, a gift shop, picnic tables, airboat tours, and a barbecue cookhouse.

Young at Art Children's Museum (ages 2 to 13)

11584 West S.R. 84, Davie; (954) 424-0085; www.youngatartmuseum.org. Open 10 a.m. to 5 p.m. Mon through Sat and noon to 5 p.m. Sun. Admission is $8.00, $7.50 for seniors, children under 2 free.

The museum invites kids to participate in its interactive galleries, special exhibitions, workshops, classes, and special events.

Dania and Hollywood

Just south of Fort Lauderdale along Hwy. 1.

Anne Kolb Nature Center (ages 5 to 13)

751 Sheridan St., Hollywood; between Hwy. 1 and Rte. A1A; (954) 926-2480; www.broward .org/parks/wlpaknc.htm. Park hours vary according to daylight; open daily. Exhibit hall is open 8 a.m. to 6 p.m. daily. Admission to parts of the park is free; $1.50 per person over age 5 at the park's south entrance and recreation area (1200 Sheridan St.) on weekends and holidays. Admission to the exhibit hall is $1 for adults and children. Canoe/kayak is $30 per person for four hours.

The center provides more than 1,500 acres for hiking, biking, birding, canoeing, kayaking (rentals available), pier fishing, picnicking, and family recreation. Narrated boat tours, a five-story observation tower, and environmental exhibits teach about the local wildlife. It's located at the lovely oasis known as West Lake Park.

Boomer's (ages 5 to 13)

1801 Northwest First St., west of Hwy. 1, Dania; (954) 921-1411; www.boomersparks.com. Open 11 a.m. to 11 p.m. Sun through Thurs, 11 a.m. to 1 a.m. Fri and Sat. Miniature golf admission is $9; kids 5 and under free. Go-kart rides cost $8.

Have a harrowing adventure on the Sky Coaster, which simulates a bungee jump. Tamer rides include bumper cars, a roller coaster, and Naskart racing. There's also miniature golf, batting cages, and video arcades.

Hollywood Beach Broadwalk (all ages)

Park around Johnson Street (off of Rte. A1A) to get closest to the restaurants and shops. Parking is metered.

Strolling the Hollywood Beach Broadwalk (not boardwalk, it's surfaced with paving stones), you're likely to hear French accents drifting from open-air cafes. French Canadians arrive here *en groupe* to winter. Year-round, enjoy a Riviera ambience under an awning at one of the French-style cafes, reasonably priced. The beach is family oriented and perfect for cycling, in-line skating, and water sports.

Top Family Beaches and Parks

1. **Crandon Park,** Key Biscayne

2. **John D. MacArthur State Park,** North Palm Beach

3. **Loggerhead Beach Park,** Juno Beach

4. **Bahia Honda State Park,** Bahia Honda Key

5. **South Pointe Park,** Miami Beach

6. **Carlin Park,** Jupiter Beach

IGFA Fishing Hall of Fame & Museum (ages 2 to 12)

300 Gulf Stream Way, Dania Beach; (954) 922-4212; fax (954) 924-4220; www.igfa.org. Open 10 a.m. to 6 p.m. Mon through Sat, noon to 6 p.m. Sun. Admission is $5 for children ages 3 to 16 and seniors, $8 for persons 17 to 61.

Toddlers to teens will love the hands-on stuff—especially the virtual marlin or tarpon they reel in. Play the computerized "Name That Fish" game. Kids ages two to seven can make fish prints and go pretend-boating in the Discovery Room. Ask about the Junior Angler Club and educational youth programs. Suave and state of the art, the museum features a school of prize fish hanging from the ceiling with plaques set into the floor to identify their world-record winners. Across the parking lot, visit Outdoor World, a football-field size sports store with a huge aquarium and Florida-style shooting range.

John U. Lloyd State Park (ages 6 to 13)

6503 North Ocean Dr., Dania Beach; (954) 923-2833; www.floridastateparks.org/lloydbeach. Open 8 a.m. to sunset daily. Park entrance is $6 per vehicle with up to eight passengers, $3 for a single passenger, and $1 for extra passengers, bicyclists, and pedestrians.

Watch the big ships coming in and out of Port Everglades from the beach. Rock jetties and a boat ramp ($5 fee) serve sportsmen, plus there are canoeing and picnic facilities at the dunes-edged park. The south end feels entirely set apart from nearby urban pressures.

Where to Eat

Dining on the water is practically required when in the area. The Intracoastal Waterway provides a scenic venue for spying on passing yachts and humbler watercraft.

Le Tub. 1100 North Ocean Dr. (Route A1A), Hollywood; (954) 921-9425; www.theletub .com. Small, out of the way, and casual. It was built from flotsam and jetsam found on the beach. Burgers, seafood, and ribs. Open noon to 4 a.m. (yes, a.m.) daily. $–$$

Where to Stay

See Fort Lauderdale listings for lodging suggestions.

Top Family **Resorts**

1. **Doral Golf Resort and Spa,** Miami

2. **Hawk's Cay,** Marathon

3. **Holiday Isle Resort & Marina,** Islamorada

4. **Cheeca Lodge,** Islamorada

5. **Sonesta Key Biscayne,** Miami

6. **Palm Beach Shores Resort,** Palm Beach Shores

For More Information

Greater Hollywood Chamber of Commerce. 330 North Federal Hwy, Hollywood 33020; (954) 923-4000 or (800) 231-5562, fax (954) 923-8737; www.hollywoodchamber.org.

Miami

About twenty minutes south of Hollywood along Rte. A1A, Hwy. 1, or I-95.

Cosmopolitan Miami sparks adventures of the ethnic and cultural variety, but it has its natural gifts to offer as well. Explore the various ethnic neighborhoods settled throughout the years by Jews and immigrants from the Bahamas, Cuba, Haiti, Jamaica, Nicaragua, and elsewhere. They combine to give Miami its own saucy style, fashion, music, and cuisine. Streets and cafes are alive with the chatter of foreign tongues.

Miami Beach is the hot spot for vacationers, especially fashionable South Beach, but other, more family-oriented attractions are scattered throughout the city, particularly south of downtown.

American Airlines Arena (ages 6 to 13)

601 Biscayne Blvd.; (786) 777-1000; www.heat.com. Tickets cost $10 and up.

The Miami Heat National Basketball Association team plays at this state-of-the-art arena, connected to Bayside Marketplace by bridge.

Aquatic Rental Center and Sailing School (ages 9 to 13)

1275 Northeast Seventy-ninth St., Pelican Harbor Marina; (305) 751-7514; www.arcmiami .com. Open daily. Rentals run $85 for two hours, $150 for a half day, $225 for a full day.

It rents sailboats and teaches certification classes.

Bayside Marketplace (ages 4 to 13)

Off the island via MacArthur Causeway, turn south on Biscayne Boulevard (Hwy. 1); 401 Biscayne Blvd., R-106; (305) 577-3344; www.baysidemarketplace.com. Open 10 a.m. to 10 p.m. Mon through Fri, 10 a.m. to 11 p.m. Sat, and 11 a.m. to 9 p.m. Sun (extended hours at some restaurants and bars). A parking ramp charges $4 the first hour and up to $10 maximum.

For dining and shopping, head to this open-air, festive waterside mall. It is also a good place to find a boat tour of the glamorous homes of Star Island, where celebrities of all kinds have homes. Two popular boats are the *Island Queen* (305-379-5119; www.island queencruises.com) and *Schooner Heritage of Miami*, a tall sailing ship (www.heritage schooner.com; 305-442-9697). Both do daily tours; *Schooner Heritage* operates only September through May.

Bill Baggs Cape Florida State Park (all ages)

1200 South Crandon Blvd., Key Biscayne; (305) 361-5811; www.floridastateparks.org/ capeflorida. Open 8 a.m. to sunset daily. Park entrance is $8 per vehicle with up to eight passengers, $3 for a single passenger, and $1 for extra passengers, bicyclists, and pedestrians. Lighthouse guided tours take place at 10 a.m. and 1 p.m. Thurs through Mon. Limit is twenty people; register at the gate. Must be 8 years or older to climb the tower.

South of the island's commercial area, you'll find another beach and picnic spot that families love. Bring your own food or eat at the Cuban-style restaurant. The park holds the added attraction of a historic site—Cape Florida Lighthouse, south Florida's oldest structure, built in 1825, which you can climb by tour only.

Crandon Park (all ages)

4000 Crandon Blvd., Key Biscayne; (305) 361-5421. Open 8 a.m. to sunset daily. Parking is $5 a day ($10 for recreational vehicles and buses).

This is Miami's best outdoor venue for families. The causeway toll limits crime, the view of cruise ships coming and going is great, and the vast recreational area contains a variety of activity arenas—a wide beach, an amusement center, a golf course, tennis courts, baseball fields, soccer fields, a bike path, volleyball courts, a playground, and a marina.

Orange Blossom

Miami owes its existence, legend has it, to an orange blossom. In the winter of 1894–95, freezing temperatures in Palm Beach had developer Henry Flagler all aquiver. Guests at his posh resort were complaining, while oranges were dying on the tree. Miami pioneer Julia Tuttle, interested in putting her backwoods town on the map, sent a bouquet of fragrant orange blossoms to Flagler's Palm Beach home. The ploy worked. By 1896, work had begun on Miami's Royal Palm Hotel.

Little **Haiti**

Bounded roughly by Northeast Second Avenue and Forty-first and Eighty-third Streets, the neighborhood designated Little Haiti bursts with the color and spirit that is Haiti.

Families spend their weekends here, barbecuing, beaching, and relaxing, with lifeguards on duty.

Enchanted Forest Elaine Gordon Park (ages 2 to 9)
1725 Northeast 135th St., North Miami; (305) 895-1119. Open daily, one hour after sunrise to sunset. Admission is **free.**

Just like the name says, this place is enchanted: A park where swans, storybook thickets, nature trails with wood bridges, a tot lot, and horseback riding stir magic. One expects Robin Hood to come charging in at any minute. Bring carrots and apples to feed the horses. Pony rides start at $3 but call (305) 891-9512 for times and price list.

Haulover Park (all ages)
10800 Collins Ave., North Miami Beach; (305) 947-3525. Cost for all-day parking is $5 per car, $10 per recreational vehicle.

This is a huge center for recreation, with a pretty beach, picnic shelters, grills, food concessions, trails, bike path, lifeguards, tennis, golf, and a marina with boat rentals. The 1,103-foot pier sells bait and rents tackle. A portion of the beach is designated clothing optional, Florida's only legit nude beach. It is patrolled to discourage oglers.

Historical Museum of Southern Florida
101 West Flagler St.; (305) 375-1492; www.hmsf.org. Open 10 a.m. to 5 p.m. Mon through Sat, 10 a.m. to 9 p.m. on the third Thurs of each month, and noon to 5 p.m. Sun. Admission is $8 for adults, $5 for children ages 6 to 12.

Hands-on displays and changing exhibits trot you along the local time line. Children can try on pirate costumes, play with pioneer toys, and hop aboard an old-fashioned streetcar.

Holocaust Memorial (ages 8 to 13)
1933–1945 Meridian Ave., Miami Beach; (305) 538-1663; www.holocaustmmb.org. Open 9 a.m. to 9 p.m. daily. Admission is **free.**

See an inspirational monument to Jewish victims of the Holocaust in a park setting marked by a dramatic sculpture.

Key Biscayne

South of downtown and east off Hwy. 1 onto Rickenbacker Causeway (toll $1.50 from Miami, **free** on return).

South of downtown Miami, take a turn for the more natural, upscale Miami when you veer toward Key Biscayne. The island attracts families with its lovely parks and other attractions. Along the causeway, windsurfers congregate at sands known as Hobie Beach. You can usually rent equipment there from mobile vendors.

Key Biscayne Boat Rentals (ages 7 to 13)

3301 Rickenbacker Causeway, Key Biscayne; (305) 361-7368.

Stop here for power and jet boats and Wave Runners, rentable by the hour or for half and full days. All-inclusive packages are available for fishing, waterskiing, snorkeling, diving, and sightseeing.

Land Shark Stadium (ages 6 to 13)

2269 Dan Marino Blvd.; (305) 626-7400 for Marlin tickets, www.flamarlins.com; Marlin tickets cost $9 to $105; (305) 452-7000 for Dolphin tickets; (305) 620-2578 for Dolphin information, www.miamidolphins.com. Dolphin ticket prices vary.

This stadium is home to two professional sports teams: the Florida Marlins and the Miami Dolphins. The Florida Marlins baseball team plays April through October. August through December, watch the Miami Dolphins kick off. In 2012 the Marlins will move to a new stadium nearby.

Little Havana

Miami's Cuban culture, strong as a *café con leche,* centers along Southwest Eighth Street (Hwy. 41), known locally as *Calle Ocho,* site of the annual whopper Carnaval Miami each March. Calle Ocho, one of the festival events, is billed as the world's largest block party with the world's longest conga line.

Southeastern **Climes**

Temperatures average 77 degrees year-round. January is the coldest month, with an average low of around 66 degrees. August and September are the hottest, when daytime temperatures reach into the mid-90s. The east coast benefits from breezes off the ocean, which keep things cooler and less buggy than the west coast.

The Keys are as tropical as it gets in the continental United States. You'll never see freezing here, yet summer breezes manage to keep it climate controlled.

Miami in **the Movies**

Movies filmed in Miami: *Stuck on You* (Matt Damon), *Bad Boys II* (Will Smith), *Heartbreakers* (Sigourney Weaver), *Any Given Sunday* (Al Pacino), *Random Hearts* (Harrison Ford), *Analyze This* (Billy Crystal), *There's Something About Mary* (Cameron Diaz), *Wild Things* (Kevin Bacon), and *Miami Vice* (Jamie Foxx). More than 1200 movies and TV shows have been filmed here.

Miami Seaquarium (all ages)

4400 Rickenbacker Causeway, Key Biscayne; (305) 361-5705; www.miamiseaquarium.com. Open 9:30 a.m. to 6 p.m. daily (ticket sales end at 4:30 p.m.). Admission is $35.95 plus tax for adults, $26.95 plus tax for children ages 3 to 9. Parking is $8. Swim with Dolphins program is $139 per swimmer and $45 for observers and includes tour of aquarium.

See Flipper the dolphin, along with Lolita the killer whale, Salty the sea lion, lovable manatees, and feeding sharks. The killer whale show is the most impressive. Tour the alligator exhibit, reef aquarium, and rain forest habitat. Swim with Flipper (must be 52 inches or taller).

Parrot Jungle Island (ages 2 to 18)

1111 Parrot Jungle Trail; (305) 400-7000; www.parrotjungle.com. Open 10 a.m. to 6 p.m. daily. Admission is $29.95 for adults, $27.95 for seniors, $23.95 for children 3 to 10; under 3 **free.**

Parrot Jungle Island opened in June 2003 as an animal attraction, featuring trained birds, a serpentarium, Manu Encounters in its aviary with 200 free-flying birds, dance and musical presentations in the Jungle Theater, a flock of real pink flamingos glamorizing Flamingo Lake, a rare plant nursery, a petting barn, and a kids' area called Monkey Bars.

South Beach

This erstwhile bastion of winter-sun tourism has rerisen to its former glory, thanks to the redemption of South Beach's Art Deco district.

SoBe, as it's known in shorthand, is a place most suitable for adults. It makes for a fun morning drive (come late afternoon, Ocean Drive traffic slows to a crawl and parking is near impossible), and Lummus Beach provides a lot of action for older children with its water-sports rentals and sidewalks perfect for biking and in-line skating (rentals are available on the beach). There are two playgrounds for the younger kids. Topless sunbathing occurs with frequency.

The Tennis Center at Crandon Park (ages 8 to 13)

7300 Crandon Blvd., Key Biscayne; (305) 365-2300. Open daily 8 a.m. to 9 p.m. The public can use its courts (seventeen hard, eight clay, and two grass).

Hard court per-hour use fee is $4 for adults, $3 for children. Clay is $7 and $3.

THERAPY-IV (ages 5 to 13)

Haulover Park Marina, 10800 Collins Ave., Miami Beach; (305) 945-1578; www.therapy4
.com. Open daily. Half-day fishing costs $180 per person.

Go deep-sea fishing for a half or full day. Catch shark, sailfish, marlin, and other game species.

Coral Gables

Lies south of Hwy. 41 and east of Rte. 959 (Southwest Fifty-seventh Street).

Coral Gables is a special place, a respite from the anonymity of city life. One of the
nation's first planned cities, it was built in Mediterranean Revival style back in the 1920s.
It is known for its art galleries, theaters, and fine restaurants. To get a taste of the town's
Old European flavor, follow the scenic route along Old Cutler Road north to Riviera Drive,
then west on Anastasia Avenue, looping back south along Granada Boulevard. A bike
path follows most of the route. For a more detailed map, download a visitors' brochure at
www.citybeautiful.net/CGWeb/visitors.aspx.

Actors' Playhouse at the Miracle Theatre

280 Miracle Mile, Coral Gables; (305) 444-9293; www.actorsplayhouse.org. Children's theater performances Sat at 2 p.m.

It presents award-winning children's musical theater, among other offerings.

Venetian Pool (ages 5 to 13)

2701 DeSoto Blvd., Coral Gables; (305) 460-5356; www.coralgablesvenetianpool.com.
Opens 11 a.m. Mon through Fri, 10 a.m. Sat and Sun. Closing time varies with the season.
Admission is $10.50 for adults, $6.00 for children ages 3 to 12. No kids under 3 permitted.

Why take 'em to any old swimming pool when they can splash around the Venetian Pool?
Carved from a coral rock quarry, this 1923 landmark features caves, lush foliage, stone
bridges, and waterfalls.

Coconut Grove

East of Coral Gables at the south end of Bayshore Drive.

If South Beach is the free-spirited youth of the family, then Coconut Grove is the
matured ex-hippie. With its chic shopping arenas and burgeoning arts scene, it is one
of Miami's more fashionable neighborhoods. Try to visit during its Coconut Grove Arts
Festival in February, zany Bed Race in May, or colorful Goombay Festival in June. The
Goombay festival is the largest African-American festival in the United States, featuring
Bahamian Junkanoo bands and a sailing regatta. It recalls the district's roots as a community for migrating Bahamian seafarers. On Charles Avenue, you can see many of their
early homes, ca. 1890.

"The Grove's" shopping district takes on a holiday atmosphere around Grand Avenue.
(Take McFarlane Road off Bayshore Boulevard.)

Barnacle Historic State Park (ages 6 to 13)

3485 Main Hwy; off McFarlane Road; (305) 442-6866; www.floridastateparks.org/The Barnacle. Open 9 a.m. to 5 p.m. Fri through Mon, with tours at 10 and 11:30 a.m. and 1 and 2:30 p.m. Admission is $3 for persons age 6 and older.

Tour the unusual cone-shaped home built in 1891 by Coconut Grove's founding father, Commodore Ralph Middleton Munroe.

Matheson Hammock Park (ages 2 to 8)

9610 Old Cutler Rd.; (305) 665-5475. Parking is $5.

Families with small tots like this little-known park for its calm, protected Atoll Pool Beach. It also provides picnic facilities, lifeguards, showers, dressing rooms, concessions, a marina, and a nature trail.

Miami Metrozoo (all ages)

12400 Southwest 152nd St.; (305) 251-0400; www.zsf.org. Open 9:30 a.m. to 5:30 p.m. daily (ticket booth closes at 4 p.m.). Admission is $15.95 for adults, $11.95 for children ages 3 through 12.

Komodo dragons, koalas, wallabies, white Bengal tigers, and Himalayan black bears are among the 225 species of animals that call this 300-acre habitat home. To hold the interest of the tiny, there is a playground, rides, a petting zoo, and a meerkat exhibit. Ecology and wildlife shows take place all day long. An air-conditioned monorail helps you get around the vast grounds.

Miami Museum of Science and Planetarium (ages 4 to 13)

3280 South Miami Ave.; south of Rickenbacker Causeway; (305) 646-4200; www.miamisci .org. Open 10 a.m. to 6 p.m. daily; the box office and wildlife park close at 5:30 p.m. Admission to the museum planetarium shows and wildlife center is $18 for adults, $16 for seniors and students with identification, $13 for children ages 3 to 12. Free planetarium show presented the first Fri of the month.

Birds of prey are one of the specialties of this modest but popular facility. Known for its work rehabilitating predatory birds, it keeps more than 175 live animals and features permanent and special natural history exhibits. Indoors, see the Smithsonian's Latin America–Caribbean exploration exhibit, play virtual basketball, and surf the Internet. The planetarium hosts astronomy and laser shows.

Monkey Jungle (ages 2 to 8)

14805 Southwest 216th St.; off Hwy. 1; (305) 235-1611; www.monkeyjungle.com. Open 9:30 a.m. to 5 p.m. daily. Admission is $29.95 plus tax for adults, $27.95 for seniors, $23.95 for children ages 3 to 9.

You're in the cage and the animals run free in an Amazon rain forest and other settings. Kids love dropping food in their cups and watching them pull it up from overhead.

Vizcaya Museum and Gardens (ages 7 to 13)

3251 South Miami Ave.; across the street from the science museum; (305) 250-9133; www
.vizcayamuseum.com. Ticket office is open 9:30 a.m. to 4:30 p.m. daily; the house closes at
5 p.m., the gardens at 5:30 p.m. Admission is $15 for adults, $6 for children ages 6 to 12; 5
and under **free.**

It allows the curious a peek at the lifestyles of Miami's early rich and famous. Chicago
industrialist James Deering built this Italian palace and its gardens in 1916. Its thirty-four
rooms of richly ornate furnishings and artwork date from the fifteenth to the nineteenth
centuries. Guests can wander the home's second floor and gardens on their own.

Wings Over Miami Museum (ages 6 to 13)

14710 Southwest 128th St.; in Tamiami Airport; (305) 233-5197; www.wingsovermiami.com.
Open 10 a.m. to 5:00 p.m. Thurs to Sun. Admission is $10 for adults, $6 for seniors and $7
for children under 12 years of age.

Immerse yourself in wartime aircraft. The museum features planes from the world wars
and keeps a video collection for your perusal.

Where to Eat

You'll find a wide selection of restaurants in
Miami, which has developed its own rising
style of local cuisine, known popularly as
Floribbean or Miami New World—a fusion of
Florida, Caribbean, and global styles. Legends
in dining are created here, but many are not
for families. Try these.

Picnic's. 6500 SW 40th St. Miami. (305) 665-
6964. Sandwiches, homemade meals, banana
splits at the thirty-year-old soda fountain.
Breakfast, lunch, and dinner weekdays; breakfast and lunch weekends. $–$$

Tap Tap Haitian Restaurant. 819 Fifth St.;
(305) 672-2898. Wholesome, inexpensive,
authentic Haitian stews and fish in a bright
setting off Ocean Drive. Open Thurs through
Sun noon to 11 p.m. $–$$

Where to Stay

Doral Golf Resort and Spa. 4400 N.W.
87th Ave.; (305) 592-2000 or (800) 71-DORAL;
www.doralresort.com. Known for its great
golf, spa, and Blue Lagoon Recreation Park.
Kids' program teaches golf and undertakes
other creative endeavors. Eleven hard and
clay tennis courts and stadium, kiddie pool,
security gate. $$–$$$$

Sheraton Bal Harbour. 9701 Collins Ave.,
Bal Harbour; (305) 865-7511 or (800) 325-
3535; www.sheraton.com. Fantasy swimming
pool, beachfront, water-sports rentals, tennis,
workout gym, restaurants, 645 rooms and
suites, and kids' program. $$–$$$$

Silver Sands Beach Resort. 301 Ocean
Dr., Key Biscayne; (305) 361-5441; www.silver
sandsbeachresort.net. Minisuites and cottages with kitchenettes looking out onto the
pool or beach. $$$–$$$$

For More Information

**Greater Miami Convention and Visitors
Bureau.** 701 Brickell Ave., Suite 2700, Miami
33131; (305) 539-3000 or (888) 766-4264;
www.miamiandbeaches.com.

Homestead

About 25 miles south of Coral Gables–Coconut Grove area. To avoid city congestion, take the Florida Turnpike (toll) from Cutler Ridge to Homestead.

Fruit and Spice Park (ages 6 to 13)

24801 S.W. 187th Ave.; (305) 247-5727; www.fruitandspicepark.org. Open 9 a.m. to 5 p.m. daily. Admission is $7 for adults, $2 for children 6-11. Under six free. Guided tram tours, 11 a.m., 1:30 p.m. and 3 p.m. daily included in price.

Homestead is known as Florida's capital of exotic fruits. In this 37-acre garden you can see more than 500 varieties of rare fruit, herb, nut, and spice trees and plants and 70 kinds of bamboo in the setting of a historic farm community known as Redland.

Homestead-Miami Speedway (ages 6 to 13)

Off Canal Drive (Southwest 328th St.); 1 Speedway Blvd.; (305) 230-5000; www.homestead miamispeedway.com.

It is home to NASCAR and Indy Car events.

For More Information

Greater Homestead–Florida City Chamber of Commerce. 43 North Krome Ave., Homestead 33030; (305) 247-2332.

Weekend Jaunt: Biscayne National Underwater Park and Everglades National Park

Primal wilderness lies less than an hour away from the skyscrapers and bright lights of Miami. Homestead is the threshold between two unique federal parks. At the juncture of Palm Drive, head east for Biscayne's marine life, or west for the wetlands and hammocks of the Everglades.

Biscayne National Underwater Park (ages 5 to 13)

9 miles east of Homestead on North Canal Road; 9710 Southwest 328th St./Route 9336, Homestead; (305) 230-1100 for park information and (305) 230-7275 for tour reservations; www.nps.gov/bisc. Majority of park open 24 hours, visitor center, 7 a.m. to 5:30 p.m. daily. The three-hour family snorkeling tour departs at 10: a.m. and 1:30 p.m. daily. Tour fare is $45 regardless of age, snorkel equipment is included. There are also glass-bottom boat tours, island camping, canoe and kayak rentals, and SCUBA dive trips. Contact the

Florida Trivia

Extent of the Everglades First called River Glades by early intimidated explorers who penetrated no farther than the open saw grass expanses, *Everglades* refers generically to a wetland ecology that spreads far to the north of park boundaries.

Everglades National Park encompasses 2,100 square miles and contains the largest mangrove forest and the slowest-moving river in the world.

concessioner for reservations at www.biscayneunderwater.com; 302-230-1100. Advance reservations are recommended.

For a truly remarkable day that is full of experiences unique to Florida, head for Biscayne National Underwater Park. The park comprises 181,500 acres, 95 percent of which is underwater. The remaining acreage dots the seas with a cluster of keys that form a chain, which heads the Florida Keys. Mangrove and magnificent coral habitat make up the underwater portion. You can see much of the same marine life here as you would in the Keys, Bahamas, and Caribbean. The beautiful Convoy Point Visitors Center provides exhibits, breezy picnic grounds, and a nature trail. For primitive overnights, you can camp on Elliott or Boca Chica Key, which are part of Biscayne National Park and are accessible only by boat. Facilities include showers, restrooms, and drinking water on Elliott Key only. You must haul your own trash off the island.

Everglades Alligator Farm (ages 4 to 13)

40351 S.W. 192nd Ave., Florida City; en route to Everglades National Park; (305) 247-2628; www.everglades.com. Open 9 a.m. to 6 p.m. daily. Admission is $15.50 for adults, $10.50 for children ages 4 to 11. With airboat ride included, cost is $23.00 and $15.50.

If you spend time in the Everglades, you'll have no problem spotting alligators. Here, you can see how they are farmed and handled. Snakes add to the creepy crawliness of the place. A thirty-minute airboat ride provides opportunity to observe hawks, ospreys, roseate spoonbills, and, of course, alligators in their natural habitat. The farm also introduces you to caged bobcats, cougars, and an American black bear and presents alligator and hourly wildlife shows.

Everglades National Park (ages 6 to 13)

About 15 miles south and west of Homestead on Rte. 9336; 40001 Rte. 9336; (305) 242-7700; www.nps.gov/ever. Admission is $10 per car (good for seven days), $5 for pedestrians or cyclists. Park is open 24 hours.

The Everglades' main visitor center lies outside the park's entrance gate and provides a thorough and state-of-the-art examination of 'Glades critters and the factors that influence them. One exhibit that kids like identifies the calls of cricket frogs, limpkins, and other noisy park residents. A map directs visitors to trails and other facilities along the 40-mile road on the park's east access (for western access, see Southwest Florida chapter). There are only a few vending machines here and there, so plan to bring your own snacks and drinks.

Two short interpretive trails depart from the Royal Palm Visitors Center, 4 miles inside the park. Anhinga Trail is best in the park for wildlife—lots of gators and birds. Others penetrate slash pine, hammock mahogany, saw grass prairie, and cypress environment. At Pa-hay-okee Overlook, 13 miles inside the park, a boardwalk leads to an observation tower. Eco Pond on Flamingo Road is another good place to spy wildlife—alligators, otters, roseate spoonbills, egrets, and other wading birds.

The Flamingo Visitors Center and Marina features natural history exhibits and information on camping, sightseeing cruises, charter fishing, canoeing, and boat, houseboat, and bicycle rentals. (Some services are limited after the high season ends.) The park hosts interpretive programs, including a weekend family session, in season.

Miccosukee Indian Village and Airboat Rides (ages 5 to 13)

About a quarter of a mile west of Shark Valley Information Center; at mile marker 70 on U.S. 41; (305) 552-8365. Open 9 a.m. to 5 p.m. daily. Admission is $10 for adults, $5 for children ages 5 to 12. Airboat tours cost $10 per person.

Alligator wrestling gets top billing at the Miccosukee village. Tribesfolk also sell their crafts and host thirty-minute airboat tours. The Miccosukee Restaurant offers a taste of local ethnic cuisine, including fry bread and alligator tail, as well as family favorites.

Shark Valley (ages 7 to 13)

From Homestead, follow Krome Avenue (Route 997), 20 miles north to Tamiami Trail and head west for about 20 miles; (305) 221-8455; www.sharkvalleytramtours.com. Open 9:15 a.m. to 5:15 p.m. daily. Admission is $10 per car. Bike rentals are available from 8:30 a.m. to 3 p.m. for $6.25 per hour. Two-hour tram tour costs $16.25 for adults, $15.25 for seniors, $10.00 for children ages 3 to 12, under 3 free.

Other east-end access to the Everglades National Park lies along Hwy. 41. From here, you can catch a tram tour, rent a bike, or begin a hike to explore the quiet natural infrastructure of the Florida Everglades via a paved 15-mile loop road into the Shark Valley Slough. Watch for alligators (lots of them, often quite close to the path), roseate spoonbills, wood storks, snail kites, panthers, and other rare inhabitants of the saw grass marshes and hardwood hammocks. An observation tower gives you a heightened view. It's best to try the hike or bike trip in cool weather, when mosquitoes are less likely to carry off the little ones. There are only a few vending machines here and there, so plan to bring your own snacks and drinks.

Glades Critters

The alligator and Florida panther are the stars of the Everglades critter show. Snakes, river otters, manatees, mosquitoes, and more than 600 types of fish and 300 bird species inhabit the teeming wetlands.

Upper Keys

About 45 minutes south of Homestead along Hwy. 1.

You are now leaving Florida and the United States as you know it and entering the world of the Florida Keys—part Bahamian, part Caribbean, and part plain unclassifiable. This becomes especially apparent the farther south you travel, the farther you range from what dictates and concerns life on the mainland.

Incidentally, the farther south you drive, the smaller the numbers become on green markers alongside the road. These mile markers (MM) are the Keys' answer to street addresses along Hwy. 1, also referred to as the Overseas Highway. The numbers tell you how far you are from Key West, which lies at the end of the road.

Since all waters surrounding the keys were designated as the Florida Keys National Marine Sanctuary in 1990, they are protected, making them a diver's paradise where angelfish, barracuda, octopuses, conch, and lobsters hang out at the local coral bar. (NOTE: Conch collecting is not allowed in Florida.)

Fish are prime tourist bait in the Keys. The area is particularly noted for its bonefish, tarpon, dolphinfish, grouper, sailfish, and marlin. Fishing charters and party boats are found at most large resorts and marinas. Party boats charge about $30–50 per person for a day on the high seas; small charter boats charge about $550 per day for four to six persons.

Cheeca Lodge and Spa

Mile marker 82 (P.O. Box 527), Islamorada 33036; (305) 664-4651 or (800) 327-2888; www
.cheeca.com.

If you're looking for lodging where all of your needs are met on-property, you'll like this. It's a classy place, but its reputation is built primarily on its environmental awareness. Kids do outdoors stuff, such as snorkeling and fishing, and learn how to be environmentally responsible. Even the restaurant menus are benevolent to the environment. The resort has a nice private beach; a historic cemetery; swimming, tennis, a spa, boat charters, golf; and all the makings of a self-contained vacation. Ask about family packages. $$$$ NOTE: Damaged by fire in early 2009, but is reopening in December 2009.

John Pennekamp Coral Reef State Park (ages 6 to 13)

Mile marker 102.5 (P.O. Box 1560), Key Largo 33037; (305) 451-1202 for park information; (305) 451-6300 for concession information and tour reservations; www.floridastateparks .org/pennekamp. Open 8 a.m. to sunset daily. Park entrance is $8.00 per vehicle with up to eight passengers, $3.50 for a single passenger, and $1.50 for bicyclists and pedestrians. Glass-bottom boat tours cost $24 for adults, $17 for children under age 12.

First stop for underwater enthusiasts: Its most popular sea-bottom sight is the 4,000-pound bronze statue called *Christ of the Deep*. Besides snorkeling and diving charters, you can keep busy canoeing, hiking, sailing, motorboating, and setting up camp in the campground. A concession rents all the necessary water-sports equipment and operates a glass-bottom boat tour three times daily. Stop by the visitor center to see the 30,000-gallon aquarium 9 a.m. to 5 p.m. daily. **Free.**

Long Key State Park (all ages)

Mile marker 67.5; 67500 Overseas Hwy, Long Key; (305) 664-4815; www.floridastateparks .org/longkey. Open 8 a.m. to sunset daily. Park entrance is $6.00 per vehicle with up to eight passengers, $3.50 for a single passenger, and $1.50 for bicyclists and pedestrians. Camping fees are $31.75, tax included, per night.

You can camp or picnic right on the beach here. The lanky key hosts abundant birdlife, which you can observe on nature trails and canoe trips. Reservations are accepted for campsites.

Theater of the Sea (all ages)

Mile marker 84.5, Islamorada; (305) 664-2431. Shows run continuously 9:30 a.m. to 4 p.m. daily. Admission is $25.95 for adults, $18.95 for children ages 3 to 10 and **free** for children 2 and under, including a guided tour and bottomless boat ride. Cost for swimming with dolphins is $175 per person; for swimming with a sea lion, $135; for swimming with stingrays, $55.

A longtime sea critter attraction, it will delight little ones with dolphin, sea lion, and shark shows. Anyone age five or older can arrange to swim with a dolphin, sea lion, or stingrays if you call in advance. Snorkeling tours and other programs are also available.

Where to Eat

Islamorada Fish Company. 81532 Overseas Hwy at Mile Marker 81.5; (305) 664-9271; www.islamoradafishco.com. Open daily 11 a.m. to 10 p.m. Fish, fried, grilled and raw, plus some turf items too. If the stone crab claws are in season, they are to die for. $$

Key Largo Conch House (that's pronounced "conk"). Mile Marker 100.2, Key Largo (look for the Victorian house behind the trees); (305) 453-4844; www.keylargocoffeehouse .com. Open daily 7 a.m. to 10 p.m. Traditional American flavored with Caribbean and Keys cuisine, and great coffee. $–$$

Where to Stay

Lodging is plentiful and varied in the Keys, with options in every price range. See also Cheeca Lodge and Spa.

Holiday Isle Resort and Marina. Mile marker 84, 84001 Overseas Hwy, Islamorada;
(305) 664-2321 or (800) 327-7070; www .holidayisle.com. Marina with rental boats and fishing and diving charters, pools, restaurants, shops, playgrounds, and endless entertainment. Rooms, efficiencies, cottages, and suites are available. $–$$$$

Key Largo Bay Marriott Beach Resort. Mile marker 103.8, 103800 Overseas Hwy, Key Largo; (305) 453-0000 or (800) 932-9332; www.marriottkeylargo.com. Lush resort with 153 rooms overlooking the bay. Man-made beach, pool, restaurants, tiki bar, dive shop, kids' club, and fitness room. $$–$$$$

For More Information

The Florida Keys and Key West. P.O. Box 866, Key West 33041-0866; (800) FLA-KEYS; www.fla-keys.com.

Key Largo Chamber of Commerce. 106000 Overseas Hwy, Key Largo 33037; (305) 451-1414 or (800) 822-1088; www.key largo.org.

Marathon

About a half hour south of Long Key on Hwy. 1.

Crane Point Museum & Nature Center (ages 2 to 10)

5550 Overseas Hwy (bayside at mile marker 50.5); (305) 743-9100; www.cranepoint.net. Open 9 a.m. to 5 p.m. Mon through Sat and noon to 5 p.m. Sun, with shortened hours in summer. Admission is $11 for adults, $9 for seniors, $7 for students; 5 and under **free.**

Small and homey, this is a must-stop, free of the commercialism of a lot of other attractions. Be sure to see the simulated coral reef. Children may dress up as pirates and play on the pirate ship. Nature trails lead to more discovery, including an aviary for bird rehabilitation.

Hawk's Cay Resort and Dolphin Connection (all ages)

Mile marker 61, north of Marathon; 61 Hawk's Cay Blvd., Duck Key; (305) 743-7000 or (888) 313-5749; www.hawkscay.com. Forty acres of water-oriented activities and luxurious relaxation. One of its finest assets is the Dolphin Connection; (888) 814-9154; www .dolphinconnection.com (reservations required). The Dolphin Connection is open to the public.

This facility enables families to observe dolphins from the dock (they come up to you to be petted) for $60 per person. Swim with the dolphins for $155 per person or be a trainer for a day for $295. Four pools (one with an interactive pirate ship run aground), a sheltered beach lagoon, a tree-house playground with climbing wall, and an adventure kids' program get high marks from young guests. Older ones can take advantage of the resort's fly-fishing and offshore sailing schools. $$$$

Pigeon Key (ages 6 to 13)

Visitors Center at mile marker 48 (1 Knight's Key Blvd.), oceanside right before the Seven Mile Bridge on Knight's Key; (305) 743-5999; www.pigeonkey.net. Tours depart from the center hourly 10:30 a.m. to 4 p.m. daily. Admission and ferry is $11.00 for adults, $8.50 for ages 5 to 13; under 6 **free.** Ferry shuttle is included in the price.

You can see the tiny key as you cross the bridge, but you can reach it only by the old bridge, which allows no car traffic. The key is significant for the role it played during the building of the railroad in 1905 and for its surviving Bahamian architecture. The museum,

Florida **Trivia**

Seven Mile Bridge The Seven Mile Bridge that connects Marathon and the Lower Keys, also known as the Eighth Wonder of the World, affords a magnificent view and is the longest segmental bridge in the world. It was built in 1982 in pieces in Tampa and shipped to the Keys to be assembled.

occupying the assistant bridge tender's house, holds old postcards, paintings, photographs, and memorabilia.

Where to Eat

Herbies. Mile marker 50.5, 6350 Overseas Hwy; (305) 743-6373. Casual, picnic-table atmosphere. Choice seafood and beef. Lunch and dinner Tues through Sat. $$

Where to Stay

See also Hawk's Cay.

Conch Key Cottages. Mile marker 62.3 oceanside, 62250 Overseas Hwy, Walker's Island; (305) 289-1377 or (800) 330-1577; www.conchkeycottages.com. Twelve ocean-side self-sufficient cottages with small beach, pool, and boat docks. $$–$$$

For More Information

Greater Marathon Chamber of Commerce. 12222 Overseas Hwy, Marathon 33050; (305) 743-5417 or (800) 842-9580; www.floridakeysmarathon.com.

Lower Keys

Continue south along Hwy. 1.

South of the Seven Mile Bridge, the temperament changes. Activity level drops a notch. Wildlife and vegetation heighten.

The second largest of the Keys, Big Pine Key remains one of the most undeveloped, gratifying adventures with its abundant opportunities for fishing and nature exploration.

Offshore of Big Pine Key, diving hits its spectacular peak at Looe Key National Marine Sanctuary. Technicolor reefs attract tropical fish of sheer dazzle, mostly in less than 30 feet of aquarium-clear water. Summer is the favorite time for divers. The waters are warm, and the season is open for lobster. No spear or lobster fishing is allowed within the sanctuary, however.

Bahia Honda State Park (all ages)

Mile marker 37, south of the Seven Mile Bridge, north of Big Pine Key; 36850 Overseas Hwy, Big Pine Key; (305) 872-2353; www.floridastateparks.org/bahiahonda. Open 8 a.m. to sunset daily. Park entrance is $8 per vehicle with up to eight passengers, $3 for a single passenger, and $1 for extra passengers, bicyclists, and pedestrians, plus a county surcharge of 50 cents per person 6 years and older.

If you're craving a nice beach, something you don't find much of in the Keys, head to Bahia Honda for a day, overnight, or as long as you can get away with it. It has two beaches, actually, one on the ocean side, another bayside. The bayside beach is favored by families because of its calm waters and extensive facilities, including shaded picnic tables with grills, food concessions, and a nearby marina and concessions that rent kayaks, sailboards, and snorkeling equipment and offer snorkel boat excursions. Off the beach, you can stake a tent or rent a cabin, go on a fishing charter, or hike a nature trail that leads over an old railroad bridge.

National Key Deer Refuge (ages 4 to 13)

Entrance on Key Deer Boulevard (Route 940), off Rte. A1A at mile marker 30.5; (305) 872-2239; www.fws.gov/nationalkeydeer. The visitor center is off to the right in the Big Pine Key Shopping Plaza (P.O. Box 430510, Big Pine Key 33043); it conducts tours in the winter. The center is open 9 a.m. to 4 p.m. Mon through Fri. The refuge is open sunrise to sunset daily. Admission is free.

The tiny Key deer, a subspecies of the white-tailed deer, survives in the far-off reaches of Big Pine Key and is protected at the 8,000-acre refuge. Best times to spot one of the 800 or so deer is on a slow drive during the morning or evening hours. Visit the refuge's Blue Hole (a lake formed by quarry digging) to see alligators, turtles, and fish in the see-through waters and hike two self-guided nature trails.

Reflections Nature Tours (ages 7 to 13)

P.O. Box 431373, Big Pine Key 33043; (305) 872-7474; www.floridakeyskayaktours.com. Open daily. Cost is $50 per person for three-hour guided tour. Tours at 9 a.m. and 1 p.m.

Explore National Key Deer Refuge, the Everglades, and other wilderness areas by kayak. Half- and full-day tours and rentals with backcountry ferry are available.

Underseas Inc. (ages 10 to 13)

Oceanside at mile marker 30.5 (P.O. Box 430319, Big Pine Key 33043); (305) 872-2700 or (800) 446-5663; www.underseasinc.com. Open daily. Snorkeling charter cost is $33.95 per person, including gear.

Conducts snorkeling and scuba charters and instruction (ages twelve and older) and rents equipment. Half-day charters take you to two different sites.

Where to Eat

Mangrove Mama's. Mile marker 20, 19991 Overseas Hwy, Sugarloaf Key; (305) 745-3030. Stop for a typically Keys casual bite hidden among the banana trees. Ribs, steak, fresh shrimp and fish, and legendary Key lime pie in an atmosphere of color-splashed fun. Lunch and dinner daily. $$–$$$

Where to Stay

Big Pine Key Fishing Lodge. Oceanside at mile marker 33 (P.O. Box 430513, Big Pine Key 33043); (305) 872-2351. Well-maintained park with campground and mobile home, motel, efficiency units, complete marina, boat rentals, fishing charters, a pool, and bait and tackle shop. $

For More Information

Big Pine and Lower Keys Chamber of Commerce. P.O. Box 430511, Big Pine Key 33043-0511; 31020 Overseas Hwy (mile marker 31); (305) 872-2411 or (800) 872-3722; www.lowerkeyschamber.com.

Key West

At the end of the road.

In 1982, Key West symbolically seceded from the Union, dubbing itself the Conch Republic in honor of its Bahaman background (residents of Bahaman heritage are known as Conchs). Though the act was not official, Key West remains a land with its own rules and free-spirited attitude. Expect somewhere totally different. You won't be disappointed.

Old Town is the center of activity and attractions. Look for a copy of the *Walking & Biking Guide* for a historic self-guided tour. Plan to stay for sunset to get a taste of what the town is all about. Each evening at Mallory Square, sword swallowers, human statues, tightrope walkers, other street performers, food vendors, tourists, and residents gather to celebrate the day's finale.

Conch Tour Train (all ages)

Departs from station at 303 Front St.; (305) 294-5161; www.conchtourtrain.com. Open 9 a.m. to 4:30 p.m. daily. Admission is $29 for adults, $14 for children ages 4 to 12. Package tours are available for added fees that can get you into almost all Key West major tourist attractions.

To get to know the town and its history in short order, take the Conch Tour Train ninety-minute tour. Learn how Key West became the richest city in the United States from salvaging ships wrecked on yonder reefs. **Free** reboarding is allowed.

Fantasy Fest (ages 8 and up)

(800) FLA-KEYS; www.fantasyfest.net.

Key West takes Halloween dress-up seriously, with ten days of costumed carnival, including a Children's Day and Pet Masquerade. Be prepared to see partial nudity (usually covered with body paint) on the street at any time.

Fort Jefferson (ages 5 to 13)

Garden Key, Dry Tortugas; www.nps.gov/drto; but contact (305) 294-7009 or (800) 634-0939; www.yankeefreedom.com for passage to the island. The Yankee Fleet ferry service from Key West (at 240 Margaret St.) will take you there and back for $160 for adults, $150 for seniors, $120 for children ages 4 to 16 (includes breakfast, picnic lunch, tour, and snorkel gear). Park entrance is $5 for ages 17 and up.

Now, to really get away from it all, plan a trip from Key West to Dry Tortugas, where you can snorkel and explore Fort Jefferson, which once served as a prison that held Dr. Mudd, the physician who patched up Lincoln assassin John Wilkes Booth. Restrooms are the only facilities.

Fort Zachary Taylor State Historic Park (all ages)

End of Southard Street on Truman Annex (P.O. Box 6560) Key West 33041; (305) 292-6713; www.floridastateparks.org/forttaylor. Open 8 a.m. to sunset daily. Park entrance is $6.00

More Things to See and Do
in Southeast Florida

- **Ancient Spanish Monastery,** North Miami Beach; (305) 945-1461
- **Audubon House,** Key West; (305) 294-2116
- **Children's Museum of Boca Raton,** Boca Raton; (561) 368-6875
- **Dolphins Plus,** Key Largo; (305) 451-1993
- **East Martello Museum & Gallery,** Key West; (305) 296-3913
- **Environmental Center,** Miami; (305) 237-2600
- **Everglades Holiday Park,** Fort Lauderdale; (954) 434-8111
- **Everglades Safari Park,** Miami; (305) 226-6923
- **Ernest Hemingway Home and Museum,** Key West; (305) 294-1575
- **Fairchild Tropical Gardens,** Miami; (305) 667-1651
- **Fun Depot,** Lake Worth; (561) 547-0817
- **Indian Key State Historic Site,** Long Key; (305) 664-9814
- **International Swimming Hall of Fame,** Fort Lauderdale; (954) 462-6536
- **Little White House Museum,** Key West; (305) 294-9911
- **Perky Bat Tower,** Lower Sugarloaf Key
- **Scott Rakow Youth Center Ice Rink,** Miami Beach; (305) 673-7767
- **Wreckers' Museum and Oldest House,** Key West; (305) 294-9502

per vehicle with up to eight passengers, $3.50 for a single passenger, and 50 cents for extra passengers, bicyclists, and pedestrians, plus a 50 cent county surcharge per person 6 years and older. Bicycle rental $1.50.

Beaches are not Key West's strong suit. This one is man-made and fringed with shade trees. When it's time to get out of the sun, a history refreshment awaits in the form of a fort that was built before the Civil War. Living-history tours are conducted the last weekend of the month during winter season. Join a ranger-guided tour of the fort at noon or 2 p.m. daily year-round.

Key West Aquarium (all ages)

1 Whitehead St.; (305) 292-8990; www.keywestaquarium.com. Open daily 10 a.m. to 6 p.m. Shows and feeding at 11 a.m. and at 1, 3, and 4:30 p.m. daily. Admission is $12 for adults, $5 for children ages 4 to 12.

On the waterfront near Mallory Square, this is a small, open-air, Key West–style aquarium, meaning it's kind of funky, nothing plastic or dressed up. You can watch shark and turtle feedings and feel around the touch tank.

Key West Lighthouse Museum (ages 7 to 13)

938 Whitehead St.; (305) 294-0012; www.kwahs.com. Open 9:30 a.m. to 4:30 p.m. daily. Admission is $10 for adults, $9 for seniors, $4 for children and students.

Climb the 150-year-old, 90-foot, 88-step structure, walk inside a 12-foot prism lens, and have a look at the photos and memorabilia inside the reconstructed Keepers Quarters.

Key West Shipwreck Historeum (ages 4 to 13)

Across the street from the aquarium at 1 Whitehead St.; (305) 292-8990; www.shipwreck historeum.com. Guided tours with a show commence every half hour 9:40 a.m. to 4:40 p.m. daily. Admission is $12 for adults, $5 for children ages 4 to 12.

It will thrill young adventurers with tales of salvaging, using actors, films, and lasers. The kids can even climb the 65-foot captain's observatory to watch for reefs and wrecks and get a feel for the danger and excitement involved in Key West's most prosperous industry of yore.

Mel Fisher's Maritime Museum (ages 4 to 13)

200 Greene St.; (305) 294-2633; www.melfisher.org/museum.htm. Open 8:30 a.m. to 5 p.m. Mon through Fri, 9:30 a.m. to 5 p.m. Sat and Sun. Admission is $12 for adults, $6 for children.

One of Key West's most recent finds was a spectacular trove of treasure aboard the sunken seventeenth-century *Atocha,* displayed here.

Where to Eat

El Meson de Pepe. 410 Wall St.; (305) 295-2620. Indoor-outdoor traditional Cuban restaurant. Lunch and dinner daily. $–$$

Kelly's Caribbean Bar and Grill. 301 Whitehead St.; (305) 293-8484. Owned by Kelly McGillis (of *Top Gun* fame), in the historic Pan Am building and its courtyard. Island atmosphere and cuisine, home-brewed beer. Lunch and dinner daily. $$–$$$

Where to Stay

Key West is known for its intimate guesthouses, but many of them do not accommodate children. Families should try the larger hotels and resorts.

Hyatt Key West Resort & Marina. 601 Front St.; (305) 809-1234 or (800) 233-1234. Close to the action at Mallory Square and Duval Street, but safely removed and gated, Hyatt Key West offers families water-sports rentals and charters, an on-site restaurant, and pool in a compact 120-room complex. $$$–$$$$

For More Information

Greater Key West Chamber of Commerce. 402 Wall St., Key West 33040; (305) 294-2587 or (800) LAST-KEY.

Annual Events

Old Island Days. Key West; (305) 294-9501. A celebration of Key West's multifaceted past and architecture with activities for the whole family. **Free.**

Carnaval Miami. Miami; (305) 644-8888. Miami's most lively celebration at Mardi Gras time. Ten days of sports, concerts and Latin food, music, and dance at the world's largest block party.

Fantasy Fest. Key West; (800) FLA-KEYS; www.fantasyfest.net. A live street fest in October that lasts for ten days and includes a costumed carnival, Children's Day, and a Pet Masquerade.

Junior Orange Bowl International Youth Festival. Coral Gables; (305) 662-1210; www.jrorangebowl.com. Youth athletic and fine art competitions and parade, October through January.

Miccosukee Indian Arts Festival. Miccosukee Indian Village; (305) 223-8380. Representatives from about twenty tribes perform in July and December. Call for dates and times.

Index

About the Authors

Adele Woodyard has been writing on Florida travel, people and places since 1988. Her articles have appeared in such publications as *Backpacker, Family Fun, History Channel Magazine, AARP the Magazine,* the *St. Petersburg Times, Miami Herald,* and *Providence Sunday Journal,* among many others in print and online. She has contributed to a guidebook and wrote a regular column on Florida travel for one magazine for over three years. A member of the American Society of Journalists and Authors (ASJA), she coauthors www.vacationfunflorida.com.

Stephen Morrill came to Florida in 1970. An Army brat who had also served in the Army, he had no roots anywhere in the U.S. and simply decided to live where everyone else dreamed of retiring to. He chose the Tampa Bay area for its plethora of water-oriented activities and then worked in the maritime trade for many years. He's been writing about Florida business and travel since 1984 and today cohosts, with fellow travel writer Adele Woodyard, the Web site www.VacationFunFlorida. Steve also operates the www.Tampa BayOnTheCheap.com Web site. When not writing about Florida, Steve is out canoeing, sailing, camping, and visiting the weird and the wonderful of Florida. It's a tough job but someone has to do it.